Mercade

Hamlet

Or Shakespeare's Philosophy of History

Mercade

Hamlet
Or Shakespeare's Philosophy of History

ISBN/EAN: 9783743400115

Manufactured in Europe, USA, Canada, Australia, Japa

Cover: Foto ©Thomas Meinert / pixelio.de

Manufactured and distributed by brebook publishing software (www.brebook.com)

Mercade

Hamlet

HAMLET;

OR,

SHAKESPEARE'S PHILOSOPHY

OF

HISTORY.

A STUDY OF THE SPIRITUAL SOUL AND UNITY OF HAMLET.

BY

MERCADE.

The extreme parts of time extremely forms
All causes to the purpose of his speed,
And often at his very loose decides
That which long process could not arbitrate.
LOVE'S LABOUR'S LOST.

WILLIAMS AND NORGATE,
14, HENRIETTA STREET, COVENT GARDEN, LONDON,
AND 20, SOUTH FREDERICK STREET, EDINBURGH.
1875.

HERTFORD:

PRINTED BY STEPHEN AUSTIN AND SONS.

CONTENTS.

HAMLET.

		PAGE
PREFACE	. . . .	vii
INTRODUCTION	. . . .	xi
A SUGGESTIVE KEY TO HAMLET	. . . .	xxxi
CHAPTER I.	. . . .	1
CHAPTER II.	. . . .	51
CHAPTER III.	. . . .	90
CHAPTER IV.	. . . .	113
CHAPTER V.	. . . .	130
CHAPTER VI.	. . . .	135
CHAPTER VII.	. . . .	155
CHAPTER VIII.	. . . .	167
A FEW WORDS UPON OTHELLO	. . . .	187
APPENDIX.	. . . .	201

PREFACE.

THE author offers no apologies for his little work, nor for his opinions. If true, then truth can need no apology; although we know, thanks to Rosencrantz and Guildenstern, it is "dreadfully attended," even in these days. If, on the other hand, they are insane delusions, then the author will be happy to have so illustrious an example as Hamlet, and say with him, "His madness (*if 't be so*) is poor Hamlet's enemy." The play of Hamlet is not merely a piece of exquisite writing; it is a practical and every-day affair. Hamlet is being acted on the world's stage, by humanity, at this present hour. And every momentous epoch in the world's history only realizes some line or prognostication of the play itself. Finally, we have to remark, the interpretation of Shakespeare's plays is not an affair which will remain for ever at the dispensation of fancy or of carping criticism. Our Poet's own words will finally lift the veil off his works, and then let those who think they know him best beware of eating their own words.

It is high time some attempt be made to show Shakespeare was a *thinker*, and not alone an *artist*. We can imagine the rage such a question may excite ; but, nevertheless, we know absolutely nothing of Shakespeare's *own thoughts*. The fragments of beautiful mosaic in thought, which are all we at present grasp, must not be mistaken for our Poet's beliefs. Nor has any systematic attempt been yet made to seize in synthesis the unity and symbolism of one of his works. The sole way of meeting any counter-charge to this fact, is to enunciate some questions like the following. Do we know Shakespeare subjectively? Are we intimate with the man himself as we are with Milton, with Goethe, or with any other genius? Do we know what Shakespeare's political, philosophical, or historical opinions were? In short, can we as yet venture to separate the author from his works, detecting in the unity of the objective art the subjective man? Answers to questions of this sort (which might be multiplied *ad infinitum*) are not to be found. Where shall we search for them? Echo answers, where indeed? We are quite aware there are plenty of people who would attempt to answer these questions readily. But let us assure them, no extracts from the text will satisfy the problem. Shakespeare was far too objective in his art to confound his own thoughts with anything short of unity of idea. Besides, if we appeal to the text, we could easily find negations to almost every positive thought somewhere else. No, it is alone in the unity of the symbolic and spiritual soul of art that we can find the true thought and inspiration of its creator. With this opinion deeply rooted within us, we offer the hypothesis worked out in this little work, as help and suggestion towards final solution.

LONDON, *February 18th*, 1875.

INTRODUCTION.

THIS little work is not addressed to those who see no mystery in the works of Shakespeare. Those who can read his plays, his poems, and his ambiguous language, without any misgivings or further conjecturings, are only to maintain this attitude always, and everything will remain plain to them. In this world, where stale custom reduces everything (to all but philosophers or poets) to the level of the common-place, nothing but novelty succeeds. Idealists and materialists quarrel over their narrow shibboleths, forgetting that their criterions are such as mere blindness alone prevents them from seeing to be as groundless and unreal as the very questions they attack. Realism, that hopeless chimera of philosophical debate, imagines that it has grasped substantiality when it has only removed the question a step further back. Thus we persist in calling things supernatural and spiritual because uncommon, and neglect the common itself, failing to see the transcendental in it around us; which defies comprehension in itself beyond measurement, order, and relation. Perhaps we should do well to take a lesson from Shakespeare, who refused to acknowledge to names a reality existing beyond the ways we look at things. If we turn to "The Tempest," we find we are told in one breath :

" . . . . We are such stuff
As dreams are made on."

And a little before :

> " . . . . The great globe itself,
> Yea, all which it inherit, shall dissolve
> And, like this insubstantial pageant faded,
> Leave not a rack behind."

There is neither materialism nor idealism here. Only the great mystery, the great unknown, of which we know nothing but our poor one-sided and limited views. As Mr. Lewes truly says, in his "Problems of Life and Mind," the world is mystic to man. Beyond relation it is probable we can never pass. Indeed it will ever grow more questionable whether mind and thought are in any way true guages of this universe in itself. And this leads us to the comparison of Shakespeare and the mysteries which philosophy seeks to solve. Mr. Swinburne has well compared our Poet to the ocean. May we not apply Mr. Lewes's dictum about the world to Shakespeare with as great felicity? Are not the works of Shakespeare mystic to man? Who can deny this? Who knows anything of Shakespeare himself? We know a Goethe, we know a Milton; but we do not equally know the greatest of all poets.

Fortunately, to those we address, there is no need of such a question. The growth of Shakespearian societies, and of the literature which at home and abroad is ever swelling around the works of our Poet, are sufficient proof that we are beginning to realize the nature of the problem in down-right earnest. What is that problem?

That problem, we answer, is the realization of the man himself—of Shakespeare as a thinker, not alone as an artist. When we study a painting, we try and enter into its creator's mind, to see what he thought and what he intended in his work. We do not ignore the conception because the execution is perfect. That is generally secondary, or it ought to be so. If there is no conception, only a mere copy, we may admire the artist, but the creator, the genius, is wanting. Thought is at the bottom of all things, and thought alone is the true measure of genius. Thousands possess the artistic gift, thousands execute like automatons. Witness the artisan, it is he alone who builds the ship or rears the house; but who conceives it?—the architect. And we like to know what manner of man the architect was. We wish to learn what he thought; and from his house or his ship we trace the man in the unity and breadth of his design alone. We do not take each column of a temple, each section of a ship, and say this shows the man. It is the whole conception alone which satisfies us. Now the nature of Shakespeare's art is much of this character. We see a mosaic of beautiful passages, love-stories, romances, tragedies, comedies, etc. We read them, and we think we know Shakespeare. It is as if we read "Gulliver's Travels" as a child, swallowing the story oblivious of its irony, its philosophy, and its bitterness. Suppose we were to see nothing in "Don Quixote" but a lunatic? Or in "Zanoni" but a magician? We do not commit these errors here; yet we transpose them easily to that giant Shakespeare. Nobody thinks that Dante's work contains no allegory. Readers are not so dense as not to see the "Divina Commedia" requires a key before it can be understood. And we maintain that every creation of genius in literature is more or less of this character. No matter how early we go back, be it to the Bible or the earliest poetry, we find the prevalence of word-painting, of metaphor, and imagery. Now we contend these latter contain the principle of symbolism in them. They are not direct; on the contrary, they avoid harshness by substituting one picture to call up another, by its likeness and suggestiveness. The germs of rationalism are hidden under this similarity, calling out identity from out diversity. Art, we maintain, is easily described as one large metaphor. It images the thoughts, not by signs, but by pictures which resemble those thoughts; and, whilst touching the feelings, appeals to the mind also. If we were to follow the steps of art in all its growth, we should find the symbolism growing wider, deeper, and more intricate. As we ascend into the realms of dramatic literature, we find in " Prometheus," " Œdipus Rex," and the Greek drama generally, attempts to picture the relations of man to destiny. This is the subject of the drama—the struggle of man with fate. Already we have made a gigantic stride; we have passed from poetry, say, like the Psalms with its beautiful imagery, to unity of conception. The universal verity of Prometheus is a gigantic symbol. Here we have man tied to the rock of inexorable destiny, fate, or law. In " Œdipus Rex" the Sphinx-like mysticism of this world is well pictured. Like the King, we are hurried to our doom irrespective of ourselves. We have no control over circumstances, chance, or fate. Indeed, as we proceed upon our ascent into modern literature, we find a greater and greater differentiation taking place.

Let us arrive at once to Shakespeare, who may well stand for all art in himself alone. And we naturally ask ourselves, what has Shakespeare symbolized ? There are thousands of people who deny the symbolism of art. And let us ask them if art can be direct ? As it can only speak to our feelings and to our thoughts by a species of dumb language, must it not be symbolical ? Is there no thought lurking in the spire ? Does it not, like a silent and solemn finger, point heavenward ? What is the aim of art ?—the ideal. What is the ideal but the voice of the absolute, the perfect, the eternal ? Each man finds a different utterance for it ; but whatever be that utterance, it must be symbolical. Is not all mythology of this character ? The ideal is the ideal, because it is not the real. But it is based upon thought, and that thought is conception from abstractions. Out of large generalizations in the philosophic world, gigantic thoughts arise, which cloud-like would roll away, if genius Titan-like did not embody them in types which fascinate us for ever.

Hamlet is such an ideal, not real as a character, but ideal as a creation, and real as a symbol and a thought. When we rationalize the typifications of art into their symbolical ideas and significations, we are in the land of thought and reality once more. That is to say, of a reality in keeping with the possible and the knowledge of this earth. If it is true genius is above this every-day world, it is also true it cannot leave it. Its force exists in its breadth of view. It embraces the centuries in its gaze, and unrolls them like a scroll. When it typifies them into characters, they are gigantic indeed.

Independently of knowing nothing of Shakespeare's life or his opinions, we know nothing of his works. As a genius we know less about him than of any other genius. His Sonnets are before every one; we have but to read, yet who understands them? It is as yet undecided to whom they are addressed. Some say a woman, others a man. Let us turn to his plays. What do we know of them? Not one alludes in any way to the topics of their day. We can apparently find no thought of the author behind them. Like an invisible abstraction, the creator is not to be seen. The works are there, but the man who conceived them is unapparent. Now there is something about Shakespeare's works which persuades us he *is* there. The profundity of his art, and probably the width of his conceptions, in their gigantic unity and design, prevents us from seeing the truth. Shakespeare is so much above every other genius that he is perhaps out of the range of ordinary criticism. We see his hands, his feet, his legs, but we are too near the Colossus to see the whole in perspective. Time will alone gradually heighten our view of him. "He who wants the wealth of the Indies should take wealth to the Indies," is an old saying. Do we take anything to Shakespeare? And can we carry as yet a measure sufficiently large to guage in any way this giant?

That Shakespeare is behind his works is undoubted.

Everything points towards this truth. In the first place, no genius can so disassociate his works from himself in the subjective design, as not to betray himself, if the unity of the idea, hidden under the objective garb, is once seized. That Shakespeare's works are not exhaustive on their mere exoteric side, who can question? Does not a profound idea peep all through Hamlet? And can we not say the same for almost every play?

The theory we are about to enunciate in rationalizing Hamlet is as follows.

Shakespeare has employed art (after the manner of all genius) as the vehicle for his ideas and conceptions upon the greatest and profoundest of subjects — History. He has idealized in Prince Hamlet the spirit of truth-seeking, which realizes itself historically as progress. In that profound and philosophical character of the hero of the tragedy we read a typical idealization of humanity, impelled by that divine sense of justice, truth, and liberty, which, with its still voice, unrolls itself as that divine evolution called progress. The whole tragedy of Hamlet is therefore a Dramatic Philosophy of History. Hamlet himself is progress. Truth is not a concrete entity, but solely a relation; and its only expositor is history. Therefore it is alone in the latter that we must seek for the history of Prince Hamlet. There we find, as in the play, that the battle is not to the swift, nor to the strong, but to time alone. Hamlet's history is therefore the history of man during his apprenticeship of conflict. With the end of that conflict Hamlet's mission is accomplished, since he represents the spirit *warring* for truth alone.

On the other hand, the King represents Hamlet's antithesis. As error, opposition to truth, injustice, and stagnancy, Shakespeare has idealized in Claudius a gigantic type of evil and historical oppression. To kill Claudius and revenge his father is the sole aim of Hamlet. This, in our eyes, is symbolically to redress wrong, establish truth, and secure liberty. The whole action of the tragedy revolves upon the conflict of the King and Hamlet. That struggle is accordingly the antinomy of past and present, or truth and error. It is impossible to treat these abstractions by themselves. Therefore, under that law which overrules social development, and which Shakespeare evidently solved and divined three centuries ago, we must seek for the interpretation of Hamlet.

Ever mindful of the double unity of art and idea, which must be wedded to each other in exquisite harmony, Shakespeare has embodied in the central figures the qualities or sum totals of which their respective followers and supporters are the very constituents. Thus the King is a fiction, necessary for dramatic unity alone, and who is represented by his Lord Chamberlain and courtiers. Hamlet again symbolizes the action and progress of truth in history: He is also the sum total of his partisans.[1] Thus the irresolution and apparent inaction of Hamlet become constant action and continual destruction of the King, as each of his organs is successively killed by Hamlet. We at once recognize the weakness of Hamlet, to be remedied by time; and we notice that the death of the King can only be accomplished with the whole tragedy, since the latter is the history of the continual death of the King alone. It is here we notice the marvellous skill of Shakespeare. By embodying the King in several characters, he has succeeded in representing the gradual process and continuity of historical progress. Critics are impatient because Hamlet fails to kill the King at once. We would ask them, why truth does not realize itself at once?

---

[1] Shakespeare has evidently endeavoured to embody in characters the conflicting forces of history, which emerge in that resultant called Progress. Hamlet is this resultant.

Progress and truth are synonymous, and the former, as Mr. Herbert Spencer has assured us, is a very gradual movement. Hamlet, we again assert, is killing the King all through the play. Polonius, Rosencrantz, Guildenstern, Laertes, are successively destroyed; and, with his last support, the King has vanished. Thus, as Hamlet grows in strength and power, the King is proportionally weakened.

The action of the tragedy becomes first the detection of error by the birth of Hamlet.[1] Secondly, the action of Hamlet and its results. The latter is another expression for the growth of Hamlet; which Goethe has so wonderfully realized in those memorable and oft-quoted but misunderstood words: "Here is an oak planted in a vase fitted for the most delicate flowers, the roots strike out, the vessel flies to pieces."

In short, the growth of Hamlet is the growth of man, of progress—the expansion of thought. Hamlet is the oak, the King and his supporters the vase. The death of Polonius is the result of the growth of Hamlet, and thus the vase is broken. Let us be clearly understood. The King is slowly *dying* all through the play, because Hamlet is *acting* all through the tragedy also. Hamlet's monologues are the expressions of fresh impetus, of action and reaction gained from the growth of liberty, knowledge, and progress in general. The whole play is a picture of some of the past and a pure prophecy of much of the future. Let us now realize the character of the King through the detail of his supporters.

In Polonius Shakespeare has philosophically summed up certainty and absolutism; he is therefore the very backbone of the King. With his death the climax of the tragedy is reached. From that moment things take a new direction. Polonius is the authority which antiquity and tradition,

---

[1] This is the revival of learning.

when united with autocratic Ophelia (or the Church), form,
and admit of no question nor misgivings. Polonius represents broadly the past. Hamlet pictures in like manner the
present and future. Polonius is approached through Ophelia.
Hamlet first criticizes the latter. By doing this he is criticizing and inspecting Polonius. Father and daughter are
one—Church and State before the Reformation. With the
death of Polonius certainty is dead. Ophelia is the daughter
of tradition and of certainty. As the latter becomes shaken,
so she becomes incoherent, dissents, drowns herself, and is
buried. Laertes is a continuation of Polonius in a modified
form. Since error cannot be questioned until certainty be
shaken, the growth of Hamlet is pictured in his satire of
Ophelia and Polonius. Polonius is everything which resisted the Protestant Reformation. His death historically
is the accomplishment of that Reformation. From that
moment the past has been shaken by the present. Rationalism has more and more encroached its domains upon
the claims of antiquity and belief in tradition. Two forces
were face to face at the Reformation. On the one hand
reason, asserting itself through the growth of learning,
advanced its claims in the teeth of ignorance and the
voice of antiquity. On the other, custom resisted this
new and unprecedented assertion of the fallibility of the
past.

We now turn to two more of the King's supporters.
They are the two courtiers Rosencrantz and Guildenstern.
Here Shakespeare's genius has italicized itself. In these
two we recognize the great passive opponents of progress
and truth. They are indifference, opposition of the self-
interested in power, and that optimism which, benefitting
by error, maintains things to be at their very best. They
evade truth, or Hamlet, by means of sophistry and casuistry.
As long as they come between the King and Hamlet, the
latter can effect nothing permanent. Nothing in our whole

exposition is less ambiguous and less equivocal than Shakespeare's meaning here. He has distinctly realized the opposition which compromise and the languid indifference of the children of fortune would put in the teeth of progress and truth, or Hamlet. In continually dogging Hamlet, we find how Shakespeare has made them come between the King and our hero as a sort of shield. Hamlet effects nothing whilst with these two sycophants; and when he escapes them for the first time, we have the term *naked* in connexion with him. In these two characters Shakespeare has epitomized hypocrisy and the abuse of reason, by that immense privileged body who have thriven upon abuses in history, if they do not do so to-day. If we only turn to the opposers of free trade and of reform in this country, we realize, in the long struggle for justice and truth, the recent opposition of Rosencrantz and Guildenstern. Every true student of history will recognize their significance as hardly second to that of Polonius.

The next constituent of the King is Laertes. Here, again, Shakespeare's genius reveals itself. Having artistically to kill Polonius, Shakespeare felt he must yet continue him symbolically, as his power gradually and slowly decays. His son not inaptly takes his place as opponent to Hamlet. But he represents party, not a sole autocratic and tyrannical power. Laertes defends Ophelia as supporter of Church and State. The travels of Laertes, like the growth of Fortinbras, are understood by us as silent. Laertes represents not only his father, as the conservative and stable principle, but the growth of that principle by education into a party. Similarly Hamlet, by the aid of Horatio, represents the opposite, and progressive or liberal party. Thus the whole play is the conflict of the two forces, statical and dynamical, whose resultant is progress; and who are respectively individualism and authority.

As caution, Rosencrantz, by means of Guildenstern,

banishes Hamlet. They themselves provide. When our hero returns, it is as naked and alone. Shakespeare's meaning is undoubtedly as follows. Hamlet, as truth-seeking or progress, having in the death of Polonius fulfilled the death of intolerance and interference, has accomplished a great political mission. But before rationalism can again gather itself for another crisis, it must free itself from Guildenstern and Rosencrantz. This it does by means of Fortinbras or liberty, who rises with Hamlet, and is part of him. Fortinbras rises, in the very opening of the play, as abortive attempts at liberty. He disappears, to grow with Hamlet silently. This growth is typified in his sudden appearance as a large army in the centre of the play. Finally he comes in as conqueror at the end of the tragedy. He is part of Hamlet, and we are directly told in the Church-yard-scene that liberty and progress (or truth-seeking), were contemporary and identical births. The First Clown and Hamlet are one. Thus Hamlet is turned in upon himself. The monologue which follows the interview with the army of Fortinbras gives us to understand Hamlet benefits by liberty (accruing from the death of Polonius), to use his reason. In that use he gradually kills or escapes sophistry, casuistry, and indifference. We therefore believe England to typify science. The text is not unfavourable to such an hypothesis. For the Ambassadors of England are part holders of the dramatic situation at the end of the play. But this is a part we do not feel so certain of as the rest. We venture only to offer suggestions.

We may now turn to Hamlet and his partisans. Our theory here is the same as that we have enunciated with regard to the King. Hamlet is a synthesis of qualities. He is evolved in the first act as a force. His birth is the result of Bernardo, Horatio, and Marcellus, furthered by the Ghost. The play opens in the depth of the night. This typifies ignorance and the undoubted reign of corruption,

which is given in the words "Long live the King."
Presently Francisco is relieved. In short, scholarship arrives
in the shape of Horatio. But he is the product of those before
him, whom we suspect to be reading and printing. Doubt,
as a Ghost, illuminates this revival of learning. And the
whole go far to form a young Hamlet. Liberty arises with
Fortinbras contemporary with these events; and we are
thus given to understand that Hamlet is liberty, justice, and
knowledge in co-partnership. Truth or progress is thus
epitomized in Prince Hamlet.

In Hamlet's father we hear the ideal voice of Christianity. The Queen is simply human belief and custom.
Her marriage to Claudius is the corruption of Christianity
—the union of error in belief or belief in error. Hamlet is
son of belief, and of that unadulterated union of ideal justice
prior to the second century. Thus the gradual detection by
Hamlet of the murder of his father at the hands of his uncle,
is the artistic history of the Reformation. The Interlude
is actually and undoubtedly an artistic parallel of Luther
pointing out the corruption of the Romish Church. The
Ghost represents the revival and shadow of ideal truth and
justice, which, as scepticism, becomes a revelation in itself.
When the heart of the Queen is cleft in twain, we may
recognize Shakespeare's attempt to realize artistically the
Reformation completed in its Protestant schism. Thus
Hamlet's father is typical for truth as ideal justice, and
the divine spirit of Christianity itself. This may account for the references of Horatio and Hamlet in connexion with him. However, this interferes very little,
whether accepted or not, with the whole character of the
tragedy, or with its signification.

The most important and confirming solution of the tragedy
will be found in our treatment of the Churchyard-scene.
Here we find the very key of the play contained in the
contemporary origin of Clown, Hamlet, and the rise of

Fortinbras. Here we gasp for breath at the miraculous ingenuity and genius of Shakespeare. This scene has been a
veritable stumbling-block to all criticism. The introduction
of Clowns, and the curious conversations, are apparently out
of harmony with the rest of the play. But, by our solution,
the play comes out in double its striking clearness and
spiritual interpretational force. For this Churchyard-scene,
we maintain, is an epitome of progress and of the whole
play. The two Clowns are Time and Progress. The First
Clown is Hamlet himself. Shakespeare is laughing at us
when he says, " *Every fool can tell that.*"[1] Hamlet and the
Clown are one. Our hero is studying himself, and at once
parallels historical criticism and the study of historical
philosophy in general. In short, man learns how progress
arose, and what it signifies. It is this part of our solution
of Hamlet which we particularly insist upon, and which we
claim as exposition of the extraordinary ingenuity of Shakespeare's genius and art. By turning Hamlet in upon himself, by means of another character, artistically separate
but symbolically *identical*, Shakespeare gives us a sublime
picture of the present day as pure prophecy. Progress is
epitomized in this Churchyard-scene, where the ridicule
which kills by criticism, metaphysical discussion, and satire,
are given in two Clowns. They are actually Time and Progress, or Hamlet himself reforming over great space of time.
Finally, Hamlet begins to study the science of history or
progress, and in doing this he studies himself. When he
learns how he was born, and that he is related to liberty
and knowledge in general, we may not be thought too bold
if we parallel such a recognition with Mr. Buckle's "History
of Civilization." However, there it stands, as a question
which criticism will finally decide to be the most marvellous

---

[1] The wit lies in Hamlet asking the Clown (himself) *when he (himself) was
born.* " *Every fool can tell that.*"

piece of art and prophecy ever conceived and forestalled by genius, or let it perish as the wild chimera of a madman.

In conclusion, feeling how out of place it would be to carry into detail an interpretation of Hamlet, which might be rejected by criticism altogether, we have refrained from expanding this little work into those dimensions which could alone do justice to the subject. Sufficient for us if we have thrown a new light over this sublime tragedy.

Hastily written, our essay requires a few remarks in the Introduction, if not in the Preface. Hamlet is a subject which is always developing: it never stands still. We fancy we have not sufficiently insisted upon the nature of the hero himself. To us Hamlet represents humanity and the growth of rationalism. He is both progress, truth-seeking, and liberalism. In the history of Hamlet we read the history of man.

We wish to insist also upon the identity of Hamlet with Horatio. The latter seems the scholarship of the Hamlet school of thought. Progress, liberty, and knowledge are the constituents of Hamlet. They give birth to the latter in simultaneous interaction. The Players, therefore, are Hamlet himself in action. And they act and react upon each other. These Players are undoubtedly typical for the Reformers.

Again, we would call notice to the revival of learning, which we imagine is the main cause in the birth of Hamlet. That revival is pictured in the speech of Polonius to Reynaldo. Reynaldo is to combat all unorthodoxy. Whilst Laertes well represents his father in literature. This speech, coming immediately after the first act, when Hamlet and his friends determine "to go in together," shows us what Laertes typifies. It is the step which Polonius takes to combat the spread of learning and rationalism. To have neglected it would have been to overlook the direction Laertes takes. And the travels of Laertes represent that learning itself very well. Hamlet and Laertes both represent two branches which the revival of learning split itself into. One was inquiry, reason, rationalism, resulting in progress, science, and liberalism. The other, theological orthodoxy and toryism; opposing Hamlet, and leading into the mild conservatism of to-day, which threatens some day to coalesce with the principles of Hamlet (in all but name). Laertes defends tradition, antiquity, authority, *the past.* Hamlet attacks all the above. The result is a question of time alone.

We would remark here, that Hamlet is, in short, not only a political play, but essentially a philosophical one. For its philosophy is the philosophy of development, of the growth of knowledge, liberty, and progress. It is highly optimistic if so taken, as it looks upon time as the friend of man in the long run. Therefore we have termed it the "Philosophy of History" of our Poet. The Philosophy of History embraces two principles, individualism and authority. Their mutual interaction is progress. We quote from the recent volume of Professor Flint upon the Philosophy of History :

"As soon as political thought comes forth into life, it is found to oscillate between two poles—between despotism and anarchy—the extreme of social authority and the extreme of individual independence. Before political thought awakens, social authority predominates. The man as an individual does not exist, but is merged in the family, the clan, city, or nation. But in every progressive society there comes a time when its stronger minds feel that they are not merely parts of a social organism, that they have a life and destiny, rights and duties of their own, and simply as men. There are then two principles in the world—the principle of authority and the principle of liberty, the principle of society and the principle of individualism. These two principles co-exist at first in a few individuals ; but, in process of time, they come not only to co-exist in some degree in all, but to manifest *themselves apart*, and then *there are not only two principles in the individual, but two parties in the state; the one* inclining more to the side of *social authority*, and the other more *towards individual independence —a conservative* and a *liberal party;* each party existing in virtue of its assertion of a truth, but existing only as a party, because it does not assert the whole truth—each conferring its special services—each having its special dangers —*each being certain to ruin any society in which it succeeds in crushing the other—but the two securing both order and progress*, partly by counteracting each other, and partly by co-operating with each other."—(Introduction to first volume of Philosophy of History.)

The italics in the above wonderful masterpiece of political philosophy are our own. We claim for Hamlet the principle above illustrated. And Hamlet is built as a tragedy upon such principles. On the one side we have Hamlet, who, with his friends, represents liberty, individualism, progress —the rights of man. On the other, we have authority, certainty, and the whole array of the social forces. The history of the story of Hamlet is the history of the conflict of these two parties ; the result is order, yet progress, without anarchy, and the whole is the largest generalization upon the Philosophy of History as yet extant. We have identified our hero (Hamlet) with truth, the King with error. Critics may quarrel over the distinction, but the principle is the same. Truth is ultimately with Hamlet. And the whole of historical progress is the rejection of past errors hitherto considered truths, and the adoption of the latter in their place. Thus truth and error are at the bottom of all the great questions which agitate humanity. In conclusion, we offer the whole more as a suggestion and an hypothesis than as a solution, and we are quite ready to acknowledge the insufficiency of some of the evidence adduced.

Shakespeare has embodied in the characters of the play
the collective essence of the principles of society and the
principles of individualism. In Hamlet we recognize progress, truth, and liberty. The latter is expressed through
the triumphant march of Fortinbras, which is going on all
through the play. His introduction in the middle of the
tragedy is to give expression to this march of liberty.
Horatio expresses the growth of liberal knowledge in Hamlet.
His scholarship is born through Bernardo and Marcellus,
and, when expressed in the symbol of Hamlet, is the growth
of rationalism. Justice, freedom, rationalism, and thus progress, are condensed in the character of Prince Hamlet and
his friends.

On the other side, we have the King and Queen as mere
symbols of error in belief and belief in error. Superstition,
tyranny, falsehood, and every form of despotic authority and
oppression, are contained in the character of the King. His
death is therefore gradual, and contained in the death of his
Lord Chamberlain and courtiers. Polonius sums up the
principle of authority, bigotry, and tradition. Certainty
and infallibility are his characteristics. He thus embodies
the chief essence of social stability and order. He is the
continuation of history, and he is the very backbone of the
King. In his son Laertes we notice the same principle,
only modified and expressed through literature. Ophelia is
also the heir of tradition and of infallibility. The two
courtiers, Rosencrantz and Guildenstern, fill up the vacuum,
and represent perhaps the greatest opponents Hamlet has
to deal with. In the indifference and sophistry of these
courtiers we recognize the great enemies to truth and liberty,
and we are struck especially here with Shakespeare's genius.
He has succeeded in embodying in these characters the very
essence of that great body which, whilst professing to love
truth, are generally indifferent to it (whilst they remain un-
affected by it), and are its deadly enemies when it touches

them in any degree whatever.[1]   The whole of history, and particularly the history of opposition to reform, is alive with them. We have only to turn to the history of the early part of this century in England to realize, in the opposition to the Repeal of the Corn Laws and Reform in general, the power and activity of this party in their persistent action of hindering and embarrassing Hamlet. Rosencrantz and Guildenstern are the representatives of those who thrive upon abuses and injustice, who hate Reformers, and who make them suffer for their love of justice and truth. Their means of action are sophistry, casuistry, hypocrisy, cunning, and evasion. Naked truth alone can crush them, and naked truth attains a rigid exposition and unequivocal demonstration in the growth of knowledge, rationalism, and science alone. England serves this purpose in the play, and Hamlet having escaped them, returns *naked*.

The conflict of individuality and authority continues in a modified form between Hamlet and Laertes. Osric represents the criticism of society, which, as opinion, is the sole referee. Finally man's apprenticeship is accomplished, and Hamlet (expressing the action of the conflict alone), having performed his mission, dies.

This, in our opinion, is the main outline of the solution and rationalistic interpretation of Hamlet. The play is thus the battle-field of two political and historical parties. Those are the weak out of power and the strong in power. The subject of the conflict is that of liberty, truth, and

---

[1] " Who does not know this temper of the man of the world, that worst enemy of the world ? His inexhaustible patience of abuses, that only torment others ; his apologetic words for beliefs that may perhaps not be so precisely true as one might wish, and institutions that are not altogether so useful as some might think possible ; his cordiality towards progress and improvement in a general way, and his coldness and antipathy to each progressive proposal in particular ; his pigmy hope that life will one day become somewhat better, punily shivering by the side of his gigantic conviction that it might well be infinitely worse."

justice—rationalism and individuality—against ignorance, authority, and falsehood. Time alone is the friend of Hamlet, and the King dies slowly through his supports. The madness of Hamlet is the artistic expression of his evil in the eyes of his enemies. His irresolution is another artistic expression for weakness, which Time alone can rectify. The monologues and soliloquies are the effects of action and reaction, expressed through time in the growth of knowledge, liberty, and crises.

Finally, we may observe, two interpretations are open to the student. One is to identify the play with much of the history of the last few centuries, or to merely embrace the more general and catholic views of a Philosophy of History alone. In the latter case Polonius must stand for the principle of certainty, and with his overthrow the climax of a Philosophy of History would be well expressed. The growth of knowledge, liberty, are expressed in the word *Truth*. And this growth is the history of Prince Hamlet. Although we have adopted a historical parallelism in our interpretation, we are not inclined, upon such a profound subject, to dogmatize, and we disclaim any pretensions beyond hopeful and fruitful suggestion.[1]

---

[1] The reader will think perhaps we have fitted history to Hamlet, and begged the whole question. But this is the astounding character of the play—it does parallel modern history up to this very hour. Why? Because Shakespeare *probably* seized the secondary laws of historical science. Through the modification and continuity of authority, resulting from the growth of individualism or liberty, Shakespeare has anticipated the future.

A SUGGESTIVE
KEY TO HAMLET.[1]

DRAMATIS PERSONÆ.

HAMLET—A little History of Man.

Claudius } Error, injustice, etc.   { (Marriage) corruption
Gertrude } Human belief and custom {   of Christianity.

Hamlet's Father—Unadulterated Christianity prior to the second century, ideal truth and justice.

BULWARKS OF ERROR OR CONSTITUENTS OF THE KING.

Orthodoxy and machinery prior to the Reformation.

Polonius { (Weight of many). Certainty or infallibility, authority, antiquity, and tradition. Bigotry, intolerance, absolutism.

Reynaldo { (Probably inquisition) (discouragement of learning) (orthodox bias).

Relations of Norway } *Voltimand*—Repression by force, persecution (?). *Cornelius*—Hard-heartedness (?).

Indifference and hatred to truth } *Rosencrantz*—Opposition of those who benefit by abuses. *Guildenstern* — (Method of defence) — Sophistry, casuistry, hypocrisy, and evasion.

Children of Polonius { *Ophelia*—Church. *Laertes*—(Modified Polonius)—Historical continuity of authority, orthodox literature, conservatism.

Osric—Society and criticism.

King and Queen, Error in Belief (Allied by Custom). } KING.

BULWARKS OF TRUTH OR HAMLET.

Soldiers (Whole workers, body and mind) { *Francisco* *Bernardo* *Marcellus* } End of Dark Ages, first movement of the growth of knowledge (revival of learning), probably reading, criticism, inquiry, and printing.

Horatio—Spirit of justice, independence, and scholarship, resulting from above.

Born the same day (*Vide* Act v. Sc. 1) { (*Fortinbras*—Might and right—Liberty. *First Clown*—(Artistic double to Hamlet)—Progress. *Hamlet*—Progress.

Ghost of Hamlet's Father—Revival of Christianity—Doubt.

} HAMLET.

Interlude—Reformation.

---

[1] This key is of course absurdly crude and partial, but it simplifies the right study of the play by not embarrassing us with too many abstractions. It is ideal.

"I am very far from censuring the plan of Hamlet; on the other hand, I believe there never was a grander one invented; *nay, it is not invented, it is real.*"— *Wilhelm Meister's Apprenticeship.*

"In Hamlet we are taught another lesson: the hero is without a plan, but the piece is full of plan."— *Wilhelm Meister's Apprenticeship.*

"Genius has but little concern with the moment; the 'eternities are its seed field.'"—*Dr. Maudesley's Essays.*

"The characteristic of genius of the first order is for each to produce a copy of man. All present humanity with her portrait, some laughing, some crying, some thinking. The latter are the greatest. Plautus laughs and gives man Amphitryon. Rabelais laughs and gives man Gargantua. Cervantes laughs and gives man Don Quixote. Beaumarchais laughs and gives man Figaro. Molière weeps and gives man Alcestis. Shakespeare thinks and gives man Hamlet. Æschylus thinks and gives man Prometheus. Æschylus and Shakespeare are immense."—*Translated from Victor Hugo's Shakespeare.*

"Every play of Shakespeare is a true poem, and has the spiritual unity that is in every great work of art. Each play has its own theme in some essential truth of life, which is its soul expressed in action, and with which every detail is in exquisite accord."—*Professor Morley's History of English Literature.*

HAMLET;

OR,

SHAKESPEARE'S PHILOSOPHY OF HISTORY.

CHAPTER I.

IT has often been remarked that the greatness of great
men consists in their living before their age. They
are in advance of their contemporaries. If this holds true
in every case, it must be true of that giant of all giants,—
and whom could we mean alone by this except William
Shakespeare? Was our Poet in advance of his age? Did
he peer into Futurity? Did he foresee, through the dark
avenues of Time, the events which would be delivered from
the womb of centuries? What opinions had he upon all
those questions which are the prerogatives of all genius?
Did he realize Progress in the sense that we do in this age?
What were his political and historical prognostications?
These are questions which cannot at present apparently be
answered. Nothing is absolutely known of our Poet's
private life. His works are Sphinxes, which, ever propound-
ing riddles, have as yet in *no one* case received any satisfactory solution.

SHAKESPEARE was born the same year Galileo was born
(1564). He was in the full tide of his manhood when
Giordano Bruno suffered at the stake for maintaining the
Heliocentric doctrine (1600). And Shakespeare, of all men,
must have realized most forcibly what the age he lived in

meant. He must have settled in his own mind, with genius-like prescience, whether Authority, Antiquity, and Bigotry were to crush out Reason, Inquiry, and Truth; or whether the latter, taking a fulcrum in the glorious movement of the Reformation, would finally emancipate man from the thral-dom of the Night of Ignorance. Here was our Poet living in a most marvellous age: one in which darkness was be-hind, and all was crescent, though faint, light in front. The world re-echoed with the triumphs of the Reformation, with the wonders of the New World, with the scientific truths of the "world moves." Perhaps the sixteenth century is the one most important in man's history to man. In it was contained the birth of all that liberty, of all that enterprise, and of all that individuality, which has developed into the nineteenth century. Of course all history is con-tinuous and unbroken. But some ages sum up the silent work of centuries. Such an age was the sixteenth. Blow after blow had been dealt against that tyrrany of man over man, which had kept authority in a state of stagnancy, and individualism in a state of thraldom. Light had been steal-ing in during the last three centuries, to accumulate at last in the glorious sun of the Reformation. Such was the strength of this movement, that it infected every department of human thought. It was simply pure air and light after darkness and corruption. No wonder this age abounds in illustrious men. Like caged birds, they realized their free-dom in bursts of rapturous song. Spenser, Shakespeare, and Ben Jonson are singers of that age; Raleigh and the discoverers of the New World are the men of action of that age; whilst we have science represented by Coperni-cus, Kepler, Galileo, and Bruno. The world had simply, after some six centuries of torpor and night, awakened itself out of its lethargy, and was realizing the birth of Rationalism and its growth. But the very fact that England enjoyed, under Elizabeth, such a great amount of toleration, must have forced itself, in contrast, upon the mind of our Poet. How his great mind must have sympathized with the Copernican system, and with the glowing description of

Bruno (in England), upon the hypothesis of "a plurality of worlds"! Is it possible, we have to ask ourselves, Shakespeare escaped the enthusiasm of the age? We feel at once how absurd such a question sounds. But, at the same time, we are face to face with another question, and one which requires an emphatic solution: and we immediately wonder why his plays contain nothing which seems to point in any way to those times and those conflicts which were the birthright of his age. The question is easily put upon two footings, which admit of no equivocation whatever.

Either we do not comprehend the Plays of Shakespeare, or he has taken no literary interest in the great topics of his day. These topics are, wonderful to say, exactly the ones calculated to attract genius. They were topics of Reason *versus* Authority and Tradition. Dante had prophesied the Reformation: has one greater than Dante prophesied anything? Bacon sat down and prophesied: surely one greater than Bacon has done the same. And the topics which were agitated in the age of William Shakespeare were of an absorbing kind. Religion and dawning science were at deadly feud. The latter was in the throes of a re-birth; struggling for its very life. Liberty, Knowledge, and Progress—ever co-partners and co-heirs—had embraced, had shaken hands, and were beginning their endless march in the van of humanity. These are topics which interest most the greatest minds.

On the one side, we have to confess that our age has not grown up to our Poet's height. On the other, we are met with the astounding necessity of showing Shakespeare's mind to be deficient in all those qualities which go in other men towards greatness and comprehensiveness. For what is a great mind? Largeness of view upon all those subjects which must be eternally absorbing to man. Those are—the nature of man, of the future life, of his destiny below, and of his destiny hereafter,—philosophy and history,—man in the macrocosm, and man in the microcosm;—these are topics which genius never fails to handle. But, if we are not entirely mistaken, the text of Shakespeare, taken simply verbatim, gives us no positive views upon these subjects. Splendid as the language, magnificent as the poetry of thought, we still fail to find any definite opinions. Nothing is to be found which we could call a discovery. Shakespeare (as yet) has added nothing but beauty to man's store of literature ; his own opinions, upon all those subjects which have agitated and will continue for ever to agitate mankind, are not to be found in the mouths of his characters. He was far too great an objective genius to identify himself subjectively with his *dramatis personæ*. He identified himself with his meaning in quite another way. And to that we shall arrive by and by. Had Shakespeare any opinions upon history? Of course he had. But where are they then? Had he a philosophy of history of his own? Had he a philosophy pertaining to himself concerning religion, concerning politics, concerning the future of man? We reply, with the greatest confidence, that he had; and those who read his plays may find them there.

We have a distinct charge to bring against all Shakespearian criticism. And this charge consists that Shakespeare has been robbed of the principles which underlie all works of the imagination. Critic after critic, with the exception of Goethe (who plagiarized from his discovery), deny tacitly to William Shakespeare what they willingly grant to a Cervantes or a Swift. Nay, to come down to modern times, we find novelists like Hawthorne, the late Lord Lytton, and George Eliot, enjoying their literary rewards based upon true principles. Every great work is a creation. It does not copy individualities. It creates or copies universalities. What is permanent in man in the abstract, either ridiculous or sublime, that is copied alone. It may be an age is thus exemplified, or it may be an age is ridiculed. Again, it may be the decay of a great empire, or the rise of a great power. Voltaire, who ridiculed Hamlet (because it was beyond him and his age), wrote his plays upon such principles. Witness Alzire, Mahomet, etc. And shall we deny to William Shakespeare what we grant, without a murmur, to his very inferiors? Our Poet, it will be found, was the sole master and originator of the principles which underlie all Dramatic Art. Goethe, who discovered them in Shakespeare, has given us a complete exegesis of the same. And what are they? The typical representation of generalities clothed in the particularization of idealized art. The difference between a great work of art and a work of no art is—in one, the grandeur of the conception and its faultless execution; in the other, the want of any conception, or its poverty united to faulty execution. When we have poorness of conception, and good execution, we recognize that finish, or that the technic itself has solely run away with the whole. A great conception may be faulty in workmanship, and yet, on account of its grandeur, may be redeemed from oblivion. For example, Bunyan's Pilgrim's Progress is a work whose conception is most grand; but the whole, as a work of art, is most imperfect. Indeed it cannot be classed as a work of art; for unity of plan is the essential of art: whereas we have no unity; half is plain allegory, and half is here half-finished art. A work of art has its two sides. These are the esoteric and exoteric. An artist, no matter whether in the Catholic sense, or in the narrower sense of painter, sculptor, or musician, finds in art the vehicles of his ideas. The better they are expressed, the more perfect the art. But one side, instead of revealing the other at a glance, serves rather to obscure it at first sight, though at a profounder view to reveal it. Mere copying is not creation. Our ideas are our own, and when we have clothed them in art, we are then alone worthy of being styled artists. God is alone the artist of artists. How simple is all in this world to the uninquiring! How self-evident does the realism of the every-day world appear! Yet philosophy, on deeper inspection, is still at variance upon this same realism. Let us turn to Shakespeare, and apply all this to him. If art, and his art particularly, was simply histrionic, why has he plagiarized, for example, Hamlet from an old story in Saxo-Grammaticus? Why not create something quite original? We maintain that in the same play he has created something quite original. But it is not the exoteric and text side alone of the play. It is the esoteric and symbolical idea upon which the play is alone in its originality based. The story from which our Poet borrowed served as a mere peg whereon to hang his great drama of the Philosophy of History.

Why is it we are all fascinated by Hamlet? Because, being an attribute of human nature generalized, we feel a portion of him in ourselves. Through his artistic garb we instinctively feel something which we dimly recognize—a great truth which we cannot express. We are all true to ourselves in something, if not in everything; and Hamlet strikes this chord. The same may be said of Polonius. Impossible to point him out individually, yet we are all well acquainted with him. And this sort of ambiguous recognition puzzles us, and we ask ourselves vaguely where. Again, who does not recognize Guildenstern and Rosencrantz, and again the same sort of intimate acquaintanceship and doubtful whereabouts. As in all great art, the generalization holds good, but the individualization is nowhere in particular. This constitutes the greatness of Shakespeare—a greatness hitherto unrationalized; but a greatness which every age recognizes. For Shakespeare's characters are the essence and generalized attributes of collective humanity in all times and throughout history. A great artist imitates God. He creates a mystery. This mystery fascinates whilst it perplexes. Like all problems, it is wooed by humanity as long as it remains a mystery or a marvel. This mystery is created with a two-fold purpose. First, to convey to posterity truths that are prematurely born; and secondly to obey the canons of true art, which admit of no one-sidedness. Again, an artist is compelled, by his love of the beautiful, to clothe and paint his ideas, be it in poetry, in stone, or in canvas; but he feels there is little pause between true art and rationalization. In fact, all art is the harmony of instinctive, and often unknown, rationalization. The greater the rationalization, the greater the art, if art it be. But the poetic or dramatic mode of expression may be lacking, and then we have prose, science, logic. As Professor Ribot aptly says, "the metaphysician is only a poet who has missed his vocation." Thus the artist, like Shakespeare, feels his work only perfect when the union of the esoteric and exoteric sides are most perfect. When the art stands perfect as art alone, and the truth of the work is in perfect harmony with it, it is, as Shakespeare repeatedly tells us in his sonnets, the marriage of Truth and Beauty. And we feel the truth mysteriously, and vaguely, peeping out everywhere in Hamlet.

We are, through all our criticisms upon Shakespeare, driven to one inevitable conclusion. That is, his works are still a mystery to man. The art of reading them is still unborn; or, though appearing to possess the greatest comprehensiveness, and the subtlest brain ever possessed by mortal man, he refused to employ it any other way, but embellishing plagiarized stories for merely histrionic and dramatic purposes. But who can believe this? It is essentially the prerogative of great minds to prophesy. In the law of the present they surmise the law of the future. Dante foretold the coming Reformation. Bacon sat down and prophesied the marvellous mechanical fecundity of the present day. Jomini, imbued with military genius, forestalled the battle of Jena. Minds are not so much unlike in quality as different in degrees of power. We may depend upon it, if Shakespeare did prophesy, he prophesied more surely and more splendidly than any man before or after him. What did he foresee? Here is the question which drives men over and over again to make his life and works the subject of their own toil.

What we profess to do in this pamphlet is to offer an hypothesis upon the subject of Hamlet. Every one has a conception of his own concerning this play. But it is one which is growing more and more positive every day. That conception is that Hamlet is a sort of philosophy of our Poet. It is so in one sense, but it is a Philosophy of History. Men are beginning to grasp the fact that there is more in Hamlet than meets the eye. That Hamlet is not an individual is also gaining ground. As Dr. Maudesley says, he is an "idealized creation" of humanity. We begin to recognize the symbolical character of Shakespeare's works. They are Sphinxes, which have been unread for three centuries, and they still offer as yet insolvable problems. The Germans have been long before us in this direction. Following the leadership of Goethe (who of all men has furnished, as yet, the most exhaustive and profound criticism upon Hamlet), they recognize in Hamlet's character analogies which have paralleled their own country's history. But Goethe's work of the Wilhelm Meister is, as yet, another enigma to be solved. As Lord Lytton justly remarks, it is undoubtedly the apprenticeship of man in life, and of man in art. But the criticisms which it contains upon Hamlet are of too searching a nature to be quite understood as yet. The Wilhelm Meister's apprenticeship is a plagiarism of Hamlet. It is a prose Hamlet; not written as an exegesis of the play alone, but as a creation upon similar lines, and in many respects the same. This will be thoroughly established by and by.

In the meanwhile we propose to take the play of Hamlet in hand. We shall attempt, first, to deal with the action. Then with the text in connexion with each character. And finally to contemplate its unity by the light so afforded. The most profound modern work upon Shakespeare, as yet, has been Professor Gervinus's Commentaries. But, beyond thoughtful criticisms, no new light is thrown upon the subject. The same may be said of Carl Elze's Essays. Professor Morley, in his History of English Literature, makes a very fair attempt to solve the spiritual unity of the Merchant of Venice. But the right sort of insight is still lacking.

To turn to Hamlet itself. The action of the play centres upon what may be termed the conflict of two parties. On the one hand, we have a King supported by five courtiers, a Lord Chamberlain, his son and daughter. On the other, a Prince, heir to a throne he never succeeds to, and his friends (two officers and Horatio). We have one Fortinbras, who ostensibly takes neither side. But he evidently acts powerfully upon Hamlet, and he runs, like a chorus, obscurely through the play from first to last. The whole action is thus a battle between the strong in power and the weak out of power. Mysteriously our sympathies run with the weak. It is part of the action of the play that Hamlet should only find out that his enemies have unjustly got power after they are in possession.

The whole play is the action or conflict of Hamlet and friends *versus* King and supporters. Hamlet wants power and resolution to effect his revenge. But time alone brings it; and this time is such an important element in the play, that we believe it is the groundwork of it. The action of the play, again, is one in which the King is always losing power, and Hamlet gaining it. For example: two of the King's supporters, Voltimand and Cornelius, disappear at an early period from the play. Thus, two of Hamlet's enemies are gone, and the King's power lessened. Next, the chief bulwark of the King dies at Hamlet's hands. With the death of Polonius the King is visibly alarmed. So Hamlet is banished. Next, Guildenstern and Rosencrantz disappear, and Hamlet comes back alone. Lastly, Laertes dies; when Hamlet kills the King, dies himself, and the drama is brought to a close. Let it be noticed how Hamlet gets bolder and bolder, and more resolute in every act of the play. He cannot kill the King, because he lacks power. But he kills Polonius, and that is the only way to get at the King. He is still nearer to the King when Rosencrantz and Guildenstern are dead. And nearest when Laertes dies by his own poison. We must, therefore, take these supporters of the King as indispensables to his power and evil doing. Let us begin with Voltimand and Cornelius. They evidently are only necessary at an early stage of the play. They shortly disappear. All they complete, or the part they play, is the putting down of a revolt. They are sent to Norway. They savour of direct force. They disappear. So we must take it that force disappears. Next comes Polonius, who uses cunning, stratagem, and interference. He is fond of espionage. Witness the task he sets his servant Reynaldo. He repeats himself over and over again. He is certain he can find truth anywhere. He is full of pedantic words. He is old. He is tedious. What is he? Antiquity on account

of his repetition, certainty on account of his self-conceit,
and thus infallibility. We therefore see how perfectly
Polonius realizes Tradition, which repeats over the same
monotone; and Antiquity, on account of his age; also
Pedantry, in his garrulous unmeaning jargon. He is wrong
in all his surmises, yet shows unrivalled worldly wisdom.
He is the very back-bone of the King, and does all the
spying and dirty work of that monarch. Now, the death of
Polonius is peculiar. He is killed as if by accident.
Hamlet thought he was killing the King. And he was
killed because he interfered between Hamlet and his mother.
Is this an end of interference? Is this the end of religious
intolerance? The death of autocratic authority and tradition. The text, presently, will throw more light upon this
point. Thus another of the King's chief supports is gone.
And we must be struck with the helpless way Hamlet is
obliged to kill the King's bulwarks before he can get at the
King. And this leads us to conjecture that all these supporters of the King *are the very substance of the King
himself.* This is a conjecture which the text, by and by,
will strengthen. Hamlet only gets rid of what is immediately, and at a certain period, obstructive to himself. He
only kills Polonius when driven into it by his prying interference. Until this is done he cannot speak to his mother.
Again, he only plots against his former friends, Guildenstern
and Rosencrantz, when he reads the grand commission of
the King. But we are more especially struck with the irresolution of Hamlet. Let us also remark how this irresolution gets incentives to further resolution, from epochs in the
play. One of these is the appearance and revelation of the
Ghost. Again, the Player scene is another. The march of
Fortinbras a similar one. And yet, after all, the death of
the King is almost forced upon him. What is the meaning
of this apparent contradiction? It is not one; it merely is
meant to convey the meaning that the King and his supporters are one. The death of Laertes is the death of the
King. *Law* is the power which ties the hands of Hamlet.
Time alone sets them free in the last scene of all. After the

death of Polonius, Hamlet has two more enemies, who, pretending to be his friends, are enlisted in reality upon the King's side. Let us remark how these two, who are never far apart from each other, hunt in couples. And they offer a direct contrast to Polonius. For the interference and pedantry of the latter, they substitute a form of bad logic and optimistic view of life. They directly recommend the banishment of Hamlet. At first they are his friends. Latterly in the play Hamlet first suspects, then repudiates, and finally escapes from them.

Thus the action of the play is one of unbroken continuity. It is one of progress and development. The power of the King is constantly getting weakened. With his last bulwark, Laertes, he dies himself. Hamlet is the direct means of the removal of all the King's supports. Force, hard-heartedness, authority, bigotry, tradition, sophistry, optimism, casuistry, and conservatism disappear before Hamlet, one after another. Hamlet is only set *naked* in the kingdom, when Rosencrantz and Guildenstern are gone and are dead. He is no longer hampered with false logic. He is indeed naked. The action of the drama, we repeat, is one of development, of continuity. There is no break. It is all a chain of cause and effect, over which there rests—

> "A divinity that shapes our ends, rough hew them how we will."

And we also notice how action and reaction have their legitimate and historical expression in this sublime drama.

The Players are prompted by Hamlet; and they, in their turn, react upon him, giving him further force. The march of Fortinbras, as the chorus of liberty, acts and reacts in a similar manner. But there is a long pause, whilst Hamlet is being banished.

With regard to time, we must infer that epochs of moment and movements of great strength are alone dramatically portrayed in the action. The Player scene, which we shall endeavour to show is the Reformation itself, is thus the most important point in the whole action of the play. It is the direct recognition of error, and the drawing up of the two great forces of society in Europe. These are the stationary and the progressive. Antiquity, tradition, and the past are for the first time face to face with inquiry, reason, truth, or science and modern liberalism. From this point of the play events take a new turn. Hamlet is no longer the irresolute character some believe him to be. He soon (dramatically) kills Polonius. And from the death of the latter results the banishment of Hamlet. From the banishment of Hamlet results the death of Rosencrantz and Guildenstern. And, again, their death signifies the return of Hamlet. At this point we have a rapidity of action, which defies any further elaboration of the play as hitherto. Shakespeare, in all he did, was eclectic; and the fifth act of the play is in reality a chorus of condensed time, in which great change is represented in a striking and magnificent manner. But if we go back to the beginning of the drama, we shall find little or no action. The play opens with the deep stillness and darkness of the

" Dead waste and middle of the night."

" Not a mouse stirring."

One solitary sentinel alone on his watch ; and this solitary being reports himself as cold, and sick at heart. Nothing can be more impressive, and nothing could realize better the darkness and ignorance of the Middle Ages, which are so well expressed in the word ' waste.' This solitary sentinel, Francisco, strangely disappears, at once and for ever, from the play. And we ask ourselves why ? Because, if he is ignorance, as we suspect, his relief by Bernardo would be the relief of ignorance for enlightenment. And we suspect Bernardo to mean education of some sort, or the art of reading. And our reasons for this are very strong. In the first place, the word Bernardo spells ' Born read.' Whether this is simply accidental or otherwise, we leave to others to decide. But when coupled with similar results, and when classed with other facts of the same nature, we cannot escape the conviction forced upon us. Without specifying any direct attribute as to the spiritual meaning of Bernardo, we will call him the growth of knowledge. And we must notice that he is an officer, as is also his friend Marcellus. Now Professor Morley says, in his History of English Literature, that Shakespeare employs soldiers as symbols of whole workers, body and mind. Francisco may thus stand for the first feeble inquiries and questionings, which led from the end of the Dark Ages (about the end of the tenth century) towards that ever-increasing movement which ended in the Reformation. And the whole of the first act of Hamlet is in accordance with this theory. For it is one of the accretion of doubt, and a growing certainty of the Ghost's reality and truth. It is questionable, even, if Bernardo and Marcellus do not go far to form Hamlet himself. For Hamlet does not appear until the second scene of the first act. And Bernardo and Marcellus, like Francisco, disappear from the play after the end of the first act. And why? Because they are understood in Hamlet. Hamlet himself says:

> " Let us go in together ;
> And still your fingers on your lips, I pray.
> The time is out of joint ;—O cursed spite !
> That ever I was born to set it right !
> *Nay, come, let's go together.*"

Thus we see Hamlet is himself an embodiment of many elements. And those elements are, to our minds, inquiry and doubt, a love of justice and truth, and liberty. The first scene of the first act already points to a gradual increase of light. And it ends with the beautiful words of Horatio:

> " But, look, the morn, in russet mantle clad.
> Walks o'er the dew of yon high eastern hill."

The darkness of the Dark Ages is thus typically portrayed as breaking up. The dawn of modern Europe was dispersing the vapours of credulity and superstition. Confidence in the Ghost gradually culminates into a greater and greater scepticism on the part of Hamlet. And how beautifully is all this gradually growing scepticism pictured in the play ! Seen by no one at first but Bernardo; then by Marcellus and Horatio ; it remains a mere spectre, that cannot and will not be understood or questioned. This Ghost of Hamlet's father well represents the shadows of the mind, which grow in intensity until they become a revelation itself. This doubt is communicated unto young Hamlet, who alone can understand his father's spirit, for Truth is the son of Doubt.

The whole of the first act is a growing scepticism, which accumulates into a force of itself. And the action of the play is one of silently gathering forces : forces which are quietly surveying each other's strength. Fear on the one side, hatred on the other. But still waiting for more decisive means wherewith to catch the conscience of the King.

What we merely wish to endeavour to instil into the reader's mind is, that *Time* is the groundwork of the play, and *Time* alone. Perhaps we may now announce our interpretation of Hamlet as a whole. That is, a Philosophy of the History of Europe from the end of the Dark Ages, and carried into the remote future. We are certain that the truth of this will be eventually established ; and we offer what little thought we have to the elucidation of the problem. Hamlet is thus a history and a prophecy ; but more of the latter than of the former. It is the most valuable of all Shakespeare's works, and that on account of its containing his political, religious, and social opinions and prognostications.

We lay down as unquestionable, to all profound students of Hamlet, the fact, that Time is the stage upon which the play is built. Mankind the actors. Truth and Error the action of the drama. Shakespeare distinctly recognized the great dynamical principle of Modern History in Europe. This principle is the resultant of two other principles, namely that of authority and that of liberty. The principle of society and the principle of individualism. History, to be History, and not mere Eastern stagnancy, is the product or resultant of these two forces. They may be paralleled in mechanics, as the effect of gravitation *versus* motion. One is cohesion, the other motion. One acting without the other is stagnancy or anarchy. An harmonious interaction is the result of a good constitution, which regulates the pace and position of each. The reaction of to-day is a self-adjust-

ing increase of gravitation, by which the elliptic of progress
is for the time modified. Shakespeare undoubtedly was a
firm believer in progress, and understood history better, aye
far better, than even the late Mr. Buckle, or the great Her-
mann Lotze. He clearly realized that all progress depends
upon the amount of *knowledge and liberty* an age or country
possesses. And therefore he has made Time the great ally
and friend upon whom Hamlet is dependent. Continuity of
cause and effect is seen running all through the tragedy. The
revelation of the Ghost is the key upon which the whole
play depends. And Shakespeare has made a shadow, which
grows in consistency, the means of this revelation. Scepticism is thus upheld as the liberator of modern Europe. But
how still more do we recognize in Ophelia and Laertes this
relation of cause and effect in continuity. In making these
two the descendants of Polonius, how true Shakespeare is to
actual history! Who is Ophelia? Who is Laertes? Both the
children of Tradition and Antiquity. Both the scions of
authority, they are opposed to all liberalism, which is only
individualism. Laertes is ever true to his parentage. For
what is a true conservative but a child of authority, of the
past, of antiquity. His very conservatism indorses the
authority of the past. And what is liberalism but the child
of the future, hatched in doubt, and nurtured by inquiry.
Thus the continuity of Polonius is verified in Laertes.
Polonius only dies in one form, to give rise to another modified Polonius in Laertes. And Ophelia, who is a Church,
whose very essence is the weight of authority, antiquity,
infallibility, and tradition, must necessarily go mad and
perish with the fall of these her very foundations.

Thus Time and Continuity are the basis and action upon
which the drama depends. We can already get a glimpse
at the way Shakespeare understood social evolution — a
science still in its infancy, and upon which our Poet will still
be our best instructor. Indeed no Philosophy of History
can be more perfect than Hamlet. In it are contained all
the laws of social development contributing to future equilibrium. And now what is the action upon which the play

depends? Upon the struggle between the King and Hamlet.
Rather let us be clear, and say at once *Truth* and *Error*.
Broadly this is the subject-matter of the whole drama. All
the characters are ranged upon one side or other of these
two forces. But Time is the great ally of Hamlet. There
was no doubt who would ultimately win, in our Poet's lofty
mind. He saw how ignorance and error are but twin
brothers, whom the God of time and light would ultimately
strangle. Hamlet, as we have said, is truth. He is the
direct result of doubt, of liberty, and of inquiry. And from
these he gets fresh force, and to these he, in his own turn, im-
parts fresh force. Thus the play is one vast conflict. An
historical and prophetical conflict, which at the present
moment has its counterpart in the contemporary age so well
portrayed, that it is marvellous men do not see it.

But let us now turn to the only true expositor of the
drama. That is the text. Without its overwhelming
evidence in our favour, it would be rash indeed to dogmatize
upon such a subject. But we remain firm in the conviction
that we shall carry the enlightened reader along with us.
That is to say, if history has to him any meaning, and such
a meaning as Mr. Buckle would especially give utterance.
To those who look upon history as a broken chain, as a
system of isolated facts, springing out of the conditions of
a spontaneous will, we say "Cudgel not thy brains" over
Hamlet. But let those who see in history a psychological
cause and effect, as much under law as the courses of the
stars, let them, we say, open Hamlet and read well into
futurity.

Again, we would say a word to those who repudiate the
attempt to rationalize the details of art. All imperfect art,
we grant, refuses to be so handled. But Shakespeare's was
and is perfect art, and allows itself to be examined micro-
scopically in every line and in every word. The closer the
inspection, the greater the reward. There are others, who,
by some extraordinary process of logic, consider the very
conception of there existing a further meaning to our Poet's
works as rank blasphemy. And we should ask these persons

why so? Can they furnish an answer? Does it invalidate the exoteric art of the conception, and does it lower the claim of an author to genius? We would rather reply, no man has genius in art who does not possess the quality of clothing his abstractions in the garb of idealized art. If he has no abstractions, he may be an artist, but certainly no genius, in the sense of creation alone. To proceed with the text of the play. We shall not touch yet the beginning. First, that we have already touched upon it. Secondly, that the chief characters, seized in their essential meaning, will make the earlier parts of the play speak for itself. And thirdly, that there is little in the text of a sufficiently clear evidence to be of any use in demonstrating any deduction from such a part. We therefore shall not go regularly from the very commencement of the play line for line. For it would be beyond the limits of this paper. And we believe greater light can be thrown by a less regular and more eclectic mode of criticism. Let us take Hamlet himself, and from the text alone endeavour to embody the abstraction, of which he is the idealized representative. Opening our Hamlet at the second scene, we find almost the first words of Hamlet to be:

> " *Ham.* Seems, madam! *nay it is; I know not ' seems.'*
> 'T is not alone my inky cloak, good mother,
> Nor customary suits of solemn black,
> Nor windy suspiration of forc'd breath,
> No, nor the fruitful river in the eye,
> Nor the dejected 'haviour of the visage,
> Together with all forms, moods, shapes of grief,
> That can denote me truly: These, indeed, seem,
> For they are actions that a man might play:
> But I have that within which passeth show;
> These, but the trappings and the suits of woe."—(Act i. Sc. 2.)

This excerpt seems the very key-note to the character of Hamlet. It is the essence of verity itself. Surely a poet, seeking to give expression to the beauty of truth, could not realize it more forcibly than in the above passage. Truth knows not *seems*. Verity itself is not to be expressed by "forms, moods, or shapes of grief." We are convinced at once, when we read this passage, of the depth, profundity, and thoroughness of Hamlet's character. And as everything real and true has a sympathy for us all, so the reader of Hamlet for the first time is at once enlisted with a melancholy interest upon his side. Again, Hamlet says at the end of the first act, that "the time is out of joint." And he realizes that he "is born to set it right." The profound student will find in this remark, placed as it is at the finale of an act, and that act the first, a hint of the greatest importance. Indeed, Goethe remarked it to be the key of the whole play. For if we are firmly convinced of the thorough-goingness of our hero's character, all his acts must be genuine, and must therefore be the result of truth. Whatever opposition he meets with must be from the enemies of truth alone. We shall examine their characters presently in succession.

Hamlet's first monologue or soliloquy is in accordance with our theory. As yet uninformed of the appearance of his father's Ghost, he bewails the hard destiny of life and the corruption of man :—

> " How weary, stale, flat, and unprofitable
> Seem to me all the uses of this world !
> Fie on 't ! O fie ! 't is an unweeded garden,
> That grows to seed ; things rank, and gross in nature,
> Possess it merely."—(Act i. Sc. 2.) [1]

But hardly is this monologue, the result of the King's sophistical speech, delivered, than the information of Horatio, Bernardo, and Marcellus, inform him of the appearance of his father's Ghost. Thus doubt comes fast upon doubt, strengthening the growing scepticism. And this scepticism is borne to Hamlet by three whom we believe are very ingredients of Hamlet himself. These are the growth of knowledge, the spirit of justice, and inquiry, which are the collective and separate product of those three friends he terms a little later, friends, scholars and soldiers. And let

---

[1] These lines represent a gloomy pessimism, which takes its root in a profound love of truth. They postulate gross corruption.

us mark the direct proof of all this in the decision of all four to "go in together."

The second act opens with the instructions Polonius gives his servant Reynaldo to keep a surveillance upon Laertes. And this is one of the thousand proofs of the play and its object. For the travels of Laertes[1] are the spread of learning, which, of course, is general. And Polonius, as Authority, takes care to make it as much in accordance with his tradition as possible. Hence the duty of Reynaldo. He is political espionage, who checks liberty of conscience, and puts an end to free thought. Laertes may do almost anything but one thing—*and that is be open to incontinency.*

> "*Pol.* You must not put another scandal on him.
> *That he is open to incontinency.*"

Thus we see how Laertes is to be kept in the path of his father. He will be -successively in this play all that is understood historically, by authority, antiquity, and tradition. He will stand by Ophelia. He will oppose Hamlet. He will be conservative to the backbone, no matter how modified we find his character at the end of the play. The introduction of Reynaldo was then a necessary addendum to the unity of the play. For he shows how Polonius works. Reynaldo's business is to discourage anything unorthodox. He is part of Polonius and his machinery. And his introduction gives us to understand the spread of knowledge, and the means which Polonius takes to keep it orthodox.

The first act of Hamlet's (in the second act) is the inspection of Ophelia. We maintain, contrary to ordinary criticism, that Hamlet never shows any irresolution, and is always acting. He is at the work of killing the King all through the play. And the King dies inch by inch all through the play, as each of his organs is mortally wounded and destroyed. The vulgar error is the belief that the King .

---

[1] We have taken Laertes to signify orthodox and traditional *Literature.* In this guise he returns to combat with Hamlet at the finale of the play.

is in full health at the end of the play. But a mere ghost
of the King is left in the person of Laertes. The real king
is a fiction, to represent the error[1] under which Laertes wars
against Hamlet. To return to Ophelia. Hamlet's first act
is the inspection of Ophelia ; as of a person much diseased.
She is at the bottom of all his unhappiness. For all his
happiness depends upon her favour. But her father and
her brother forbid her to have anything to do with Hamlet.
Hamlet is never really mad. His madness is only in the
eyes of others. And of whom, let us ask ? Of his enemies.
Ophelia thinks him mad, because she is a true daughter of
her father. But Horatio does not think him mad. Hamlet,
like all truth, seems mad to those to whom he appears anything but truth. It is the old stoical idea of the world being
mad to a philosopher ; and the philosopher appearing mad
in the world's eyes. There is a good story of some person,
questioning an inmate of a lunatic asylum upon the reason
of his incarceration. The reply was witty : " I thought the
world mad. But they say I am mad. And being the
stronger party, of course I am locked up ! "

There is hardly a great discovery before its time, which
does not receive the character of a mad scheme. Instances
might be numbered *ad infinitum*. The discovery of the
circulation of blood by Harvey, was derided and execrated
in his day. And we know he lost practice by it. Indeed,
for even a century after him, it was not universally accepted
by the Faculty. The dreams of a poor conchologist in the
eighteenth century were laughed at by Voltaire as the
evidence of madness. Yet here was the great science of
geology being silently born. We are almost persuaded, after
great historical study, to exclaim of the world—

> " Her all, most utter vanity ; and all
> Her lovers mad, insane most grievously,
> And most insane, because they know it not."—*Pollok*.

---

[1] For the sake of clearness we term the King Error. He is everything contained in the falsehood, injustice, and superstition of social authority and oppression.

But we deny Hamlet to be mad. He disclaims it,[1] and leaves it an opinion of his adversaries alone. For in no single line does Hamlet utter an incoherent word. There are many passages which, being misunderstood, are looked upon as the gibberish of a dangerous lunatic. But they are not sounded by the general students of Shakespeare, who dive no deeper than the text surface, and bring neither historical nor speculative philosophy to aid in the solution of the question. Those that have no science and no powers of comprehending truth, by its own light, will always adhere to the old, and call every innovation madness. No doubt the theory of Darwin is madness to thousands, who, imbued with tradition, are true descendants and cousins-german of Polonius and Laertes. No generation is therefore fit to judge of the truth of new theories. Time alone will be their patent. But to return to Hamlet's supposed madness. What does it mean artistically? It signifies profound art by which Hamlet's madness serves the purpose of the union of double plot, so essential in such difficult art. It was necessary that our Poet should keep the artistic side of the drama free from being too one-sided. To make his spiritual meaning too apparent was not his object. It was to be carefully veiled under the form of perfect art. Thus Hamlet's madness *artistically* (feigned or otherwise) serves to express his wildness and evil in the eyes of others. How exquisitely Shakespeare has escaped contradictions, almost inevitable in such a subject, is worthy of a great work of its own. Let us clearly define our position. Hamlet is no more mad than the sanest of Her Majesty's subjects in our eyes. His madness[2] in our eyes, once for all, is only his badness in the eyes of others, and an artistic cover under which he may utter the most profound truths to Polonius and Ophelia. As we have before remarked, it is merely an artistic ruse, by which the fear of his adversaries

---

[1] " If 't be so;" and again, " Hamlet is of the faction that is *wrong'd*."
[2] At the end of the play Hamlet identifies his madness with his enemies—"his madness is poor Hamlet's enemy."

is expressed by calling him mad, and which puzzles those
who, criticizing the play, cannot grasp the meaning of
some of his speeches. The first act of Hamlet, we repeat,
is the criticism of Ophelia. This criticism she describes
herself. It is an examination, by long perusal and inspection. It will simply lead to the Reformation, which is
dramatically pictured in the Player-scene. Ophelia is
diseased. And let it be particularly noticed, after the
Interlude or Player-scene, Hamlet is never seen with
Ophelia again. Hamlet is described by Ophelia as one
in a deplorable state of mind.

> " *Oph.* My lord, as I was sewing in my closet,
> Lord Hamlet, with his doublet all unbraced;
> No hat upon his head; his stockings foul'd,
> Ungarter'd, and down-gyved to his ancle ;
> Pale as his shirt; his knees knocking each other;
> And with a look so piteous in purport
> As if he had been loosed out of hell,
> To speak of horrors,—he comes before me." [1]

In the above passage we have a great many touches which
illuminate the whole conception. We are bound to remember the historical facts which preceded the Reformation,
and which accompanied it. Prison was the place, if not
the stake, to which the disciples of truth, of inquiry, or
what were termed heretics, went. Truth might well, at
such a time, have a

> " Look so piteous in purport
> As if he had been loosed out of hell."

Hamlet is a prince; an heir who never comes to the
throne. Truth is the prince of thought—its goal, its prize ;
but it never comes to the throne of mankind. So Hamlet
is pretty clearly criticizing severely a love who receives his
truth so unkindly. No wonder he

> " Raised a sigh so piteous and profound
> As it did seem to shatter all his bulk
> And end his being."

---

[1] Mr. Tyler, in his " Philosophy of Hamlet," has commented well upon this
passage.

Hamlet is clearly recognizing his great enemy, in the whole of the scene from which these excerpts are made. And Polonius is alarmed. For, as he remarks, this ecstasy of love may

"Lead the will to desperate undertakings."

What is the cause of all this? The repulse of Hamlet by Ophelia, at the instigation of Polonius. A Church which, under an autocratic rule, will allow no room for truth, must either keep her followers in ignorance, or consent to part with some of them. And presently we have more direct intimation of what Hamlet means. For we have a letter written by Hamlet to Ophelia. And this letter is merely a summary of the polity of the Church of the period. It is as follows:

> Doubt thou the stars are fire;
> Doubt that the sun doth move;
> Doubt truth to be a liar;
> But never doubt I love.

O dear Ophelia, I am ill at these numbers; I have not art to reckon my groans: but that I love thee best, O most best, believe it. Adieu.

> Thine evermore, most dear lady, whilst
> this machine is to him, HAMLET." [1]

The above is as plain as plain can be. The lines to Ophelia are Ophelia's own policy. That is, the policy of the Church. It is the old conflict of to-day — Religion and Science. No wonder Hamlet is ill at these numbers. For on one side Science tells him to doubt, and on the other Religion to believe the opposite. Already Hamlet is getting dangerous. He cannot believe two things at once. Let us remember the continuity of the action of the play. Growing discontent has caused Laertes and Polonius to warn Ophelia against Hamlet. But Hamlet is ever gaining in strength. Polonius cannot explain why Hamlet is mad. He says:

> "Madam, I swear I use no art at all.
> That he is mad, 'tis true: 'tis true 'tis pity;
> And pity 'tis 'tis true: a foolish figure;
> But farewell it, for I will use no art."

---

[1] The essence of the above is its principle of contradiction, as contained between religion and science.

What we gather from the above is the art and cunning
of Polonius, and the danger of Hamlet, which Polonius
explains by reading his letter to Ophelia. Let us mark
how Polonius repeats and blunders pedantically over the
same thing in words, and nothing but words. This is the
essence of Tradition and Antiquity. And we are told in-
directly that the lines of Hamlet to Ophelia are actually
Ophelia's :

" In her excellent white bosom, these."

And what are "these" in her excellent white bosom? Nothing shorter than an emphatic denial of those questions
of the day, which are matters of fact in this day. For
Copernicus, Galileo and Bruno[1] established the Heliocentric
system, as against the Geocentric, which latter was the
orthodox one of the day. Everything was to be doubted
that interfered with the life of the Church. And Hamlet
is of those who did believe in these new facts of discovery.
Therefore, in Polonius's eyes, he is bad and mad; and he
denies him access to his daughter. The whole of this letter
to Ophelia is one of the simplest and amplest pieces of
evidence in the whole play. Polonius is explaining to the
Queen the evil and heresy of her son Hamlet. And
that heresy is his enmity to the tenets, traditions, and
doctrines of the Church. The latter was autocratic, and
explained the whole system of the universe. That system
was, that the world was a flat plane, round which the sun
moved. Bruno and Galileo destroyed for ever this delusion ;
but the former died at the stake in 1600 for his opinions.
Shakespeare must then have been thirty-six:[2] a period

---

[1] Thinking men disbelieved the Geocentric system in the fifteenth century·
Let it be remembered that though Copernicus did not publish his work until
1543, it was completed in 1507, prior to the Reformation. The three great
voyages of Columbus (1492), Magellan (1519), and Vasco de Gama (1498), had
destroyed the old Geocentric tradition prior to the Reformation, by proving the
earth's rotundity. And the Reformation was, in truth, in full progress the whole
of the sixteenth century.

[2] As a Philosophy of History expresses general movements, in the place of
particular facts, so here we contend our parallelism is only meant to be suggestive.

when the whole of his faculties of historical judgment must have been singularly mature. He was alive during the whole of that period when the old cosmogony was being destroyed by men who dared to think for themselves. In the lines from Hamlet to Ophelia we have these very questions mooted. The old movement of the sun is or is not to be doubted. The ancient theory that the stars were lights, made especially to illumine this particular earth, had received its death-blow at the hands of Bruno, who discussed the subject of a Plurality of Worlds.

Can one doubt truth to be anything but truth, and not a liar? Yet the Church, Hamlet tells us, says:

> "But never doubt I love."

No wonder Hamlet has not "art to reckon his groans," upon the horns of such a dilemma. And he is, indeed, "ill at these numbers." For the Church says, "Doubt all these things; though they seem true, yet they are not truth." But Hamlet is still (though invisibly in the play) accompanied by Bernardo, Horatio, and Marcellus. Inquiry, study, reason, is part and parcel of Hamlet's constitution. He says, later in the play:

> "What is a man,
> If his chief good and market of his time
> Be but to sleep and feed? a beast, no more.
> Sure, he that made us with such large discourse,
> Looking before and after, gave us not
> That capability and god-like reason
> To fust in us unused."

No, Hamlet will rationalize and philosophize, as he does from the first, whether he will or no. It is his idiosyncrasy to use his reason. But this constitutes his badness in the eyes of Polonius. He is especially dangerous to Ophelia. For he threatens her very foundations, which are Infallibility. Again, we have the address of Hamlet's letter to Ophelia. It is as follows:

> "Pol. 'To the celestial and my soul's idol, the most beautified Ophelia,'—
> That's an ill phrase, a vile phrase; beautified is a vile phrase."

Now why does Polonius object to the word *beautified?* Because it has a reproach of manufacture about it. There is a want of nature about such a word. It suggests artificial means, by which Ophelia has been made. She is not truly beautiful; she is made so by unnatural aids. We believe this word to mean Bigoted. We shall arrive, by and by, to facts of such similar nature, as to leave no question upon the subject. Hamlet calls himself a machine. He is indeed one, under the tyranny of intolerance and persecution. But there may be reference to torture in this satirical remark, that truth is only Ophelia's, whilst the rack enforces obedience. However we may quarrel over details, there can be no doubt of the relations which exist between Ophelia and her father. Polonius says :

> " I have a daughter—have while she is mine—
> Who, in her duty and obedience."

She is only the daughter of Polonius whilst she is obedient and servile to authority and to tradition. Polonius is full of certainty :

> "*Pol.* Hath there been such a time—(I'd fain know that)—
> That I have positively said '*'Tis so,*'
> When it proved otherwise ? "

This is part of his infallibility. Polonius is positively sure of the madness, or, as we take it, the errors of Hamlet. We now have the entrance of Hamlet reading. He is evidently gathering force from a criticism of the past. And we are told he walks for hours in the lobby. Is not a lobby an ante-chamber, where people have to wait before they can find an entrance, or gain a hearing ? Hamlet is as yet in this predicament. He is outside, and his princely right to the throne a mere mockery and the deepest irony.

Hamlet greets Polonius with the epithet of " God-a-mercy." Polonius is a God of mercy with a vengeance. What satire ! This is the thin edge of the wedge. Hamlet will soon ridicule him. Polonius is termed by Hamlet a fishmonger. Again, Hamlet says:

"Ay, sir; to be honest, as this world goes, is to be one man picked out of ten thousand."

Hamlet recognizes the character of those that deal in dead fish; and that Polonius falls short even of this standard. What does all this mean? We reply, it is a scene in which the relations of Hamlet to the Church, and to authority generally, are portrayed. It is part of the continuity of the play. It is the ridicule and satire which will lead ultimately to the death of Polonius. Shakespeare has done everything art can do in this play to bring out the continuity of the characters and the modification of their powers. The play begins with "Long live the King." The existence of wrong-doing is recognized first by Hamlet in the passage commencing:

"This heavy-headed revel."

And it is followed by the appearance of the Ghost. Thus do doubt and certainty succeed each other, to be followed by greater doubt and greater certainty.

Polonius, as authority, is always getting robbed of some of his power by Hamlet. This is the result of the revelation of the Ghost. And the Ghost is the result of Bernardo, Marcellus, Francisco, Horatio, and Hamlet.[1] Ophelia has been severely criticized by Hamlet. Polonius is now being ridiculed. Hamlet tells him that what he reads are merely

"Words, words, words!"

That is, the whole of Polonius is a mass of words, without sense or meaning. Hamlet mocks Polonius upon the subject of his daughter:

---

[1] The reader is begged to remember our theory, viz.: Fortinbras (liberty), Hamlet (progress and truth), Horatio (knowledge), all work together.

"*Ham.* For if the sun breed maggots in a dead dog, being a god kissing carrion,—Have you a daughter?

Pol. I have, my lord.

Ham. Let her not walk i' the sun: conception is a blessing: but not as your daughter may conceive. Friend, look to 't."

The whole of the above is profound scorn and the bitterest irony. It is a recognition by Hamlet of the fear in which Polonius holds all inquiry and knowledge. The sun we take to be typically knowledge. Hamlet actually says to Polonius: "If you let your daughter have liberty, she may conceive or think, or she may bring a new birth to light; and everything shows that knowledge can give new life and new direction to what is old and corrupt."

Hamlet is thus giving us a hint of those thoughts which filled the minds of men imbued with reforming principles. Polonius begins to see method in the apparent delusions of Hamlet. And Hamlet has begun to ridicule and satirize authority, through the Church. Polonius replies by similar taunts, and ironically asks Hamlet if he will walk out into the air. But Hamlet knows this is his grave. Hamlet has recognized already the emptiness and the dotage of Polonius. Hamlet says:

"*Ham.* You cannot, sir, take from me any thing that I will more willingly part withal: except my life, except my life, except my life.

Pol. Fare you well, my lord.

Ham. These tedious old fools!"

Here, then, we are assured that Polonius is thoroughly appreciated by Hamlet. The latter would willingly part with him. But he still lacks power. Polonius is in the eyes of Hamlet a "tedious old fool."

Let us be clear as far as we have followed our chain of continuity. Hamlet repudiates Polonius. But two friends step in now, who play an important part throughout the whole drama. Let us thoroughly realize them if we can. These two are the courtiers Rosencrantz and Guildenstern. They are sent to Hamlet by the King and Queen, and Hamlet has been brought up in their society. Indeed, he seems to be at first partial to them. But he soon gets suspicious, and finally fully recognizes both their emptiness and their significance. Hamlet is some time in finding out if these two courtiers are on the King's side or upon his. We, who are readers of the play, and thus behind the scenes, know more than Hamlet does, at some stages. For we have the following words to reassure us :

ACT II. SCENE II.

" *Enter* King, Queen, Rosencrantz, Guildenstern, *etc.*

King. Welcome, dear Rosencrantz and Guildenstern!
Moreover that we much did long to see you,
The need we have *to use you* did provoke
Our hasty sending."

In those two words " *use you*" we have a key of the character of Rosencrantz and Guildenstern. They are part of the succession in the continuity of the play, or what we would rather term a Philosophy of History dramatized. These two courtiers have one quality in common, and they hunt in couples, being only once apart (and only for a few lines) in the whole play. They fill the places of the now vanished Voltimand and Cornelius. Everything in their conduct suggests smoothness, caution, and craftiness. They are going to be *used* by the King, and their use is to come between Hamlet and himself. Now we shall realize by the text alone in what their common quality consists; and we shall see that they are complements to each other, as indispensable as are the Siamese twins to each other's existence. Polonius directs them to Hamlet; and it is necessary we quote in full the meeting between Hamlet and them, to thoroughly seize their full meaning :

" *Enter* Rosencrantz *and* Guildenstern.

Pol. You go to seek the Lord Hamlet; there he is.
Ros. [*To* Polonius.]   God save you, sir!   [*Exit* Polonius.]
Guil. Mine honoured lord!
Ros. My most dear lord!
Ham. My excellent good friends! How dost thou, Guildenstern? Ah, Rosencrantz! Good lads, how do ye both?

Ros. As the indifferent children of the earth.
Guil. Happy, in that we are not over-happy;
On fortune's cap we are not the very button.
Ham. Not the soles of her shoe ?
Ros. Neither, my lord.
Ham. Then you live about her waist, or in the middle of her favours ?
Guil. 'Faith, her privates we.''

Here we pause in the quotation to see what we have gained
so far; and that is no small part of the sum of the characters
of these two courtiers. In reply to Hamlet, Rosencrantz
says that himself and Guildenstern are "*as the indifferent
children of the earth.*" They represent indifference, and care
not for those questions which agitate Hamlet. Again, we
know they live in the middle of the favours of Fortune. This
is what makes them indifferent. Hamlet tells Rosencrantz
later—

"Aye, sir, that soaks up the king's countenance, his rewards, his authorities.''

Rosencrantz and Guildenstern thrive upon abuses and
errors. And why ? Because they soak up the means, the
rewards, countenances, and authorities of error or the King.
Every innovation, every change, is a positive evil to people of
such a temper ; and that temper is the temper of the man of
the world. They are therefore staunch bulwarks of the King,
and the profoundest enemies of Hamlet. The characteristic
they hold in common is, as we have already said, indifference ;
an indifference which arises from circumstances which make
them the privates of Fortune. They consist of that large
body of every age, who have everything to lose by progress,
and everything to keep by stability. But now we have to
define their method of dealing with Hamlet ; and that is by
the means of *sophistry, casuistry,* and a species of optimism,
which tries to maintain that everything is at the very best
possible point it can be. Henceforward we shall term Rosencrantz and Guildenstern[1] as *representing indifference, sophistry,*

---

[1] Rosencrantz, by himself, seems to represent the optimism of those who are
the friends of fortune, and who benefit by error. Guildenstern is more the method
by which the truth is evaded.

casuistry, and optimism. And let us first see to which these respective terms individually apply. To both indifference and a carelessness, if not hatred of truth. To Guildenstern, especially, the art of trying to make the worse side appear the better :

> " *Guil.* What should we say, my lord ?
> *Ham.* Why anything, but to the purpose." [1]

This is exactly what Rosencrantz and Guildenstern succeed in doing. They evade all truth and good logic, and "never say anything to the purpose." Everything they say is as wide from the point in hand as possible. See how Shakespeare has brought this out, in their argument with Hamlet. The trenchant logic of Hamlet is contrasted with the evasive and false sophistry of theirs. They see things utterly differently to Hamlet. To the latter the world is a prison; but to the two sycophants of the King the world is actually honest :

> " *Ham.* . . . . . What's the news ?
> *Ros.* None, my lord, but that the world's grown honest.
> *Ham.* Then is doomsday near : but your news is not true. Let me question more in particular : what have you, my good friends, deserved at the hands of fortune, that she sends you to prison hither ?
> *Guil.* Prison, my lord !
> *Ham.* Denmark 's a prison.
> *Ros.* Then is the world one.
> *Ham.* A goodly one; in which there are many confines, wards, and dungeons, Denmark being one o' the worst.
> *Ros.* We think not so, my lord.
> *Ham.* Why, then, 'tis none to you : for there is nothing either good or bad, but thinking makes it so : to me it is a prison.
> *Ros.* Why then, your ambition makes it one ; 'tis too narrow for your mind.
> *Ham.* O God, I could be bounded in a nutshell,[2] and count myself a king of infinite space, were it not that I have bad dreams.

---

[1] In some editions there is a full stop after "*anything.*" In either case (*comma* or *fullstop*), we read Shakespeare's real meaning to be Hamlet's recognition of the evasive character of the two courtiers.

[2] The word *nutshell* suggests Hamlet as the *kernel.* Thus truth is the *core* of things.

Guil. Which dreams indeed are ambition, for the very substance of the
ambitious is merely the shadow of a dream.
Ham. A dream itself is but a shadow.
Ros. Truly, and I hold ambition of so airy and light a quality that it is but a
shadow's shadow.
Ham. Then are our beggars bodies, and our monarchs and outstretched heroes
the beggars' shadows. Shall we to the court ? for, by my fay, I cannot reason."

In the above we notice the aim and drift of Shakespeare
in enforcing the contrast between Hamlet's perfect logic,
which annihilates the arguments of the two courtiers, and
their sophistry. Hamlet has been brought up with Rosencrantz and Guildenstern ; but it is the first time he disagrees
with them upon views of life. Hamlet is taking stock of
Rosencrantz and Guildenstern, as he has done of Polonius ; and
he will by and by repudiate and escape their claims upon
him. Let us notice the different views which Hamlet holds
to these two courtiers. To our hero the world is a prison ;
to the other two the world has grown honest. The views of
the former are decidedly pessimistic ; those of the latter optimistic. And the cause of this difference has much to do with
the circumstances in which both are respectively placed.
Hamlet, as we have already seen, knows more of the gyves,
of the prison, and of the stake, than do the other two. These
only are intimate with the rewards and countenances of the
King, upon whom they thrive, and by whom they alone exist.
Denmark to Hamlet is a prison ; and Denmark is identified
with the world by Rosencrantz. But what is Denmark ?
In our opinion Denmark is literally *dark men*, of which it
is an anagram ; and it thus stands for ignorance, of which
Hamlet is the only light and the only prince—Truth. As
Hamlet remarks :

" Why, then, 'tis none to you : for there is nothing either good or bad, but
thinking makes it so : to me it is a prison."

In the above we recognize that the world is a prison to all
truth. That good and bad depends, according to the dis-
crepancy between the views of Hamlet and the courtiers,
either to difference of thinking, or to their obliquity. Of

course we feel the latter powerfully forced upon us. For we feel there is something far more real than a mode of registering our particular circumstances. There is not one law for the good, and one for the bad; but one for both. And Hamlet soon shows us how poorly these two courtiers can rationalize upon the simplest subject. How magnificently grand is Hamlet's logic! And what a thorough collapse for Rosencrantz and Guildenstern! But we must always remember that it is part and parcel of these two gentlemen to say nothing to the purpose. The whole drift of Rosencrantz and Guildenstern is to run down ambition; and ambition is desire for promotion. Hamlet himself says he lacks advancement—

"Sir, I lack advancement." [1]

Again, ambition is the result of bad dreams and dissatisfaction. But if ambition is nothing, as the courtiers insinuate, then those who realize the dreams of ambition, as monarchs and outstretched heroes, are nothing also.

The argument is too absurd to need even Hamlet's refutation. For if ambition is nought, how is it that the aspirations of beggars are so substantially realized? The whole discussion is one in which Rosencrantz and Guildenstern employ their talents to argue down and oppose Hamlet's dissatisfaction and liberal impulses. We must clearly comprehend the relations of the two parties. Everywhere, for the future, we shall find Hamlet fettered by these two tools of the King. And when, for the first time, he escapes from them and returns to England alone, we have his letter to the King, beginning—

"High and mighty, You shall know I am set *naked* on your kingdom."

We have no hesitation in thus understanding our Poet's meaning; and we are convinced that Hamlet, having got rid of sophistry, casuistry, optimism—*hoc et genus omne*—is

---

[1] This *advancement* we read as the liberal and reforming ambition of Hamlet.

set naked in the play. Truth is at last unalloyed, and we
owe this blessing to England. We have somewhat anticipated the gradual development of the play; but it is necessary we should endeavour clearly to realize the meaning of
the two courtiers Rosencrantz and Guildenstern. The last
we hear of them is as follows :

> " *Hor.* So Guildenstern and Rosencrantz go to 't.
> *Ham.* Why, man, they did make love to this employment;
> They are not near my conscience; their defeat
> Does by their own insinuation grow :
> '*Tis dangerous when the baser nature comes*
> *Between the pass and fell incensed points*
> *Of mighty opposites.*"

What could express the essence of our friends better than
the above! Is not sophistry, is not indifference, and an optimistic philosophy, based upon plunder, the baser nature which
comes " between the pass and fell incensed points of mighty
opposites "? Those opposites are Truth and Error. We shall
arrive by and by to an explanation of England. The latter
is the direct instrument of the disappearance and extinction
of these two " adders fanged." Our end at present is to
establish the nature of their characters plainly in the
reader's eyes; and to do this it has been necessary to quit
the order of our advance with the text. Therefore, we now
return to the relations, and continuity in those relations, of
Hamlet and these two. We have seen how cheerfully
Hamlet greets them. And not only this, we hold direct intimation of Hamlet's childhood being spent in their society.

> " *King.* . . . . . I entreat you both,
> That, being of so young days brought up with him,
> And sith so neighbour'd to his youth and haviour," etc., etc.

But in the first interview between Hamlet and them we
find, first, disagreement in their views of life; secondly,
mistrust and suspicion upon Hamlet's side —

> " *Ham.* [*Aside*] Nay, then, I have an eye of you."

And, lastly, we have positive hatred and a determination to
outmanœuvre them in their own line.

> "*Ham.* There's letters seal'd : and my two *schoolfellows*,
> Whom I will trust as I will adders fanged,
> They bear the mandate; they must sweep my way,
> And marshal me to knavery. Let it work ;
> For 'tis the sport to have the enginer
> Hoist with his own petar : and 't shall go hard
> But I will delve one yard below their mines,
> And blow them at the moon : O, 'tis most sweet,
> When in one line two crafts directly meet."

So we perceive the same continuity with regard to Rosencrantz and Guildenstern as we have seen in Polonius. We
can never insist sufficiently upon this continuity and development of character which Shakespeare has so profoundly
realized. The whole play is the continuity of history; and
this continuity is so interwoven with time and each part of
itself, that no one part should be taken alone. Everywhere
Fortinbras is slowly gaining ground. The reason of his
abrupt appearance in the midst of the play is thus an underground basis of action and reaction. But to proceed. Rosencrantz and Guildenstern are perhaps Hamlet's greatest
enemies; for they hamper all his movements, and on every
occasion of note in the play, up to his actual escape from
them, they are the direct means of allowing Hamlet no
standing room. He is actually suffocated and oppressed by
their intense servility and apparent obsequiousness. They
profess to love truth ; but they never look it in the face.
At the best, their whole spirit is that of compromise.
Timidity and a constant fear of any change is their
characteristic. As Guildenstern remarks :

> "*Guil.*   We will ourselves provide :
> Most holy and religious fear it is
> To keep those many many bodies safe
> That live and feed upon your majesty.".

Nothing could express their whole policy better.. They
are themselves the "many many bodies that live and feed
upon error;" and let us particularly take note of the part

they take in Hamlet's banishment. *They are the direct cause
of it.* As we have before said, the King is a fiction. He is
contained in Guildenstern and Rosencrantz. And to prove
this Hamlet says :

> "*Ham.* The body is with the king, but the king is not with the body. The
> king is a thing—
> *Guil.* A thing, my lord!
> *Ham.* Of nothing: bring me to him. Hide fox, and all after."

Thus we see the King is a thing "of nothing ;" and error
and falsehood are by their very nature in themselves nothing.

> " The body is with the king."

Authority is on the side of error, but error is not for
authority. Hamlet, as we know historically, when banished,
owes his exile to public opinion ; and that opinion is often of
the following description :

> " *Ros.* The single and peculiar life is bound,
> With all the strength and armour of the mind,
> To keep itself from noyance ; but much more
> That spirit upon whose weal depend and rest
> The lives of many. The cease of majesty
> Dies not alone ; but, like a gulf, doth draw
> What 's near it with it : it is a massy wheel,
> Fix'd on the summit of the highest mount,
> To whose huge spokes ten thousand lesser things
> Are mortised and adjoin'd ; which, when it falls,
> Each small annexment, petty consequence,
> Attends the boisterous ruin. Never alone
> Did the king sigh, but with a general groan."

Putting aside the marvellous knowledge displayed in the
region of social psychology and the phenomena of belief, we
would call attention to the distinction our poet makes between the individual and the social life. Hamlet is then
dangerous to the weal of the latter, and Rosencrantz not
only advocates his banishment, but accompanies Hamlet in
his exile, together with Guildenstern. Let us clearly realize
our position. The exile of Hamlet, which will come after the
effects of the Player-scene, will be exemplified by his being
hampered by the two courtiers. As long as our hero is with

them, he is not Hamlet "*naked*," but a Hamlet who has Rosencrantz and Guildenstern to come between him and truth. This is his true exile, and England alone will break the bondage, and set him "*naked*," for the first time, on the King's kingdom.   He will be more a prince then than when mockingly called a prince, who has no followers.   Hamlet knows this, for he says to our two friends:

"*Ros. and Guil.* We 'll wait upon you.
Ham. No such matter: I will not sort you with the rest of my servants, for, to speak to you like an honest man, I am most dreadfully attended."

Whatever way we interpret the above, it remains still to the purport.   Hamlet does not consider the courtiers his friends.   He knows their business, and he is most poorly attended, or shall we say, most cruelly attended, by the inquisition, the stake, and the torture-chamber.   But Rosencrantz and Guildenstern bring Hamlet some good news. That news is the rumour of the players.   Who are these players?

"*Ham.* . . . . . . What players are they?
Ros. Even those you were wont to take delight in, the tragedians of the city."

These players are, in our opinion, the growing knowledge and literature which led towards the Reformation.   They are the children of the revival of learning, the heirs of the Renaissance.   To define them would be to write a history of the causes of the Reformation.   But we need not doubt historical criticism and philosophy played a great part in that movement.   The schoolmen had long accustomed men to the subtlest discussions.   Indeed, we are far too apt in these days to underrate their subtlety and ability.   Many questions are now being discussed, which were centres of fierce discussion in the Middle Ages.   Luther was the product of his times.   He merely gave, like all great men, direction to the movement of those times.   And we perceive what joy it gives Hamlet to hear of the arrival of these Players.   Their coming is the first gathering of the storm.   A storm which is the result of greater knowledge.   A knowledge which the Players

most fitly represent. Whatever in the mind of man produced the Reformation must be understood by these Players.
We have had reference to Wittenberg early in the play :

> "*Ham.* And what make you from Wittenberg, Horatio ?—Marcellus?
> *Mar.* My good lord,—
> *Ham.* I am very glad to see you. Good even, sir,
> But what, in faith, make you from Wittenberg?
> *Hor.* A truant disposition, good my lord."

Here we have Wittenberg mentioned twice. And Wittenberg is the very birth-place of the Reformation. Here it
was begun, and here it culminated. For here Martin
Luther burnt the Pope's Bull, as every school-boy knows.
Why does Horatio come from Wittenberg? Because Horatio
is a scholar, and in our eyes represents the spirit of justice
and independence.

> "*Ham.* Horatio, thou art e'en as *just* a man
> As e'er my conversation coped withal."

It is through Horatio, the staunch friend of Hamlet, that
our hero finds true support to carry out his ends. What is
a spirit of doubt or truth without an accompanying spirit of
justice, independence, and firmness ? Horatio's character
may be gathered from the speech of Hamlet to him ; and we
may be sure he is everything which is the essence of a bold
spirit of truth-seeking.

> "*Ham.*   Nay, do not think I flatter;
> For what advancement may I hope from thee,
> That no revenue hast but thy good spirits,
> To feed and clothe thee? Why should the poor be flatter'd?
> No, let the candied tongue lick absurd pomp,
> And crook the pregnant hinges of the knee
> Where thrift may follow fawning. Dost thou hear ?
> Since my dear soul was mistress of her choice,
> And could of men distinguish, her election
> Hath seal'd thee for herself: for thou hast been
> As one, in suffering all, that suffers nothing,
> A man that fortune's buffets and rewards
> Hast ta'en with equal thanks : and blest are those
> Whose blood and judgment are so well commingled,
> That they are not a pipe for fortune's finger
> To sound what stop she please. Give me that man
> That is not passion's slave, and I will wear him
> In my heart's core, ay, in my heart of heart,
> As I do thee."

In the last lines of this quotation we have the actual fact. Our hero wears Horatio in his heart's core. And what he wears is, as he has told us, independence, " *good spirits,*" a mind to endure all things, and an intense love of justice. These are some of the qualities of a Luther. They are not the more cautious ones, which go to form an Erasmus. However, Erasmus was a tragedian of the city. He laid the egg, and Luther, or Hamlet, hatched it. After this necessary parenthesis upon Horatio's attributes, let us return to the text in hand. Horatio has come from Wittenberg. And Hamlet asks him what he makes from there. Hamlet half answers the question himself; for he says, " Marcellus? " And Marcellus represents a spirit of inquiry, of search and discovery, to whom it was given, with Bernardo[1] (reading), to see the Ghost, or Doubt. Luther, studying the Bible, is a fit emblem of Bernardo, Marcellus, Horatio, and Hamlet. And how ? In reading, he uses the gift Bernardo brings into the play. In criticism and examination, that of Marcellus. He is impelled by a spirit of independence,—that is, Horatio. And, finally, the love he holds for Hamlet is at the bottom of the whole affair. And Luther soon saw the Ghost. Thus Hamlet's question is one of interrogation, and half surmisal of the inquiry coming from Wittenberg. And we then remark the answer of Horatio, which is, " a truant disposition." Are we to understand that Horatio only sees fickleness, and a truant disposition, where Hamlet surmises more. It is by the interaction of the friends, scholars and soldiers, that the Ghost is appreciated, and makes a revelation. But to proceed. The key-note of the Reformation is thus touched in this reference to Wittenberg. The very name of the place, fraught as it is with memories of the first great Rebellion of the Intellect in Europe, ought to have made critics more alive to the significance of Hamlet. And we shall presently have plenty of evidence to show how that significance may be interpreted and rationalized in the play. We

---

[1] Bernardo is not unlikely the art of printing.

ask the indulgent reader, who has accompanied us so far, to bear with any hypothesis, however wild it may appear at first sight, for the sake of further proof, which we get when deeper into the spiritual unity of the drama. Hamlet's speech to Rosencrantz and Guildenstern, beginning—

"I will tell you why; so shall my anticipation prevent your discovery, and your secrecy to the king and queen moult no feather."

—is one which has a very profound meaning. Here we recognize, again, the craftiness of the two courtiers. For they hunt with the hounds, and run with the hare. It is their temper not so much to be blind to the changes of time, as to resist them as long as they are perilous to their particular interests. And they thoroughly understand their age with regard to Hamlet. The latter is utterly in a state of deplorable dyspepsia, produced by the unhealthiness of the social atmosphere. And he has got to that point when he cannot be any worse. It is just then he hears of the Players. He wants to know why the Players travel? And he is told that it is on account of the "late innovation." Now this innovation is, therefore, the direct cause of Progress, if we so understand the word "travel." And we must bear in mind the actors are the writers and thinkers of the age. What they suffer from is criticism and direct interference of certain "little eyases." In this word we have mere spectators, and not actors, well expressed. No doubt all this refers to religious controversy and interference on the part of authority.

"*Guil.* O, there has been much throwing about of brains.
Ham. Do the boys carry it away?
Ros. Ay, that they do, my lord; Hercules and his load too.
Ham. It is not very strange, for mine uncle is king of Denmark; and those that would make mows at him while my father lived, give twenty, forty, fifty, an hundred ducats a-piece, for his picture in little. 'Sblood, there is something in this more than natural, if philosophy could find it out."

The boys we take to be the coming generation. They are the youth of the day, who carry away, of course, something original from all this throwing about of brains. And

Hamlet is surprised at nothing. For his uncle is King of Denmark. And scepticism has been so nurtured in his mind by these controversies, that he naturally expresses a desire to bring a little philosophy to bear upon the subject. His last words before the entrance of Polonius are:

"I am but mad north-north-west: when the wind is southerly, I know a hawk from a handsaw."

Now we are going to astonish the reader, if he is not already astonished. The seat of the Reformation was Germany, and Germany is situated something between north and west with regard to the rest of Europe. Hamlet is only mad in Germany. And when the wind comes from the Ultramontane side of the continent, " he knows a talk from an answer."[1] Those who look upon this interpretation as a piece of lunacy or wild imagination are requested to pause as yet in their judgment. Polonius now enters. Let us note how Hamlet no longer satirizes him covertly, but mocks him openly. He is less and less afraid of him. He will walk out into the air presently, and yet not into his grave. However, before we proceed further, we would say more as regards Rosencrantz and Guildenstern. After the great events of the Reformation, and during its growth and development, we find in contemporary literature accounts of our two courtiers : " Thus Giordano Bruno, who was born seven years after the death of Copernicus, published a work on the infinity of the universe and of worlds. It added not a little to the exasperation against him, that he was perpetually declaiming against the insincerity, and the impostures of his persecutors ; that, wherever he went, he found scepticism varnished over and concealed by hypocrisy ; and that it was not against the belief of men, but against their pretended belief, that he was fighting ; that he was struggling with an orthodoxy that had neither morality

---

[1] The reader will notice we presently read "*by lot*" as "*Bigot*." The whole of the conversation between the two courtiers and Hamlet is of the nature of talk, not direct answers, but evasion.

nor faith." We quote the above from Dr. Draper's work
upon the conflict between religion and science. And it may
be asked, what can Bruno have in connexion with our
courtiers? Simply that the substance of the above was
delivered amidst lectures in England during Shakespeare's
life. And we must ask ourselves if our great Poet has not
partly realized the hypocrisy, the indifference, and pretended
belief which Bruno rails against, in Rosencrantz and Guildenstern? Could it be possible that Shakespeare should be
indifferent, with his mighty brain, to the theories of the
Copernican system, published only nineteen years before his
birth, and furthered by Bruno? It was the greatest blow
the Church or Tradition could receive ; and it was altering
slowly men's conceptions of the world. Guildenstern is
essentially varnished over. His very name savours of a
compound of Latin and English. If we take the last
syllable "stern," we are reminded of the Latin verb *ster-
nere*, "to spread over," "to cover with." And "Guilden"
sounds very much like some *light veneer, wanting in everything
but gilt*. Thus, "to gild over," "to smooth down," "to hide,"
and finally "to pretend and deceive," is what we thus arrive
at. Taking Rosencrantz in a similar way, we have "crantz,"
clearly derived from *cranium*, "a head," and "Rosen," which
sounds very like *Rose in head*. This would be a good metaphor for optimism, namely a rosy brain, and one who, from
his easy circumstances or other causes, always saw things in
a "couleur de rose light." However, these derivations may
be true or not, but the more eclectic they are, the more
likelihood have they to belong to Shakespeare ; as in all
things, the greater the genius, the greater the eclecticism.
We can now understand why the two courtiers are so friendly
with Hamlet. They perfectly realize the times they live in.
But they lack interest, courage, and unselfishness, to make
them supporters of Hamlet. They are wanting in Horatio's
character and type, as also in Hamlet's. Nothing is more
conspicuous than their guardedness. They never venture to
do anything but play upon or obstruct Hamlet by their
own passive and hypocritical natures ; and nothing is more

natural than that they should be for a long period mixed up with him. From them he gets most of his information. And none know better than they do his complete reason and sanity. It is their especial attribute always to take care not to commit themselves to anything; and always to be on the side of the strong. What does Goethe say of them? He calls them "amateurs:"—"Out of these meditations he was roused by the other actors, along with whom *two amateurs*, frequenters of the wardrobe and the stage, came in and saluted Wilhelm with a *show* of great enthusiasm. One of these was in some degree attached to Frau Melina; but the other was entirely a pure friend of art; and both were of the kind which a good company should always wish to have about it. It was difficult to say whether their love for the stage,[1] or their knowledge of it, was the greater. They loved it too much to know it perfectly; they knew it well enough to prize the good, and to discard the bad. But their inclinations being so powerful, they could tolerate the mediocre; and the glorious joy which they experienced from the foretaste and the aftertaste of excellence surpassed expression. The mechanical department gave them pleasure, the intellectual charmed them; and so strong was their susceptibility, that even a discontinuous rehearsal afforded them a species of illusion. Deficiencies appeared in their eyes to fade away in distance; the successful touched them like an object near at hand. In a word, they were judges, such as every artist wishes in his own department. Their favourite movement was from the side scenes to the pit, and from the pit to the side scenes; their happiest place was in the wardrobe; their busiest employment was in trying to improve the dress, position, recitation, gesture, of the actor; their liveliest conversation was on the effect produced by him; their most constant effort was to keep him accurate, active and attentive, to do him service or kindness, and without squandering to procure for the company a series of enjoyments."

Nothing can surpass the keen satire and the truthful

---

[1] The stage is here meant for the *world*.

irony of the above picture. This is the man of the world.
Occupied in trifles, loving the mediocre, only acting where
public opinion is with him, and, finally, touched by the
successful and near at hand, before all things. If we have
been understood thus far, we can proceed with our hypothesis with greater confidence and assurance. If not exactly
right in every detail, still we are on the true path of discovery. A path which Goethe has only partially illuminated.
And in such a way as to substitute another difficulty for
the first. But to Goethe must be ever accorded the great
discovery of the nature of Shakespeare's works, and of the
method and principles which underlie them. But to proceed. We will now turn to Polonius, who, at the juncture we
left in the text, makes his appearance. Hamlet, as we have
already remarked, openly mocks him, and turns him into
downright ridicule.

"*Ham.* I will prophesy he comes to tell me of the players; mark it. You
say right, sir: o' Monday morning ; 'twas so indeed.
Pol. My lord, I have news to tell you.
Ham. My lord, I have news to tell you. When Roscius was an actor in Rome,—
Pol. The actors are come hither, my lord.
Ham. Buz, buz !
Pol. Upon mine honour,—
Ham. Then came each actor on his ass,—
Pol. The best actors in the world, either for tragedy, comedy, history, pastoral,
pastoral-comical, historical-pastoral, tragical-historical, tragical-comical-histori-
cal-pastoral, scene individable, or poem unlimited : Seneca cannot be too heavy,
nor Plautus too light. . . . . .
Ham. O Jephthah, judge of Israel, what a treasure hadst thou !
Pol. What a treasure had he, my lord ?
Ham. Why,
> ' One fair daughter, and no more,
>   The which he loved passing well.'
Pol. [*Aside.*] Still on my daughter.
Ham. Am I not i' the right, old Jephthah ?
Pol. If you call me Jephthah, my lord, I have a daughter that I love passing
well.
Ham. Nay, that follows not.
Pol. What follows then, my lord ?
Ham. Why,
> ' *As by lot, God wot,*'
and then, you know,
> ' *It came to pass, as most like it was,*'—
the first row of the pious chanson will show you more ; for look, where my
abridgment comes."

The last time we had Hamlet in conversation with Polonius, our hero spoke in parables, and in a state of cautious satire and irony. He was afraid of Polonius. But not so now. Polonius to Hamlet is an old tale twice told. Like a parrot, or as Goethe says: "I will speak like a book, when I am prepared beforehand; and like an ass, when I utter the overflowings of my heart."

And nothing could express the state of Polonius better than that of "a great baby," and an old one who has arrived at his second childhood. To Hamlet Polonius is nothing but words, repetition, and unmeaning ceremonies. Hamlet, after mocking Polonius, and turning him into the most painful ridicule, compares him to Jephthah. Now Jephthah is the very incarnation of the champion of a Shibboleth, and this is the likeness which Polonius and him share in common. Polonius is the champion of a Shibboleth. That Shibboleth is the Doctrine of the Church. Doctrine which, from the end of the second century, had been accumulating error upon error, and which the light, now steadily growing, was showing in all its hideousness. We quote from Dr. Draper as to the state of Europe before the end of the Dark Ages had arrived :—

"Doctrines were considered established by the number of martyrs who had professed them, by miracles, by the confession of demons, of lunatics, or of persons possessed of evil spirits : thus St. Ambrose, in his disputes with the Arians, produced men possessed by devils, who, on the approach of the relics of certain martyrs, acknowledged, with loud cries, that the Nicean doctrine of the three persons of the Godhead was true. But the Arians charged him with suborning these witnesses with a weighty bribe. Already ordeal tribunals were making their appearance. During the following six centuries they were held as a final resort, for establishing guilt or innocence, under the forms of trial by cold water, by duel, by the fire, by the Cross." Those who require weightier and more profuse evidence than this should read Buckle's History of Civilization in England, where, under the head of "The Origin of Historical Literature," they will find an almost incredible array of the credulity which existed in Europe barely three centuries ago. Putting ourselves once more under obligations to the same source as before, we have the following:—

"As the thirteenth century is approached, we find unbelief in all directions setting in. First it is plainly seen among the monastic orders, then it spreads rapidly among the common people. Books such as the Everlasting Gospel appear among the former; sects such as the Catharists, Waldenses, Petrobrussians, arise among the latter. They agreed in this: That the public and established religion was a motley system of errors and superstitions, and that the dominion which the Pope had usurped over Christians was unlawful and tyrannical; that the claim put forth by Rome, that the Bishop of Rome is the supreme lord of the universe, and that neither princes nor bishops, civil governors nor ecclesiastical rulers, have any lawful power in Church or State, but what they receive from him, is utterly without foundation, and a usurpation of the rights of man."

From this digression, necessary to keep History prior to the Reformation itself before the reader's eyes, we return to "Old Jephthah." Jephthah then will stand as a fit emblem of the Romish Church in all ages. And he, Polonius, like Jephthah, will sacrifice the life of his daughter, before he yield one iota of her tenets. His daughter, we need not repeat, is the Church; and he only loves her passing well. But how does he love her? That is the question. And Hamlet tells us—

"As bigot, God knows;"

for such is the meaning of our Poet's following words,

"As by lot, God wot."

Hamlet then points to the Players, who are his abridgments. They are impelled by Hamlet, and by love of Hamlet alone. The Reformers of Wittenberg are the abridgments of truth. Hamlet warns, nay, threatens Polonius. The first row or break out of the religious chanson or rebellion will teach

Polonius more. And, lo! here are the first stages of it at hand. The entrance of the Players is the commencement and gradual consummation of the Player-scene or Interlude. And to put our view on a clear footing before the reader, we will take it at once in hand.

Let us consider, first, a few facts. This scene is prompted and got up by Hamlet. The Players act at the request, and for the especial benefit of our hero.

They represent the murder of Gonzago. Who is Gonzago? And who is Baptista? Can we find out who is Lucianus? The whole scene is one which has been suggested to Hamlet by the Ghost. That Ghost means a succession of long doubts, aided by inquiry and research.

Marcellus and Bernardo, with Horatio, have inspired Hamlet, and he in his turn inspires the Players, and gives them the key-note in his lines beginning—"The rugged Pyrrhus."

But the Player-scene is a mere summary of all their work. In it we have the origin of error boldly thrown down in the face of the times. The whole Interlude is a direct charge ; and it is the charge which Luther brought against the Romish Church. Let us try and see how Shakespeare has realized this in the play? We have an acted copy of our hero's revelation received from the Ghost. And we shall first lay down our own interpretation of that revelation. Doubt first suggests to Hamlet with ever-increasing force, that error has supplanted truth. We have already seen from whence the source of this doubt, in the first act, and that doubt grows into a certainty that error has poisoned truth whilst sleeping in his orchard. Let us notice how typically this act of poisoning is artistically rendered—

> " *Ghost.* . . . Sleeping within mine orchard,
> My custom always of the afternoon,
> Upon my secure hour thy uncle stole,
> With juice of cursed hebenon in a vial,
> And in the porches of mine ear did pour
> The leperous distilment."

Is it not through the ears of men that truth or error find

admittance? And let us notice the poison used—"*Hebenon.*"
This word is almost "*non bene*," literally not good, or evil.
We must remember that the art of this play requires a two-
fold purpose: that of concealment, and that of yet keeping
the concealment within the bounds of discovery and the
spirit of rationalization. The mention of an orchard, and
particularly of a serpent, reminds us of the legend of the
Fall in the primeval Paradise of Scripture.

> " *Ghost.* . . . . . Now, Hamlet, hear :
> 'Tis given out, that sleeping in my *orchard*,
> A *serpent* stung me ; so the whole ear of Denmark
> Is by a forged process of my death
> *Rankly abused* : but know, thou noble youth,
> *The serpent* that did sting thy father's life
> *Now wears* his crown.

The meaning of the above may be taken as the identification by our Poet of error with the whole of the Biblical
tradition of the Temptation and Fall ; or it may not be so
taken. But when the whole play is completely worked out,
we shall find not only strong reasons for so thinking, but
ones which admit of very little choice, as far as consistency
is concerned. To return to the point in hand. Hamlet is
convinced that truth has been supplanted by error—that is,
by his uncle, the King. The Player-scene is a trick by
which Hamlet catches the conscience of the King. And
how does he effect this? By showing error its own face,
and by pointing out how he effected his crime. Let us
boldly define our position.

Lucianus in the Player-scene is Luther himself. Baptista
is human belief, and Gonzago[1] is Long-ago. The marriage
of Baptista and Gonzago is the pure apostolic faith in its
original simplicity as a scheme of benevolence ; and before
it began to be corrupted in the second century. That corruption is the effect of Lucianus. *But he is only acting what
the King has done. And Luther did this. He pointed out what
the King had done.* Lucianus (the break of day, translated

---

[1] Gonzago is an anagram upon Long-ago in all but the *z*, which is perhaps
altered on purpose.

literally), prompted by Hamlet, is pointing out artistically what the King has committed. *And Luther, studying the Bible, pointed out how the Romish Church had poured corruption* into the ears of a once pure and holy union. The whole Player-scene, we repeat, is the act of the Reformation. As Hamlet remarks:

"His name's Gonzago: the story is extant, *and writ in choice Italian.*"

Shakespeare has taken actors as the type of true action in the world. A hint which Goethe hastily seized, and reproduced in the Wilhelm Meister. And we see actually in the play what consternation and what mighty results spring from this small interlude. The reader not seizing our stand-point, may ask why Lucianus poisons Gonzago in the piece? We reply, Lucianus is only acting, and thus imitating the King's crime. He is thus exposing the King. Baptista is an image of the Queen, who, as Belief, has proved false to her first love, and married the King. This is the history of Christianity, as regards its Roman Catholic corruption. It has allied itself to error. After the death of Gonzago, or Long-ago, Luther pointed this out, and in boldly doing this he effected and consummated the Protestant Reformation. But Luther, or Lucianus, and the rest of the players are prompted by Hamlet. Hamlet is therefore the real cause of all this. And our hero is according to us the Spirit of Truth, prompted by the Ghost (Doubt), and aided by those who are part of him. The whole scene is introduced "tropically," or figuratively. And the murder was done in Vienna, which is another way of cleverly expressing Vie, or life. No wonder Ophelia says to Hamlet—

"You are as good as a chorus, my lord."

Now we can understand why Hamlet takes up his position at Ophelia's feet. It is the Church he is most interested with. Religious reform is his business. And Polonius at last has grown alarmed.

" *Pol.* [*To the King*] O, oh! do you mark that?

We can now understand why Hamlet calls himself the "only jig-maker" to Ophelia. The introduction of the word Baptista speaks for itself. And Lucianus represents not only an approximation to Luther, but in its translation, his very essence—the break of day. Luther was indeed the break of day, or rather we should say, the Reformation.

CHAPTER II.

HAVING got so far in advance of our subject as regards the text, we may return to that part of the drama which precedes the Interlude. And we will take the passage of passages—the most beautiful as well as the best known of all Shakespeare's profound soliloquies. That is, "To be, or not to be." What does it mean? To us it signifies a determination on the part of man to act. And it is a recognition of how theology has always crippled action.

> "*Ham.* Thus conscience does make cowards of us all;
> And thus the native hue of resolution
> Is sicklied o'er with the pale cast of thought,
> And enterprises of great pith and moment
> With this regard their currents turn awry,
> And lose the name of action."

Immediately after this monologue, Hamlet repudiates and insults Ophelia. The last time we have him with her, he simply criticizes, sighs, and leaves her. Now he abuses, and tells her to "get to a nunnery." The whole of this great soliloquy is the change of a passive policy to an active one. It is the determination of persecuted and oppressed humanity to have no more of it—to rise, to rebel, and to free themselves. It is the gathering thunder of the Reformation. It is indeed a question of "To be, or not to be." All the burthens of this world are summed up in it. Every calamity which man tyranically heaps upon his fellow-man is touched upon. "The oppressor's wrong, the proud man's contumely, the law's delay, the insolence of office, and the spurns that patient merit of the unworthy takes." And what is Hamlet's conclusion to all these ills? Nothing less than that they are borne because man will not take arms against them; and is hampered by those doubts which concern the future life, and are expressed by religion. The whole soliloquy is a review of two worlds: a passive one, and an active one; and it recognizes the grounds upon which the passiveness rests. Every ill of man is thus put down to a want of resolution. It is the dread of "something after death" that "makes us rather bear those ills we have, than fly to others that we know not of." "It is conscience which makes cowards of us all." Our Poet knew how plastic a thing conscience is, and he knew how much of it lay in the hands of the Church. It is this which prevents "enterprises of great pith and moment" from becoming action. And let us ask ourselves if this great masterpiece of thought uttered by Hamlet has not a deep and profound meaning, with regard to the unity of the whole drama? If it has not, what is its meaning? Why is it introduced in such an odd way, and at such a moment? Hamlet, as man, at a certain historical period and crisis, is deliberating upon action and inaction: "Whether it is nobler to take arms against a sea of troubles, and by opposing end them?"

The whole piece is in exquisite harmony with the esoteric and exoteric sides of the play. It is not too developed on either side of art. We may take it as merely a beautiful summing up of the miseries of life, and of the doubts which perplex us as to an hereafter; and thus place us on the horns of a dilemma. Or, again, we may recognize through its outer garb the profound identification of the ills of the period, and the oppressive intolerance of the Church of the age. Immediately after this soliloquy, Hamlet meets Ophelia. And we notice how changed his manners are to her. His letter to her was simply one of reproach. Now he wantonly insults her. Are we to conclude that he has decided in his mind that it is "to be," and looks firmly forwards to combat with his "arms against a sea of troubles?"

It is difficult to escape such a conclusion ; particularly when we take into consideration the correlation of the parts of the play.   At the end of the second act Hamlet has decided to catch the conscience of the King.   This decision would only be in keeping with a gradual estrangement from Ophelia.   And, finally, he must arrive at a point of determination and action in this respect.   This is the realization, in our opinion, of the necessity of immediate action ; and it is the first determined step of the Reformers themselves. But although we have endeavoured to parallel, step by step, the play with actual history, we only do so, of course (on hypothesis), for the sake of clearer exposition.   Shakespeare was far too catholic not to express rather the philosophy of history than the detail of history.   We recognize (ourselves), under the mask of the Reformation, far wider principles than the mere reform of a religion.   In it we see the first direct recognition by men of their own ignorance, of their own error, and of the delusions of the past.   Thus do we read, so far, the tragedy of Hamlet.   Let us now take a review of the first two acts.   The first is a summary of the gathering scepticism and the causes of that scepticism, which, like the break of a dawn, dispels the darkness of the midnight of past ages.   The soldier in ignorance is relieved by the officer with less ignorance, and he brings another in necessarily with him, and they together see a Ghost.   That Ghost, however, is at first very uncertain—almost an

" Extravagant and erring spirit,"

which is contrasted with the reality of the noisy cock. The cock is, by his comparison with Christmas, identified with certainty.

> " *Mar.* It faded on the crowing of the cock.
> Some say that ever 'gainst that season comes
> Wherein our Saviour's birth is celebrated,
> The bird of dawning singeth all night long :
> And then, they say, no spirit dares stir abroad ;
> The nights are wholesome ; then no planets strike,
> No fairy takes, nor witch hath power to charm,
> So hallow'd and so gracious is the time."

Thus doubt and certainty succeed each other until the first pale streaks of dawn begin to illumine the Dark Ages.

> "*Hor.* But, look, the morn, in russet mantle clad,
> Walks o'er the dew of yon high eastward hill:
> Break we our watch up; and by my advice,
> Let us impart what we have seen to-night
> Unto young Hamlet."

Thus the first scene of the first act is the epitome of a long lapse of time, and we first hear of Hamlet at the very end of it. From whom? From Marcellus, whom we can well understand is most fit to find him. Let us note the expression, *young* Hamlet. The second secne introduces us to the King, Queen, Hamlet, Polonius, Laertes, Voltimand, and Cornelius. We are informed of the position of affairs by the King. We are put *au courant* with the pith of the play. That is, the marriage of the King. A wedding which Hamlet always recognizes as a source of sorrow and regret. We are told how Fortinbras is

> "Importing the surrender of those lands
> Lost by his father." [1]

And Voltimand and Cornelius are despatched to Norway to aid in putting down the revolt. Voltimand [2] and Cornelius we suspect to- be Force and Hard-heartedness. Voltimand may mean to " put down revolt." And Cornelius is literally " stony-hearted." Who are they sent to? Norway. Him we believe to be Wrong and Tyranny. And what signifies Fortinbras? Let us remark he is nephew to Norway. Thus he represents the same relation Hamlet holds to the King. And we know Fortinbras is with Hamlet, as is Hamlet with him. We therefore shall call Fortinbras (or strong in arm) the Spirit of Liberty indispensable to the advance of Truth. And though repressed at first, and put down by Wrong, aided by Force and Hard-heartedness, he, never-

---

[1] This is the first rise of liberty.
[2] The verb *mandere* and *volt*, short for *revolt* probably.

theless, will come in triumphant at the end of the play. Error is thus making use of his tools Voltimand and Cornelius. But they soon disappear in the development and continuity of the play. The times soon become too advanced for their use. Thus, at the opening of the second scene of the first act, the King is in autocratic and uncompromised power. Hamlet is actually but just born, and even then as powerless as his early youth must make him. We now hear for the first time of Laertes. He is identified with Reason:

> " *King.* . . . You cannot speak *of reason* to the Dane,
> And lose your voice."

Laertes is accordingly Education. His travels into France are the gradual spread of learning, so indispensable to the entire development of the play. But, owing to his parentage, he always preserves a traditional and faithful bias. He is true to his father's principles, though of course modified by time, in question of autocracy. And he disappears for a long time from the play.[1] We shall meet him again by and by. We would call attention to his name, which, being connected with that of Ulysses, not inaptly reminds us of his true mission—wisdom and eloquence. His father only gives his leave when wrung from him:

> " *Pol.* . . . By slow and laboursome petition."

This shows us what difficulties authority, bigotry, and tradition threw in the way of all learning. Hamlet now gives us the key to his own character in the speech we have already quoted. His uncle tries to argue him down, and persuade Hamlet that he (the King) is a true father to him. In short, it is the effort of the age to put some stop to the rising and growing discontent and doubt. Hamlet is entreated not to go to Wittenberg. This immemorial spot not inaptly reminds us of the direction, rise, and purport

---

[1] His disappearance, like that of Fortinbras, is his silent growth.

of the Reformation. A movement which the King and Queen are not slow in using all their persuasive powers to prevent. The discontent, unhappiness, and misery of all who recognize corruption is well personified in Hamlet's first soliloquy. This is immediately followed by the action and entrance of Horatio, Bernardo, and Marcellus. They come to tell Hamlet of the Ghost. They, of course, come from Wittenberg. This is the very head-quarters of the Ghost. Presently, however, Hamlet inspires the rest, for he says :

> "Methinks I see my father."

And Horatio saw him once.

> " *Hor.* I saw him once; he was a goodly king."

Thus Hamlet acts upon the three, and they react upon him in their turn. And now they first dare to exchange suspicions and surmisals. The growing doubts gather greater certainty, from the action and interaction of inquiry,—a growing spirit of justice and love of liberty. To these must be added Bernardo, who is the very foundation-stone, as he is the slow growth of printing and reading.

The third scene opens with Laertes and Ophelia. The former warns Ophelia against encouraging Hamlet. It is the warning of traditional knowledge against the Reforming schism. Polonius now enters. In the admirable precepts he gives his son, we recognize much that applies to an education kept strictly upon the lines of orthodoxy and tradition. And education is not to be vulgar or common. It is to be only studied by those who have costly purses. How profoundly crafty and worldly-wise are these wonderful instructions. As usual, we recognize in this passage the marvellous profundity of Shakespeare's art. For we may read it without a thought of an ulterior meaning, beyond what the plain text carries upon its surface. Or we may see, without any great effort of imagination, how it applies

in every detail to the principles upon which Polonius grants
leave to Laertes to travel.

> "*Pol.* . . . Give thy thoughts no tongue,
> Nor any unproportioned thought his act.
> Be thou familiar, but by no means vulgar.
> Those friends thou hast, and their adoption tried,
> Grapple them to thy soul with hoops of steel;
> But do not dull thy palm with entertainment
> Of each new-hatch'd unfledged comrade."

In the above we have the essence of all traditional and
Tory principles. Education is not to be common or vulgar.
It is to remain faithful to its old friends and principles.
And it must "grapple them to its soul with hoops of steel."
This is all true conservatism. It is not to entertain new
ideas, or new-hatched doctrines and theories. It is to beware of controversy, as carrying danger with it. And it is,
when so provoked, to stamp out such controversy with a
strong hand.

> "*Pol.* Give every man thy ear, but few thy voice;
> Take each man's censure, but reserve thy judgment."

Cautiousness is instilled in the above. Laertes is hardly
ever to be heard. Few are to hear his voice. But he is to
keep a sharp look out upon others. Again, fancy is a thing
to be repressed. And we see how much is insisted upon in
dress, and not in the "man" himself:

> "The apparel oft proclaims the man."

Laertes is to cultivate the garb of learning, not its essence.
Style, bombast, and exterior, are to cover up an inner worth-
lessness.[1] Nor is he to borrow from others in any way.
Again, and lastly, he is to be true to himself; which means
true to Polonius and tradition.

Polonius now warns Ophelia against Prince Hamlet. She
is not to take him for sterling truth. It is the anger of the

---

[1] At the end of the play we find this confirmed in the way Hamlet identifies
Laertes with diction, etc., etc.

Church, prompted by authority, against our hero, which is beginning to make itself evident.

The fourth scene opens with the entry of Hamlet, Horatio, and Marcellus.

> "*Ham.* The air bites shrewdly ; it is very cold.
> *Hor.* It is a nipping and an eager air."

The above shows us how eager and sharp the age has grown. Humanity are getting keen-scented, and they begin to smell a rat. They are in a fit state to behold the Ghost. We have travelled in time, histrionically, perhaps barely half an hour. In time, historically, we have moved perhaps two or three centuries since the opening of the play. It is necessary to keep some such adequate proportions of the requirements of time before our reader's eyes, in order that they may endeavour to seize the right parallax of Hamlet. The age has grown so eager, and the air bites so shrewdly, that, with the aid of Hamlet, it takes direct umbrage for the first time of the " King's wake " and " wassel." And Hamlet begins to philosophize over the wrongs of the age. He distinctly recognizes wrong, error, etc., and points it out to Horatio and Marcellus. The Ghost, therefore, comes in with startling effect.[1] Nothing is more likely than a revelation :

> " *Ham.* Thou comest in such a *questionable* shape
> That I will speak to thee."

The rest of the first act is the detection by Hamlet of his father's murder. And the necessity of secrecy, due to the age, is insisted upon by Hamlet. The act ends with the joint action of the friends, scholars and soldiers. They go in together. The first act is an explanation and the dramatic action of the causes which led first to Hamlet's birth ; then doubt and final certainty of the existence of error in the King, and the murder of truth in his father's person by the former. The first act is the birth of Hamlet and his growth. The second is his growth into certainty and a determination to act. The third is the centre act of

---

[1] Goethe has powerfully brought this out in Wilhelm Meister.

the tragedy, and the axis of the play. In it the determination is effected, and its results portrayed. The fourth act deals directly with the results springing from the death of Polonius. The fifth act is a condensed chorus of time, and the end of social conflict, as pictured by our poet.

We are now again in the second act. And as we have already dealt with much of it, we will summarize the whole, only dwelling on points omitted before. The act opens with the means Polonius employs to keep Laertes true to his parentage. It is the repression of all liberty of conscience, and it is aided by the Inquisition and the " Index Expurgatorius." Ophelia is profoundly criticized by Hamlet, who is in prison, with gyves about his ancles.

> " *Oph.* . . . . No hat upon his head; his stockings foul'd,
> Ungarter'd, and down-gyved to his ancle;
> Pale as his shirt; his knees knocking each other;
> And with a look so piteous in purport
> As if he had been loosed out of hell
> To speak of horrors,—he comes before me."

Here we have a dreadful picture of the way heresy was being punished. Hamlet has long been under the ban of heresy. In the above quotation we have all the horrors of hell let loose upon us. We have the Inquisition, the rack, the long lingering imprisonment, with the " gyves about the ancles." What was this period? and where can we find an historical parallel?

Dr. Draper says :[1] " To withstand this flood of impiety, the Papal Government established two institutions : 1. The Inquisition ; 2. Auricular Confession—the latter as a means of detection, the former as a tribunal of punishment. In general terms the commission of the Inquisition was to extirpate religious dissent by terrorism, and surround heresy with the most horrible associations ; this necessarily implied the power of determining what constitutes heresy. The criterion of truth was thus in possession of this tribunal, which was charged ' to discover and bring to judgment heretics, lurking in towns, houses, cellars, woods, caves, and

---

[1] History of the Conflict between Religion and Science. .

fields.' With such savage alacrity did it carry out its object
of protecting the interests of religion, that between 1481
and 1808 it had *punished three hundred and forty thousand
persons, and of these nearly thirty-two thousand had been burnt.*
In its earlier days, when public opinion could find no means
of protesting against its atrocities, '*it often put to death
without appeal, on the very day that they were accused, nobles,
clerks, monks, hermits,* and lay persons of every rank.' In
whatever direction thoughtful men looked, the air was full
of fearful shadows. No one could indulge in freedom of
thought without expecting punishment. So dreadful were
the proceedings of the Inquisition, that the exclamation of
Pagliarici was the exclamation of thousands : ' It is hardly
possible for a man to be a Christian and die in his bed.'
The Inquisition destroyed the sectaries of Southern France
in the thirteenth century. Its unscrupulous atrocities ex-
tirpated Protestantism in Italy and Spain. *Nor did it confine
itself to religious affairs; it' engaged in the suppression of
political discontent.* Nicholas Eymeric, who was Inquisitor-
General of the kingdom of Aragon for nearly fifty years,
and who died in 1399, has left a frightful statement of its
conduct and appalling cruelties in his '*Directorium Inquisi-
torum.*' "

And again: "By the power of the fourth Lateran Council,
A.D. 1215, the power of the Inquisition was frightfully increased, the necessity of private confession to a priest—
auricular confession—being at that time established, not a
man was safe. In the hands of the priest, who, at the con-
fessional, could extract or extort from them their most secret
thoughts, his wife and his servants were turned into spies.
No accuser was named; but the thumb-screw, the stretch-
ing-rope, the boot, the wedge, or other enginery of torture,
soon supplied that defect, and, innocent or guilty, he accused
himself! Notwithstanding all this power, the Inquisition
failed of its purpose. When the heretic could no longer
confront it, he evaded it. A dismal disbelief stealthily per-
vaded all Europe—a denial of Providence, of the immortality of the soul, of human free will, and that man cannot

possibly resist the absolute necessity, the destiny which envelopes him."

The whole of the above extract realizes the position of Hamlet up to the death of Polonius. What does the Ghost say?

> " *Ghost.* Mark me.
> *Ham.*   I will.
> *Ghost.*   My hour is almost come,
> When I to *sulphurous and tormenting flames*
> *Must render up myself.*"

Here we have the martyrdom of those who dare to doubt—heretics. Again :

> " *Ghost.* I am thy father's spirit,
> Doom'd for a certain term to walk the night,
> *And for the day confined to fast in fires,*
> Till the foul crimes done in my days of nature
> Are burnt and purged away."

So doubt is " confined to fast in fires." The stake and the prison are clearly indicated here. And the " foul crimes " will only be burnt and purged away when " the days of nature," the apprenticeship of man, is past. So we see that the fifth scene of the first act represents the beginning of religious persecution—of heresy.

As regards Hamlet, we find everywhere the expression of a deep misery, as deep as is compatible with his rank as Prince. Especially is his first monologue of this character :

> " *Ham.* O, that this too too solid flesh would melt,
> Thaw and resolve itself into a dew !

These are almost the words of a man under excruciating torture. And again, later :

> " *Ham.* I have of late—but wherefore I know not—lost all my mirth, forgone all custom of exercises : and indeed it goes so heavily with my disposition that this goodly frame, the earth, seems to me a sterile promontory, this most excellent canopy, the air, look you, this brave o'erhanging firmament, this majestical roof fretted with golden fire, why, it appears no other thing to me than a foul and pestilent congregation of vapours. What a piece of work is a man ! how noble in reason ! how infinite in faculty ! in form and moving how express and admirable ! in action how like an angel ! in apprehension how like a god ! the beauty of the world ! the paragon of animals ! And yet, to me, what is this quintessence of dust ? man delights not me : no, nor woman neither, though by your smiling you seem to say so."

Here we have that profound despondency which we have had historically vouched for by Dr. Draper. And now, can we wonder at the description given by Ophelia of Hamlet? After Ophelia's report to her father of Hamlet's criticism and inspection, Polonius goes to the King and informs him of it.

The whole of the second scene of the second act is a very long one. And it is the history of the growth of Hamlet's determination to act. We have (which we have already treated at length) Hamlet's letter to Ophelia. We have Ophelia's sequestration from Hamlet on this account. And we also have the first encounter of Polonius and Hamlet. The tone of the latter is hidden satire and contempt. Then Rosencrantz and Guildenstern are recognized in their nakedness by Hamlet. And now we hear, for the first time, of the Players. Hamlet has recognized the bigotry of Polonius, and begun to mock him. We now reach a part of the text we have hitherto left untouched. We allude to his meeting with the Players. The description of the Players is one which inclines us to believe these Players are not only the knowledge of the age, but that they are prompted by Hamlet. For Hamlet makes the first speech. And they merely take up the cue he has given them. That cue is one in which Hamlet appeals to the human˙heart, and gives a picture of the times. At the end of his speech he says, " *So proceed you.*" We believe Hamlet is inciting the Players to continue in this strain. That strain is :

" An honest method, as wholesome as sweet, and by very much more handsome than fine."

The whole of this piece upon Pyrrhus is but a picture of the times. And Pyrrhus may stand for the Inquisition and persecution of the age.

" Hath now this dread and black complexion smear'd
With heraldry more dismal ; head to foot
Now is he total gules (blood) ; horridly trick'd
With blood of fathers, mothers, daughters, sons."

The persecution of the times and its horrors are admirably

painted in this classical speech. It is profoundly subtle and difficult to fathom anywhere Shakespeare's true meaning. No doubt the whole of Hamlet's intercourse with the Players is a summary of the causes immediately prior to the Reformation. We recognize how powerfully the Players react upon Hamlet. They alone give him direct force, to catch the conscience of the King. We could hazard a great deal of speculation upon this particular part of the play; but it is undoubtedly the profoundest, and requires a study beyond our time and limits. The whole speech of Hamlet and the Players, taken as a whole, is infinitely touching, and calculated to move the heart. It is probably an appeal from Genius to the human heart, by picturing the wretched state of the "mobled" Queen, and the tyranny and brutality of Pyrrhus. The latter is called a "painted tyrant." The word "mobled" is approved of by Polonius. Perhaps he considers the Queen (who probably represents the persecuted heretics) a belief which is mob-led, or only a rabble led by false principles. She runs up and down,

"Threatening the flames with bisson rheum."

Pyrrhus is thus undoubtedly intended to represent, and is held up to scorn as, the persecution and intolerance of the times. The whole piece is an appeal to the heart. The Players, who are the actors in deed and in thought of the Reformation, are prompted, of course, first by Hamlet. And so we find he starts the subject. This is the leadership of genius. This is the work of an Erasmus. The later work is that of a Luther and a Melancthon. The whole speech is a history of the Romish Church, under the artistic garb of Pyrrhus. And we are told how Pyrrhus

"Couched in the ominous horse."

—that is, corrupted through the night of the Dark Ages, has dyed his hands in blood. The old Priam, who may well stand for the first and older faith before corrupted, is killed by this younger birth, of

" . . . . Sable arms,
Black as his purpose, did the night resemble."

And then the First Player proceeds to tell us how Pyrrhus falls upon Priam.

> " Out, out, thou strumpet, Fortune! All you gods,
> In *general synod*, take away her power."

This reference to "General Synod" seems to further our criticisms. Then we have a piteous picture of the poor Queen, calculated to stir the sympathy of our hearts. This we believe is the trumpet call to arms on behalf of the persecuted. However, the effect upon Hamlet is profound. We have the first of those long soliloquies, which are full of self-upbraiding and a consciousness of weakness.[1] Our hero is acted upon most powerfully. His irresolution turns into determination to act. Yet we feel he can be aided in his entire revenge by time alone. He is too weak to do more than hope that he may grow stronger, and do what lies within his power. These soliloquies of Hamlet's are his-torical impulses. They are the actions of epochs momentous in the world's history. They are the determination of mankind to take steps, fraught with danger, but also fraught with safety. In this Player-scene we have the first appeal by man to man before the Reformation. It is an outspoken voice. And we see in the soliloquy how it lifts, how it gives force and determination to the still weak but resolute Hamlet.

Up to the end of the second act we have now arrived. How little we have done to illuminate the text, we are aware. For Hamlet is, as Goethe puts it :—" A trunk with boughs, twigs, leaves, buds, blossoms, and fruit ? Is not the one there with the others, and by means of them ?" Nothing could express the construction of Hamlet better. Every part is connected with another part. Every ante-cedent has its consequent. It is in short the evolution of history. A history which stops short with man's apprentice-ship, and is continued by Goethe in man's travels. Law is epitomized throughout the play. Nothing is spontaneous,

---

[1] These soliloquies are dramatic expressions of action and reaction.

nothing is premature. All is orderly, and everything falls into its place by the necessity of sequence.

Our great aim has been so far to throw light upon the author's signification and meaning. To give force to the leaves, buds, and twigs, requires a profundity on a par with our Poet's alone. We leave that work to those who are more fitted to the task. We must apologize for the way in which the reader is taken, at one sweep, from one part of the text to another part. For our purpose being to suggest a Philosophy of Hamlet, we think proof and connexion verified in the simplest manner more telling than an esoteric essay based upon a comprehension of Goethe's Wilhelm Meister. Let us pass over the early part of the third act, and resume our thread after the end of the Player-scene. This Player-scene is of course the turning-point of the play. From it almost directly all the other events succeed as a matter of course. The detection of error or the King is now complete. Hamlet is no longer troubled by further doubts. From this moment there is a schism. The King recognizes the power and the reality of Hamlet. Hitherto he has almost doubted Hamlet's madness. Now he is certain of it. And in this sense we mean his power and his badness in the eyes of the King. To prove this we will quote a speech of the King's prior to the Player-scene :—

> " *King.* Nor what he spake, though it lack'd form a little,
> Was not like madness."

After the Player-scene we have the King saying :—

> " I like him not, nor stands it safe with us
> To let his *madness* range."

Again (Act iv. Sc. 1)—

> " *King.* This mad young man."

From the end of the Player-scene we have a difference of attitude between Hamlet and his partisans and those of the King, to what we have hitherto found. Hamlet simply defies the King. Polonius has now begun to mock Hamlet. And though still accompanied by Guildenstern and Rosencrantz, Hamlet first repudiates the one, and then the other. He clearly points out the nature of their characters. To one he says

> "Though you can fret me, yet you cannot play upon me." [1]

To the other he says

> "You are a 'sponge,' and soak up the King's countenance, his rewards, his authorities." [2]

We must not leave out the important part Horatio has taken in the Player-scene. He has been simply critical, and although apparently passive, his work has been nobly shared with Hamlet. He claims half a share.

> "*Hor.* Half a share."

It is Horatio who has played the part of scholarly criticism. Imbued with the spirit of Hamlet, he has supplied the scholarly qualities, the earnestness, the independence of spirit, and the love of justice. He is half of Hamlet, and no mean part of the whole company of Players.

Hamlet supplies the instruction to the Players, which, let us particularly remark, is alone that of truth. Every line of his advice to the Players is to

> "Hold, as 'twere, the mirror up to nature ; to show virtue her own feature, scorn her *own image, and the very age and body of the time his form and pressure.*"

This is exactly what the Reformation succeeded in doing. The result was that men "scorned her own image," and followed "virtue" according to quite a new pattern.

Now let us try and follow what comes after the Player-scene as regards the action alone of the tragedy.

---

[1] This passage brings out forcibly our theory : that Guildenstern is Sophistry, and evasion of truth.

[2] Here we have the essence of Rosencrantz, as the self-interested alone.

The first great result is in the next or fourth scene of the act. Hamlet, for the first time, has a private interview with his mother.[1] Polonius, as usual, given to intolerance and interference, tries to prevent this conference, and in so doing loses his life. The death of Polonius is the death of intolerance; it is simply liberty of conscience. With it the Reformation is completed—not until. The Player-scene is the whole of the struggle of the Reformation. The death of Polonius is the comparative end of bigotry, gross superstition and interference. It is true that in some countries these things have lingered on into comparatively modern times. But the play is only concerned with the advanced guard of Europe. The rest must follow, sooner or later, so they are immaterial. Let us once more take a survey of the character of Polonius. He is the bulwark and backbone of the King. He is the greater part indeed in all ages of the King. He is authority based upon the past, infallibility, and bigotry. He is the Romish Church. He is everything that is old, and that is venerated, not on account of its intrinsic truth or worth, but on account of its age and its familiarity with men's minds. As if the world had socially no infancy, the adult social man would go back to his childhood for instruction. Surely this is something foolish. Individualism as personified by Hamlet is always at war with Polonius. One is liberalism, the other we call all sorts of names at different ages of its decline, and we recognize also its usefulness. It is the scaffolding, which keeps the structure firm, until it can stand by itself. When each particle is self-governed, we can remove the scaffold. And this we do bit by bit. Sometimes so fast, that we have to repair again what has been removed. And we call this conservative reaction.

The death of Polonius is only the death of one of the King's protean forms. And Polonius, though apparently

---

[1] The Queen is, in our opinion, human belief. Her marriage is error in belief or belief in error.

dead, lingers on—in a state of corruption, it is true, but still
for a part of the play. It is this continuity of the play
which makes it so difficult to fix upon the historical parallel
which accompanies it. Shakespeare has clearly realized that
there are no broken events in history. Some may seem so,
from the apparent obscurity of their causes. But on second
inspection they vanish in their causes themselves. The
King and Polonius are always dying slowly, and of an
almost imperceptible disease. And both the King and Polonius must not be separated. For one is the essence of the
other. Therefore we realize how our poet is compelled in his
dramatic art to give force to historical events, which have
occupied long periods in being brought about, by one stroke
of his pen. Such is the death of Polonius by Hamlet. Our
own interpretation of this climax of the play is, historically,
the completion and partial results of the Reformation. The
gains by man of liberty of speech, liberty of conscience,
and general independence of mind. It is realized in the
Protestant Reformation, and the freedom from Polonius
springing therefrom. Hamlet is always aiming at nothing
short but the death of the King. And who says he never
acts? Is not the death of Polonius the greatest stab Hamlet
can give the King? He has actually hacked off a large part
of him. For he has destroyed his defence, his impregna-
bility, and the fortress is both sapped and mined. Time will
now blow up the whole edifice.

The death of Polonius is the dramatic climax and centre
of the tragedy. From it events take a completely new
direction and complexion. It leads to Hamlet's banishment.
Ophelia's madness is the direct offspring of it; and her
death follows, as a matter of necessity. The revolution of
Laertes is another direct consequence of the same event.
Let us clearly understand Polonius. Upon his life and
shoulders rest two institutions. These are Ophelia and
Laertes. The former is the very essence of Polonius. Can
we say more when we say Shakespeare has done marvellously well in making her the daughter of Polonius?
Her claims to existence are upon the grounds of the

validity of tradition. Her life depends upon that of her father. As long as his integrity is preserved, she is safe; but with his fall, she is open to criticism, to inspection, and to discussion. This is how the death of Polonius brings about the suicide of Ophelia. Laertes, on the contrary, is a modified Polonius. One who is quite unable to protect Ophelia. The death of his father is a thing he is bound to revenge. We notice what a weak copy he is of Polonius. How abortive his revolution. How soon pacified he becomes, and how he takes his father's place as the supporter of the King. Laertes is the continuity of Polonius in the shape of Toryism, of conservatism, of reaction. The death of Polonius is therefore, we take it, the end of direct interference. The closet-scene of Hamlet and the Queen is a picture of man appealing to man's belief. The Queen we identify with human belief and faith. She is the credulity of the human heart, easily deceived by the King. Error and belief are one. Hamlet knows this full well:—

" *Ham.* . . Farewell, dear mother.
King. Thy loving father, Hamlet.
Ham. My mother: *father and mother is man and wife; man and wife is one flesh; and so, my mother.*"

Error only exists by the persistency of belief. And we see how particular Shakespeare is never to let us know that the Queen knows aught of her former husband's murder. Hamlet reproaches her with it, it is true. But this is only consistent with the exposure of error. The whole address of our hero to his mother is one in which an appeal is made to humanity by man. We see how the Queen is identified with custom.

"*Ham. That monster, custom, who all sense doth eat,*
Of habits devil, is angel yet in this,
That to the use of actions fair and good
He likewise gives a frock or livery,
That aptly is put on."

And the amazement of the Queen, when Hamlet says—

" A bloody deed! almost as bad, good mother,
As kill a king, and marry with his brother.
Queen. As kill a king!'"

—leads us to believe it is a novelty, that has never struck
her with any force hitherto. For her exclamation is one
of amazement, and not of guilt. A little later the Queen
says

> "What have I done, that thou darest wag thy tongue
> In noise so rude against me ?"

This does not look like the consciousness of overwhelming
guilt. And it takes a long time before Hamlet can make
an impression upon her. He says :

> " If damned custom have not brass'd it so
> That it is proof and bulwark against sense."

He uses the word *sense*, not the word *truth*. Custom is
again insisted upon as the source of all the evil.

The Queen even again protests her innocence, in words
which seem those of perfect innocence :

> " Ay me, what act,
> That roars so loud, and thunders in the index ? "

Finally, what does Hamlet point out to the Queen ?

> "*Ham.* . . . O, such a deed
> *As from the body of contraction plucks*
> *The very soul, and sweet religion makes*
> *A rhapsody of words.*"

This is exactly what the Reformation pointed out. The
Romish religion is a rhapsody of words—nothing more.

Hamlet now contrasts truth with error. He pictures his
father. And he pictures the King. The reader may ask,
Who is Hamlet's father ? We answer ideal truth implanted
in the mind of man. It is the voice of God whispering to
us. It is ideal justice, ideal liberty, ideal truth. Impossible quantities. The complements which separate man
from God. Not contained upon an earth, nor in humanity ;
but still conceived in a unity, that is divine, and as ideal
beacons to which we ever advance.

The Ghost of Hamlet's father is doubt. Doubt is the

complement to the next truth. For there is no absolute truth for us. The ideal truth is realism. And that is God alone. Doubt is therefore an active scepticism, the step from one belief to a higher one. And this is the great march of humanity. The truth of one age is the untruth of another. And yet both were true in their way. The justice of one age is not the justice of the next. Yet both seem true in their respective ages. This is no contradiction, not even a paradox. Absolute truth is not for man. Only an eternal march towards a greater perfection. This world seems almost the realization of God himself, unrolling himself in an endless march towards himself. An infinite series of terms, which, like himself, are endless.

The step, therefore, to every higher truth is by doubt. And the Ghost is the shadow of the father. Doubt is the shadow of truth. As it fades, it leaves the truth and certainty in greater relief by contrast. Doubt is only a higher reason. For who doubts, and why do we doubt? Those only doubt who have an ideal by which to criticize, and by which to contrast what they doubt. And that ideal is in itself a belief. Thus we only doubt because we believe *something else* with a much stronger certainty than the former. Doubt is thus only the son and the father of truth.

Hamlet cannot address his mother until Polonius is removed. Therefore our poet has made the direct interference of the Lord Chamberlain the cause of his own death. Hamlet at first thinks he has killed the King. But the King is not to be killed so easily. The King is mortally wounded, but not dead yet awhile for some few centuries to come.

Shakespeare has completely realized the importance of Polonius as the support of the King. He has therefore made his death the pivot upon which the climax of the drama is reached. From this time the King suffers a series of reverses. Revolution stares him in the face. He shows open fear of Hamlet. He says :—

> " Like to a murdering-piece, in many places
> Gives me superfluous death."

This is exactly what the life of the King realizes after the
end of Polonius. It is actually "a murdering-piece in many
places."

Error, superstition, hypocrisy, authority, bigotry, darkness, are all giving way before the light of modern Europe.
But we must not anticipate. We return to the Player-scene,
which we have endeavoured to show is an artistic parallel
of the Reformation. The result of this scene is the schism
which takes place between Ophelia and Hamlet. Let it be
well noted, they never meet again until Laertes and Hamlet
fight over her grave.

What a marvellous difference the Player-scene has brought
about in the character of Hamlet! We notice a similar, but
opposite change on the King's side. Hamlet says

"Ah, ah! Come, some music! come, the recorders!"

This is Shakespeare's way of expressing harmony. (See
"The Merchant of Venice," and *passim*.) The Queen is
struck into "amazement and admiration." Surely, if she
were conscious of guilt, she would not use these words!
We maintain (though perhaps not wholly without the feeling of some doubt) custom and ignorance are her greatest
faults. Belief is going at last to have an interview privately,
in a closet, with Hamlet.

The entrance of the players with the recorders is the
union of music and action, of harmony and the age? It is
perhaps the first harmony heard in Europe since the Disciples of our Lord preached the life of righteousness.

Guildenstern is no longer able to play upon Hamlet.
Sophistry cannot make what it likes of truth. The arts of
Guildenstern have not been able to prevent things coming
to this pass. And Hamlet now compares himself to a pipe,
—to harmony. And in this we recognize Shakespeare's
meaning through Hamlet. Guildenstern has no harmony
in him. He can reconcile nothing. And this is his fault,
he would reconcile the impossible, and he would play upon
truth. Hamlet therefore throws down his pipe, and magnifi-

cently exclaims with eyes of withering scorn and in a voice of thunder :

> " 'Sblood, do you think I am easier to be played on than a pipe ? Call me what instrument you will, though you can fret me, yet you cannot play upon me."

Sophistry is the art of making the worse appear the better. It is a direct evasion of truth by means of false logic. Therefore it only frets truth. Truth is an instrument, it cannot

> " Command to any utterance of harmony."

Hamlet drives Guildenstern to own this as regards a pipe. And then he applies the same argument to himself. The hypocrisy of Guildenstern is shown up and exposed for the first time. And he in common with the rest of the King's allies has felt a slight wound. Sophistry and hypocrisy, the habit of not facing difficulties, and of deception, cannot play upon truth. They do succeed for a time in keeping it in the background. But the inevitable day must come when it must die. Nothing kills like open discussion and ridicule. Voltaire is the best example of this species of warfare.

The result of the Player-scene is that Hamlet gathers sufficient force to kill Polonius. And the Player-scene, it is possible, may not express more than the criticism of Luther, which leads to the Reformation. To future criticism it must be left to decide, whether the end of the third act alone completes the Reformation. Nothing can be plainer than the recognition by Hamlet of the character of the King

> " *Ham.* For thou dost know, O Damon dear,
> This realm dismantled was
> Of Jove himself; and now reigns here
> A very, very—pajock.
> *Hor.* You might have rhymed."

What will rhyme with *was* ? Something very like *ass*. But we may have mistaken our poet's meaning. The way Hamlet mocks Polonius when he enters is very marked.

And Polonius is either humbly obsequious and servile, or
else he mocks our hero back again.

> *Ham.* Do you see yonder cloud that's almost in shape of a camel ?
> *Pol.* By the mass, and 'tis like a camel, indeed.
> *Ham.* Methinks it is like a weasel.
> *Pol.* It is backed like a weasel.
> *Ham.* Or like a whale ?
> *Pol.* Very like a whale.
> *Ham.* Then I will come to my mother by and by. They fool me to the top of
> my bent. I will come by and by."

Truth will become belief "by and by." If authority is so
weakened as to be mocked openly by Hamlet, and to echo
our hero without a significance of its own, it seems there
is no alternative.

The third scene is the advice of the cautious ones. They
are our old friends we know so much about. They are
instrumental to the banishment of Hamlet. They are the
screens between him and the King. As long as they live
Hamlet can effect nothing permanent. The advice of Guildenstern and Rosencrantz is thus characterized by the expression—

> *" Guil.* We will ourselves provide."

The fourth scene of the same act is the interview between
Hamlet and his mother. It is a very long one, and therefore we are justified in supposing its length to find some
parallel in time. It is one of great importance to the critic
of Hamlet. The entrance of the Ghost causes the exclamation of Hamlet: "a king of shreds and patches."[1] The
blindness of the Queen in not seeing the Ghost is a very
fine contrast between the Queen and Hamlet. To Hamlet
the Ghost is plain. To his mother there is nothing but
Hamlet's ecstasy to account for it.

Thus we see the death of Polonius is followed by another
stimulus. And this time it is the Ghost again.

---

[1] Error is well expressed by patchwork.

The result of all is that the Queen has her heart "cleft in twain."

"*Queen.* O Hamlet, thou hast cleft my heart in twain."

At last Hamlet has produced some effect upon his mother. And she even asks his advice.

In this expression "cleft in twain," we have the Reformation completed. One side of her heart will be Protestant, the other remain with the King. The Queen is belief, and she is now divided by schism. Part of the Queen will be now upon Hamlet's side. Finally, the whole will drink to him.

We have now arrived at the end of the third act. Up to this point Hamlet has been in active occupation. Now, however, we shall miss him for a time. Though not for long dramatically. We must realize the meaning of his banishment. As regards Church reform, Hamlet has done good work. But in history there was to be a long pause before any further important acts of Hamlet could be dramatically portrayed. We recognize Hamlet silently at work in the melancholy end and wreath-making of Ophelia. We recognize his work even in the revolution of Laertes. But our poet has thought fit to consider him dead in an artistic sense, as long as accompanied by Rosencrantz and Guildenstern. He has brought everything down to a state of what we might term the level of Rosencrantz and Guildenstern.[1] Everything above them has been cut down. But they are long-lived gentlemen, and Hamlet's banishment is exactly the length of their lives. Our hero is got rid of to give greater effect to his return. And our poet in the meanwhile takes the opportunity of working out the results which follow the death of Polonius. We have seen how the third act is made to contain the Player-scene, the death of Polonius resulting therefrom, and the free conversation which ensues between Hamlet and his mother. It would be

---

[1] Shakespeare has distinctly realized the long autocracy of the self-interested in power.

treating the intelligent reader like a child, to seek historical parallels for all the above. Probably the reader will far better find the interpretation than we could give it him.

In the fourth act we hear again of Polonius. That is, of his remains. And this is needful to that continuity of history, and the drama, with which Shakespeare has so wondrously shown us his acquaintance. The dead body of Polonius is still a witness to his former power. It will still linger on, until corruption shall have made it unfit for the senses of men.[1] It is to be hoped the reader begins to see what Goethe meant when he called the play " a trunk, branches, boughs, twigs, buds, and leaves."

And now in the beginning of the fourth act we have the recognition by Hamlet of the character of Rosencrantz. Upon that topic we have already dwelt.

> "*Ros.* Tell us where 'tis, that we may take it thence
> 'And bear it to the chapel.
> *Ham.* Do not believe it."

This reference to the chapel is of course a hint that takes us direct to the Church. Rosencrantz of course will keep the body with the Church as long as he is Rosencrantz. But Hamlet now knows the character of the courtier. He sees his relation to the King, and he tells him he can keep both his own counsel and that of Rosencrantz. If he can keep the advice of the latter, he can also keep his own. Rosencrantz however is a sponge. One who does the King " best service in the end." And the King is the last to believe in Rosencrantz.

> "*Ham.* He keeps them, like an ape, in the corner of his jaw; first mouthed, to be last swallowed."

Rosencrantz is again the King himself. And Hamlet therefore knows exactly what the advice of Rosencrantz is worth. That advice is the advice of self-interest alone, of

---

[1] We believe the allusions to the body of Polonius to be an artistic endeavour to represent the gradual decay of authority. Finally, Laertes, as a *Party*, takes up his father's policy.

those who, having everything to gain by the embalment of what is left of Polonius, would carry him into the chapel. If a change in the state of the King leaves Rosencrantz barren of his countenances, his rewards, his authorities, why here is a new Rosencrantz ready to soak them all up again. Presently Hamlet enters, accompanied by Guildenstern. This shows us how mixed truth must be at this period of the drama. Always with either both or one of these two courtiers. Though we cannot help looking upon Hamlet as a separate and particular Hamlet of our own, to do justice to the play, we must see him only through the light of those who accompany him. This makes the work of interpretation a multiplied difficulty; for we are constantly interpreting Hamlet's speeches as the speeches of a *naked Hamlet*. They are not so, and we warn the student to beware of this error, an error which we fear we are constantly falling unconsciously into ourselves. Our poet has made no confusion of this kind in his meaning. He is now, at the stage we have arrived, showing the increasing separation of truth from sophistry and hypocrisy, from that which is self-interested, from that which is mere party and that which is true in itself. This is part of the great continuity of the plan of the tragedy. Thus the advice of Rosencrantz is almost Hamlet's own advice. But Hamlet is beginning to realize the great difference between himself and Rosencrantz, and to increase that divergence.

Hamlet now comes in with Guildenstern.

" *King.* Now, Hamlet, where's Polonius?
Ham. At supper.
King. At supper! where?
Ham. Not where he eats, but where he is eaten: a certain convocation of politic worms are e'en at him. Your worm is your only emperor for diet: we fat all creatures else to fat us, and we fat ourselves for maggots : your fat king and your lean beggar is but variable service, two dishes, but to one table : that's the end."

Public opinion is at work upon Polonius. Public opinion is an emperor for diet. And Polonius is being fast eaten by a " convocation of politic worms."

Hamlet is himself pointing out the danger of a too rapid

destruction of Polonius. This is our belief, for he is accompanied by Guildenstern. We find Hamlet makes no objection to his banishment to England.

"*Ham.* Nothing but to show you how a king may go a progress through the guts of a beggar."

The whole question is one of "Where is Polonius?" The same process which has destroyed and is destroying Polonius may take a King through the guts of a beggar. No wonder the King makes up his mind to banish Hamlet. Our hero is too dangerous to be tolerated any further.

Historically we recognize the point at which Hamlet suffers banishment. We have seen what a great impulse the Reformation has given to civilization in Europe. But we also recognize the slow progress of that civilization up to the middle of the movement of the eighteenth century. We of the present day have only recovered but yesterday from a reaction following that movement. And we have even a long period from the Reformation itself, up to the beginning of the eighteenth century, when the Reformation underwent a second Reformation in dissent. All this is pictured in the wreath-making of Ophelia. But Hamlet himself only comes back after the return of Laertes. He is all this while waiting for the death of Rosencrantz and Guildenstern, a deed undertaken by science, and which is so wonderfully paralleled in the present day.

"*King.* Hamlet, this deed, for thine especial safety."

The King, as we have identified him with the courtiers and the corrupting body of Polonius, believes that the interests of truth are bound up in the exile of truth. This is expressed in the sayings, " Truth is dangerous," "A little learning is a dangerous thing," and "That truth is not for man." We have not arrived even yet at the day when outspokenness and truth, and nothing but the truth, is considered a salutary thing for humanity to practise. Not even in this wonderful age are we quite free from Rosencrantz and Guildenstern.

Let us return to the exile of Hamlet, and to the signification of England.   That signification we believe to be science, or, as we think it, the exact sciences.   What evidence have we for such an astounding assumption? We see the reader smile, and we see him lay down this work with good-natured incredulity.   But we only ask him to hear us out.

Let us note the King's speech.

> " *King.* . . . . Therefore prepare thyself ;
> The bark is ready, and the wind at help,
> *The associates* tend, and everything is bent
> For England."

The word *associates* is one that belongs to science.   It is ambiguous of course, and by itself says nothing.   But like everything else in this play, it is only a part of other evidence.

> " *King.* And, England, if my love thou hold'st at aught—
> As my great power thereof may give thee sense,
> Since yet thy *cicatrice* looks raw and red
> After the Danish sword, and thy free awe
> Pays homage to us—thou mayst not coldly set
> Our sovereign process ; which imports at full,
> By letters congruing to that effect,
> The *present* death of Hamlet.   Do it, England;
> For like the hectic in my blood he rages,
> And thou must cure me : till I know 'tis done,
> Howe'er my haps, my joys were ne'er begun."

Here two words are to be noticed—*cicatrice* and *present*. Why the *present* death of Hamlet?   As before, it is ambiguous, and may mean *immediate*.   As we are studying a play full of ambiguities, we are bound to notice that the word *present* may mean *a period* alone.   Again, why is not Hamlet banished to Norway?   Why to England?   We want to know why our poet has brought a fresh locality into the play, when, if it has no particular meaning, Norway would have served the same purpose.   Again, we have Hamlet saying, on his return from exile :—

> " Does it not, thinks't thee, stand me now upon—
> He that hath kill'd my king and whored my mother,
> Popp'd in between the election and my hopes,
> Thrown out his *angle* for my proper life," etc., etc.

Here we have the word *angle*, ambiguous, as usual ; but capable of expressing *mathematics*. The word *England*, let it be noted, may stand for the " Land of the Angles."
To quote again :

> " *Ham.* An earnest conjuration from the king,
> *As* England was his faithful tributary,
> *As* love between them like the palm might flourish,
> *As* peace should still her wheaten garland wear
> And stand a comma 'tween their amities,
> And many such like 'As'es of great charge."

All these " 'As'es of great charge," remind us of Euclid. We would ask the reader to ask himself what causes would lead alone to the deaths of Rosencrantz and Guildenstern ? Nothing but an inexorable necessity, such as implied in the exactitude and inevitable logic of cause and effect, would lead to the death of the courtiers. At the present day we are beginning to witness the results springing from the inexorable logic of Science.

The necessity of no compromise in all branches of human knowledge speaking for themselves as the law of God, must have an immense effect upon the whole mind of man. Ambiguities are rejected ; clearness, decision of outline, and facts, take the place of shadows, compromise, and a habit of self-deception, and sluggishness of thought. The nature of science is the nature of law. It admits of no rejection. It is iron-bound, and breaks the rash sophist into contradictions, when confronted by experiment and verification. Science is making the mind of man accustomed to definite answers, to definite questions. It is codifying the universe. And the day will come when anything unscientific will be considered as outside the realms of truth. For Science, a name dreaded and execrated by the ignorant as the technical name of certain branches of human learning, is nothing less than Truth itself. It is the systematization of the laws of God, or, as Oersted beautifully puts it, " the thoughts of God." There is nothing in this wide universe outside the domain of science. And science is knowledge, foreshadowing happiness. Thought is under law ; and however stupidly we may be thinking, there is a law for it contained within our organism. Not a law, we should say; for laws are not entities: but relations of cause and effect, which are invariable.

Our theory of the nature of England is one we shall stand by. For our poet lived in an age in which England was, without doubt, of all countries that in which liberty and progress were far ahead of any other contemporary nation of Europe. It was an age of greatness. A greatness partially due to the great intellect of one of the most intelligent of women—Elizabeth. And a greatness also due to that impulse which the recent events in Europe had given to all branches of learning, and thus to men's minds. It was an age which abounded in men of genius. An age which, like the present, was a boundary between the past and the future. Behind, all was dark and unsettled; in front, light, hope, and discovery were dimly seen. But genius saw this plainer than others. It was clear enough to Shakespeare. It was clear even to Bacon. And who is Bacon by the side of the swan of Avon? There were others who, like Bacon, were teaching Shakespeare what was the nature of induction. Every great intellect is a machine, in which chains of deduction and induction are established with greater exactitude and with greater rapidity than by others. They may be so rapid, so instantaneous, as to have the effect of pictures. Their next to simultaneous concatenation is wrought by a fervour of imagination which can alone find an outcome in art. This species of intellect, which is imagination, differs from the one which is content with logic, with patient search, and with experiment. The former has the deductive brain of genius, the latter the inductive one of science. But both employ more or less the methods of each other.

There were men who, like Copernicus, had given the world a work on the revolutions of the heavenly bodies, 1543. There were the discoveries of one Lippershey, a Hollander, of the telescope, 1608. There were men who, like Bruno and Galileo, were fixing men's

6

attention upon the grandeur of the universe, the insignificance of this earth, and the falsity of the Geocentric
system.

All this must have found a place in Shakespeare's heart
and mind. A place of rejection or acceptation. A key to
the future and a contrast to the past, or a change in men's
habits of thought, which must mean something. Shakespeare must have made up his mind that man knew nothing,
or everything. The validity of innate ideas, or an à priori
and intuitive knowledge underlying our consciousness, must
have been questioned by him at a very early age. Everywhere he was confronted by difference of opinion. The
watchword of the "World moves," was confronted by the
older tradition of the "World stands still." He must
have made up his mind to the fact that, either humanity
was in the earliest stage of its apprenticeship, or else that
it would never learn at all. We believe that figuratively and scientifically he believed the former opinion,
that the world moves. In Hamlet we have the social
movement of man. A movement which must have found
its origin in the mind of Shakespeare, by means of some of
those questions which were showing the instability of human
belief.

We therefore believe that the prospects and state of
England with regard to the Continent during Shakespeare's
life were such as would induce him to believe that she
would in the future be the leader of science in Europe.
And the chief reason we have to assert for this assumption
is the political liberty she enjoyed. Bruno had found refuge
in England, where he lectured. Our Poet, of course, saw
science and all physical or philosophical investigations, as
they were then termed, would flourish alone in an atmosphere of liberty and freedom from restraint. The great
freedom of our great Queen's reign must have given our
Poet a reason for believing that England would be ahead
of all other nations in such liberty and in such freedom.
The development of our Constitution since Magna Charta,
the adoption of the comparatively free religion of Pro-

testantism, all tended to make that liberty peculiar to England in the future. It was only natural then that such a brain as our Poet's should from these and innumerable other causes have forestalled the truth, and made England the type of discovery in what is now termed science.

We have now to trace to the text some of the results of the death of Polonius. One of these is the appearance of Fortinbras, with his forces, marching through Denmark. Nothing has perplexed critics more than this unexpected and apparently unconnected introduction of Fortinbras.[1] Where does he come from? And whither is he bound? In the beginning of this work we had occasion to refer to Fortinbras in the light of a chorus. Fortinbras is the chorus of liberty. Everywhere repressed in the early part of the tragedy, he has been in the background gaining and accumulating, inch by inch, forces, which now appear as an army, to give Hamlet a new impetus and fresh reaction. Therefore we have, after the conversation of the Captain with Hamlet, one of those monologues which are full of the contrast derived from resolution and irresolution. These are, as we have often already observed, the dramatic and artistic means by which Shakespeare expresses the way in which Hamlet gains power and force. Liberty acts upon Hamlet in a marvellous way. Therefore Fortinbras, with his forces, sets Hamlet to work at self-reproach and self-contrast. We have already traced a similar result with regard to the speech of the first Player, which we believe to be an appeal to the human heart from growing knowledge. The appearance of Fortinbras is only in harmony with the disappearance from the play of Voltimand and Cornelius. The death of autocratic Polonius and his gradual decay have still furthered his appearance. Liberty is so indispensable to all progress, that if our Poet

---

[1] This sudden appearance of Fortinbras is often omitted upon the stage, as being out of *harmony with the apparent* unity of the tragedy!

had omitted this scene, we should have felt that the most
important element had been left out. The sudden appearance of Fortinbras is like a revelation, and he is wonderfully
expressed in a large army. Liberty is a force. Liberty is
concentrated individualism warring for self, and recognizing
the power of union. Thus the sudden appearance of
Fortinbras is brought in shortly after the death of Polonius.
Hamlet's banishment is the freedom of thought, which,
becoming relegated to particular channels, is in too crude
a state, and in too rude a relation to men's minds, to have
any outward effect as yet. Hamlet employs his freedom; and
he works until he has escaped Rosencrantz and Guildenstern.
When they are dead, mankind are face to face with another
momentous epoch, and Hamlet is set naked in the kingdom.
Turning to the text, we find many expressions which give
us the key to the meaning of Fortinbras.

> " *Fort.* Go, captain, from me greet the Danish king;
> Tell him that, by his *license*, Fortinbras　.
> Craves the conveyance of a promised march
> Over his kingdom. You know the *rendezvous.*
> If that his majesty would aught with us,
> We shall express our duty in his eye;
> And let him know so."

The word *license* is full of meaning. It is one allied to
liberty, and may signify the character of Fortinbras himself, and the weakness of the King. Thus, the license of
liberty is expressive of its own progress. Or the license
of the King may mean the liberty extorted from him by
time. We must remember how Norway, at the request
of the King's ambassadors, Voltimand and Cornelius,
rebukes Fortinbras for his preparations against the King.
This pictures an age of oppression and tyranny, of evil and
force, which strangles every abortive attempt of liberty.
But, nevertheless, by the demand of Norway for leave " to
give quiet pass " to Fortinbras through the King's do-
minions, we infer that liberty is ostensibly checked, and
only gains ground in a wholly passive way. And we are
furthered in this opinion by the French name of *Fortinbras*,

and the French word *rendezvous*.[1] As in the case of Laertes, France stands for liberty,—for French leave and for freedom. *France* as a word signifies *freedom*. We have observed before that the relation of Fortinbras to Norway is of a similar nature to that of Hamlet and the King. Both are nephews, and both are uncles. Does this not suggest similarity in relationship of feeling and interests? Therefore Norway should be allied with the King, and Hamlet and Fortinbras to each other by community of interests. We must infer Norway does his best to hamper Fortinbras. The King gives no leave to the request of Fortinbras for "quiet pass."

> " *Volt.* That it might please you to give quiet pass
> Through your dominions for this enterprise,
> On such regards of safety and allowance
> As therein are set down.
>   *King.*   It likes us well ;
> And at our more consider'd time we'll read,
> Answer, and think upon this business."

Thus Shakespeare gives us no answer from the King that may be considered decisive. We therefore conclude that Fortinbras takes the French leave, so well in keeping with his name — *force*.[2] The march of Fortinbras is probably one which the King cannot possibly prevent.

Fortinbras is found in possession of the dramatic situation at the end of the play. Hamlet gives him his dying voice. Fortinbras comes from Poland. We believe Poland to be the symbol for "many." Liberty can alone come from the *vox populi*.

> "*Enter* Hamlet, Rosencrantz, Guildenstern.
> *Ham.* Good sir, whose powers are these ?
> *Cap.* They are of Norway, sir.
> *Ham.* How purposed, sir, I pray you ?
> *Cap.* Against some *part of Poland*."

---

[1] We suggest that Shakespeare has employed French words to hint the character of Fortinbras and his mission.

[2] The name Fortinbras, literally *strong-in-arm*, well expresses strength and force.

Nothing would be, on this hypothesis of ours, clearer than the above. The powers are here because of Norway,[1] and are only necessary from the existence of that country. For the spirit of liberty is only the antithesis of the spirit of bondage. · Again, nothing is plainer than that the spirit of liberty has to fight against part of Poland. It is only at the end that perfect liberty is summed up in the conquest of Poland. Universal assent is not conflict. Our Poet has well expressed his meaning in the words Poland, Polack, and Pole.

> " *Ham.* Goes it against the main of Poland, sir,
> Or for some frontier ?
> *Cap.* Truly to speak, and with no addition,
> We go to gain a little patch of ground
> That hath in it no profit but the name.
> To pay five ducats, five, I would not farm it;
> Nor will it yield to Norway or the Pole
> A ranker rate, should it be sold in fee.
> *Ham.* Why, then the Polack never will defend it.
> *Cap.* Yes, it is already garrison'd.
> *Ham.* Two thousand souls and twenty thousand ducats
> Will not debate the question of this straw :
> This is the imposthume of much wealth and peace,
> That inward breaks, and shows no cause without
> Why the man dies. I humbly thank you, sir."

We are told already that Fortinbras is only going to march against a part of Poland. And this part of Poland is the Polack. This little patch of ground is one of those little questions of liberty and right which are gained inch by inch, and wrested by time from authority. It is the history of progress, and thus the history of ever-gaining liberty. What is the history of England, but the defence and loss of little patches of ground, which in time will make up the whole sum of Poland ? It has no profit but the name. Yet is it vigorously defended. And if it was sold in *fee* (a word which belongs to Feudalism), it would lose nothing to "Norway or the Pole." Hamlet is astonished it should be

---

[1] Norway seems to represent autocratic force, and repression of liberty by its means.

defended. And he says, "Two thousand souls and twenty thousand ducats will not debate the question of this straw" (union). The word *debate* gives us another clue. The whole question is one of debate. And so have the liberties of the English people been a question of debate. All this Hamlet perceives is the direct heritage of wealth and peace, which silently and peacefully, like a man with a secret and internal disease, "shows no cause without why the man dies." So slow and insidious is this march of Fortinbras, that it shows no cause "outside" or "without," as it is expressed. It is the silent revolution of opinion. The slow march of liberty, which creeps almost imperceptibly along, and kills its enemies by a subtle but certain poison. How beautifully is all this expressed! Now Hamlet tells Rosencrantz and Guildenstern to "go a little before." Our Poet has meant all his soliloquies to be his own. They are the utterances of *untrammelled* truth.

> "*Ham.* How all occasions do inform against me,
> And spur my dull revenge! What is a man,
> If his chief good and market of his time
> Be but to sleep and feed? a beast, no more.
> Sure, he that made us with such large discourse,
> Looking before and after, gave us not
> That capability and god-like reason
> To fust in us unused. Now, whether it be
> Bestial oblivion, or some craven scruple
> Of thinking too precisely on the event,
> A thought which, quarter'd, hath but one part wisdom
> And ever three parts coward, I do not know
> Why yet I live to say 'This thing's to do;'
> Sith I have cause and will and strength and means
> To do't. Examples gross as earth exhort me:
> Witness this army of such *mass* and charge
> Led by a delicate and tender prince,
> Whose spirit with divine ambition puff'd
> Makes mouths at the invisible event,
> Exposing what is mortal and unsure
> To all that fortune, death and danger dare,
> Even for an *egg-shell*. Rightly to be great
> Is not to stir without great argument,
> But greatly to find quarrel in a straw
> When honour's at the stake. How stand I then,
> That have a father kill'd, a mother stain'd,
> Excitements of my reason and my blood,
> And let all sleep? while, to my shame, I see

> The imminent death of twenty thousand men,
> That, for a fantasy and trick of fame,
> Go to their graves like beds, fight for a plot
> Whereon the numbers cannot try the cause,
> Which is not tomb enough and continent
> To hide the slain ?   O, from this time forth,
> My thoughts be bloody, or be nothing worth!"

The recognition by Hamlet of the use of reason is an epoch in the play.[1] Let it stand for itself, without further comment. We would call attention to the word *egg-shell*. The word *yoke*, so expressive of bondage, is by a play of words (yolk) contained within an egg-shell. Fortinbras is fighting to break the shell, and thus the yoke, so oppressive to liberty. The last words of Hamlet are, " which is not tomb enough and continent to hide the slain." This can only be applicable to the everlasting conflict of the strong and the weak. The cause for which this Prince, as Hamlet calls him (thus identifying himself partially), fights, is one eternal in a world, where every happiness depends upon physical or mental *force*. The struggle for liberty (not alone the liberty which we understand in this day) is at the bottom of all human conflict. Money, means, power, are only instruments of procuring for us greater liberty. The struggle for liberty is the struggle of individualism against social individualism, and that is too often tyranny over the individual.

We remark the application of the word *divine* to Fortinbras. Is not the struggle for liberty a divine principle? Do we not desire in our earthly longing for a future life to realize a divine liberty? In the early stage of the tragedy we find Fortinbras making feeble and abortive attempts with

> " . . . .   Here and there
> Shark'd up a list of lawless resolutes,
> For food and diet, to some enterprise
> That hath a stomach in't ; which is no other—
> As it doth well appear unto our state—."

---

[1] It is through liberty that reason finds a fitting atmosphere to flourish in. And Hamlet in using his reason silently escapes Rosencrantz and Guildenstern.

We can understand the word *lawless* in all its meaning, as regards these early and feeble attempts.   What a vast change has come over Fortinbras since these fiascos!   Now he is a Prince, who, with a well-disciplined army, can "express his duty" in the eye of the King.   He can act powerfully upon Hamlet.   So immense is his influence upon Hamlet all through the play, that we may fairly say, without his help, our hero would never return to Denmark. Thus it is Fortinbras rises like a pyramid in the centre of the drama, giving it force and giving direction, until his triumphant entry, with drums sounding, at the conclusion of the tragedy.[1]

---

[1] Let it be distinctly understood, Fortinbras is silently marching all through the play *with Hamlet*. His sudden appearance illustrates this dramatically and purposely.

CHAPTER III.

WE now leave Hamlet to the care of England and Fortinbras. And whilst his two enemies, Rosencrantz and
Guildenstern, are being slowly killed by England, we will
follow some of the legitimate consequences which follow the
death of Polonius.

The commencement of the fourth act shows us the sad
condition of Ophelia. The distinction between her madness
and that of Hamlet is very great. She is really mad. The
latter only appears to be insane. Ophelia is intended to
be understood as *thoroughly* insane. And what does insanity signify ? Want of coherence, want of reason, or
what we term loss of rationality. Thus the madness of
Ophelia represents her want of reason and coherence. The
Queen refuses to speak with her. But at the entreaty of
Horatio she overcomes her scruples. Ophelia [1]

> " . . . . Speaks things in doubt,
> That carry but half sense: her speech is nothing,
> Yet the unshaped use of it doth move
> The hearers to collection ; they aim at it,
> *And botch the words up fit to their own thoughts.*"

Does not the last line contain the principle upon which all

---

[1] It is perhaps worth calling attention to a possible, but certainly far-fetched,
anagram upon *Ophelia's* name [HOPE (Ophe) I(n) A(fter) L(ife).]

dissent is based? Is not dissent the *collection* of "words which carry but half sense" to suit different types of mind?

The death of Polonius has, of course, produced the insanity of Ophelia. Her foundations are sapped. She carries but half sense. Nothing but the theological bias, as Mr. Herbert Spencer might term it, keeps her from utter ruin. And the Queen refuses to allow scepticism to enter her mind at first. But time, with Horatio, who is the spirit of earnestness and justice, brings Ophelia to the Queen. The latter, be it remembered, is human belief. Ophelia is the spirit of religion. She represents, in conformity to the continuity of the play, the religious beliefs of the time. And now, alas! they are very sceptical. The Queen seems quite reckless. She is not the Queen of the first act. She has modified also her character with the development of the play. If the reader does not always try and realize the parallelism of history, he will never seize Hamlet.

> " *Queen.* To my sick soul, as sin's true nature is,
> Each toy seems prologue to some great amiss :
> So full of artless jealousy is guilt,
> It spills itself in fearing to be spilt."

We can grasp the state of the Queen's mind. It is impregnated with misgiving. Doubt follows doubt dramatically. The very act of not wishing to be made sceptical brings a train of scepticism with it. The defence of a daughter, whose father is always decaying, is full of danger. The very defence exposes faults in her character.

Ophelia now enters with Horatio. The latter seems to be looking after Ophelia. And here let it be remarked, Hamlet effects little unless Horatio is with him. His exile is one in which he is bereft of his friend.

The songs of Ophelia are full of the profoundest meaning. They are different forms and stages of religious dissent, unbelief, and even materialism. Goethe has told us what her chief song conveys. Doubt once entered can never depart

again. "Never departed more." The King has the per-
spicacity to see it "springs all from her father's death."

> " *Oph.* [*Sings*] How should I your true love know
> From another one?
> By his cockle hat and staff,
> And his sandal shoon."

A cockle hat is a pilgrim's hat. Is Ophelia asking how one
faith is to be distinguished from another one? Is it, she
asks, by ritual?

> " *Oph.* Say you? nay, pray you, mark.
> [*Sings*]   He is dead and gone, lady,
> He is dead and gone;
> At his head a grass-green turf,
> At his heels a stone.
> *Queen.* Nay, but, Ophelia,—
> *Oph.* Pray you, mark.
> [*Sings*] White his shroud as the mountain snow,—
>
> *Enter* King.
>
> *Queen.* Alas, look here, my lord."

The whole of the above denotes controversy and difference of
opinion between Church and people. It is a divorcement
of beliefs. The Queen proves this in expostulating with
Ophelia. The last and next song of Ophelia is typical of
controversy over Polonius. He is authority and certainty.
It is polemical discussion over authority and certainty.
Ophelia shows great regret for her father. At the head of
Polonius, or in his place, everything is new, like green
grass.[1] Everything denotes hardness of belief — *stony-
heartedness*. Belief is growing very chilly and cold.
"White his shroud as the mountain snow." The coldness
and far-off effect of snowy mountains well represents the
increasing luke-warmness and the ever-increasing distance
of certainty and belief in tradition. The King now enters.
As scepticism, she says:

> " *Oph.* Well, God 'ild you! They say the owl was a baker's daughter. Lord,
> we know what we are, but know not what we may be. God be at your table!"

---

[1] This seems to typify new thoughts and fresh ideas resulting from scepticism.

In the last lines, "we know what we are, but know not what we may be," we read doubts as to the immortality of the soul. The King says, "Conceit upon her father." The question is one, indeed, of tradition; and he may well call it "conceit upon her father." The first two verses of the song beginning "To-morrow is Saint Valentine's day" signify increasing scepticism; a scepticism which never departs, but holds fast. They signify that once doubt has entered, and that doubt religious doubt (or Ophelia), it would never come out as it entered. Nothing less than ruin is the result.

The next two verses are an apology for nature, and the necessity of law. Can we therefore deduce our Poet's meaning to be that increase of knowledge has been the reason of the visit of scepticism? The King appears to be ignorant how long Ophelia has been in this state—

"*King.* How long hath she been thus?

Oph. I hope all will be well. We must be patient: but I cannot choose but weep, to think they should lay him i' the cold ground. My brother shall know of it: and so I thank you for your good counsel. Come, my coach! Good night, ladies; good night, sweet ladies; good night, good night."

In all the above criticisms upon Ophelia, convinced as we are of Ophelia's identity with the state of religious belief and feeling at successive epochs of history and of the play, nevertheless in all these details we only venture to suggest to the reader anything which may throw light upon the buds and leaves of the play. Every word is the touch of a painter. We may be sure no single epithet in Ophelia's lips is without meaning. In her expression, "I hope all will be well. We must be patient," we read hope for the future mixed with misgiving; and in the next we read that there are many who believe in either the virtue of time or the growth of other violets.[1] Great regret over Polonius is a notable characteristic. Lingering looks, hopeless and despairing efforts to bring him to life again. And the strong support of Laertes

---

[1] Violets typify *faith.*

in these efforts is relied upon. Thus we have a few hints which are the history of an age in itself. An age which the reader must parallel for himself.

Ophelia calls her *coach*. This word suggests her motion, and how scepticism can never stand still, but is hurried along in spite of itself. "Good night, ladies," which Ophelia repeats so often, we read as, "Farewell, belief; farewell, sweet belief; farewell, farewell!" Women in this play, of whom there are but two, seem both of the character of belief.

For the first time we find the King now beginning to get despondent. And can we wonder that his case begins to look desperate?

> "*King.* Follow her close; give her good watch, I pray you.
> O, this is the poison of deep grief; it springs
> All from her father's death. O Gertrude, Gertrude,
> When sorrows come, they come not single spies,
> But in battalions. First, her father slain:
> Next, your son gone; and he most violent author
> Of his own just remove : the people muddied,
> Thick and unwholesome in their thoughts and whispers,
> For good Polonius' death; and we have done but greenly,
> In hugger-mugger to inter him : poor Ophelia
> Divided from herself and her fair judgment,
> Without the which we are *pictures, or mere beasts :*
> *Last, and as much containing as all these,*
> *Her brother is in secret come from France ;*
> Feeds on his wonder, keeps himself in clouds,
> And wants not buzzers to infect his ear
> With pestilent speeches of his father's death ;
> Wherein necessity, of matter beggar'd,
> Will nothing stick our person to arraign
> In ear and ear. O my dear Gertrude, this,
> *Like to a murdering-piece,* in many places
> Gives me superfluous death."

Nothing can excel the art, the truth, and the depth of the above speech of the King. In it we read a summary of the tragedy itself, as far as we have arrived. The recognition of the importance of Polonius by the King is made manifest in every word. All these disasters are traceable to his death. Sorrows are compared to *spies*. This word suggests "errors," and we are thus told battalions of spies are at the work of criticizing the King. The people are muddied. This we understand us stirred up. They are "thick and unwholesome in their thoughts and whispers." The King regrets having buried Polonius so quickly. Could he help it? Ophelia is divided from herself. The Church is divided against itself. This is the result of the death of Polonius. How well does our Poet express his meaning when he points out the difference between man and beast: "Without the which we are pictures, or mere beasts." The soul is the great distinction between man and beast. Scepticism on this point reduces us to painted pictures—to mere beasts.

We are told Laertes is come from France. The growth of learning, the spread of the Arts and Sciences, are come from freedom (France); and he, Laertes, "feeds on his wonder," "keeps himself in clouds." Does the above want any interpretation? The use of wonder need not be expatiated upon; we may say the same for its origin and source—knowledge. The whole phrase is a revelation in itself.

We must try and realize what Laertes has been about since we last saw him depart into France. We must bear in mind he has been faithful to his father. He would not be his father's son, indeed, if he were not. The return of Laertes is like the return of Fortinbras—dramatic. Goethe in his novel has permitted every character to develope itself side by side. But in a tragedy this was impossible. The exigencies of effect necessitate only striking incidents. Action, and the force of destiny in respect to man's action, is the character of tragedy. A tame development, belonging to sentiments and feeling alone, would not be in harmony with the rugged outline of the tragic drama. We can only marvel how Shakespeare has managed to express the interaction of so many conflicting and developing forces. We see that, being occupied with the centralization and prominence of Prince Hamlet alone, a due subordination was to be given to all minor characters. Hamlet and the King are therefore the first two of importance. They are the lions. The rest

are merely the jackals. And our feelings are with Hamlet
of course. He is pictured as a noble Prince, full of truth,
goodness, and perfection, struggling against enormous odds.
The battle is not to the swift, nor to the strong. It is one of
time alone.

All those points which, being indispensable to the unity of
the play, would obtrude and crowd more important events,
are subordinated with marvellous skill.

Thus the introduction of Fortinbras gives us in a brief
scene the expression of liberty gaining ground and stimu-
lating Hamlet. In like manner, the return of Laertes, in
the shape of revolution, is the epitomizing of the revolutionizing effect of the spread of learning. And it is made
to follow the death of Polonius, and more particularly the
madness of Ophelia. We do not believe anything further
is meant in this temporary insurrection than the general
revolutionary effects which education and the spread of it
must inevitably bring about. But if the reader must seek
an historical parallel, let him turn to the eighteenth century,
when he will find scepticism, and attacks upon the Church,
followed by revolution, and the enthronement of Reason.
A reason well expressed in the words—

> "Laertes shall be king, Laertes king!"

The death of Polonius has upset everything. Laertes
becomes a kind of Hamlet for a time. He is thrown off
his balance at the death of his father, and he seeks wildly
to find the King. But he has too strong a bias in him to
see things clearly, and he is soon enlisted once more on the
side of the King.

Let us once more re-assert, the King is a fiction. He
is only the symbol which· is dramatically necessary to represent error in one character. The revolution of Laertes
is one then which is the direct result of a general upsetting
of principle. This revolution soon finds its equilibrium
again in an adjustment of the same parties in a more
modified form.

This revolution is the autocracy of opinion. For the first time in the tragedy, we find a new power at work, and brought into play. That is the power of party. The force of collective humanity; not a tyrannical Polonius, who directs and spies into all things. Laertes is backed powerfully by Danes. And how entirely is the Polonius of early times forgotten now?

> " *Gent.*   Save yourself, my lord :
> The ocean, overpeering of his list,
> Eats not the flats with more impetuous haste
> Than young Laertes, in a riotous head,
> O'erbears your officers. The rabble call him lord ;
> And, as the world were now but to begin,
> *Antiquity forgot, custom not known,*
> The ratifiers and props of every word,
> They cry ' *Choose we : Laertes shall be king :* '
> Caps, hands, and tongues, applaud it to the clouds :
> ' Laertes shall be king, Laertes king !' " [1]

"Antiquity forgot, custom not known." Polonius is indeed forgotten, and he made a great error when he allowed his son to go into France, for Laertes repudiates his own father. Not dramatically, but he does so symbolically. He asks for his father. He himself has been instrumental in his death. But he is too blind to see this. He can see the past is full of error, but the present is too close to him for self-criticism.

This revolution of Laertes is a momentous epoch in the play. It will take the events of the future out of the hands of chance and stagnancy, and will hurry them into equilibrium. The death of Polonius, in the true sense, is one of those historical epochs which cannot be exactly laid upon with the finger, and said to be in such and such a place. We might point to a period, we might fix upon an act, such as the act of toleration and of liberty of conscience. But this will not embody the death of Polonius. It is a gradual process. A process contained alone in a voluminous

---

[1] There is no doubt that Shakespeare signifies in this passage a complete revolution of thought.

work. One which shows the death of the protective spirit.
And one which is like the late Mr. Buckle's "History of
Civilization," exhaustive as far as it goes. So, in like
manner, it would be idleness to parallel the revolution of
Laertes with any particular revolution. It is the revolution
of thought, consequent upon the spread of knowledge, and
as such we prefer to leave it to other critics to embody in
more concrete forms. The student of the Philosophy of
History will allow this alone: that Shakespeare has shown
marvellous prescience in placing the revolution of Laertes
after the madness of Ophelia, and as one of the results of
the death of Polonius. For religion has always been the
chief and the main support of authority. We are but now
approaching an age when such a divorcement may be ex-
perimented upon. Our Poet has also done well in identifying education and the spread of knowledge with the decay of
Polonius. For it is alone through authority and the forms
of tradition that knowledge has been prevented from spread-
ing and percolating down into the lowest strata of life. The
seats of all learning have been under the control of Polonius.
The spread of all learning has been dependent upon the
weakening of Polonius. Therefore to bring revolution in
after a lapse of the decay of that power, in the shape of
a modified form of that power, is the work of a genius alone.
We need not linger upon the form which knowledge takes
under the leadership of Laertes. We have remarked over
and over again, he is the true scion of Polonius, and of
course will be faithful to his principles and the King. We
now turn to Ophelia again. In this re-introduction of this
insane girl, we have an explanation of the form she takes
with regard to her brother's return and to the popular will.
Her scepticism acts powerfully upon Laertes. Allied as he
is by ties of blood and of tradition, he is bound to combat
every stage of her dementia, and to fight to the death the
cause of it.[1] This, of course, is Hamlet. Laertes believes

---

[1] The alliance of Ophelia and Laertes is not inaptly paralleled in Church and
State.

himself in the right. He has a cause of his own,—a losing
game, as the end shows,—but no less a duty, and no less
a real and thorough one. Laertes differs from his father in
this : whereas the former was bigoted, conceited, cunning,
and more in earnest about his own interests and those of
the King than about Truth ; Laertes is in earnest, and is
more or less thorough. This is why Hamlet says to Horatio :

> " But I am very sorry, good Horatio,
> That to Laertes I forgot myself ;
> *For, by the image of my cause, I see*
> *The portraiture of his : I'll court his favours."*

The cause of Laertes is to avenge a father he believes
foully murdered. The cause of Hamlet is to vindicate, and
even justify that murder. Hamlet has every intention of
" courting the favours " of Laertes.

The words of Ophelia are—

> [*Sings*] " You must sing a-down a-down,
> An you call him a-down-a.
> O, how the wheel becomes it ! It is the false steward, that stole his master's
> daughter."

The above seems plain enough. Our Poet would signify
how fiercely the fight is carried on over the decaying body
and thus lasting power of Polonius. He will last a long
time still. Nothing is so long in dying as the traditions and
policy of centuries. They are, as Mr. Herbert Spencer might
explain to us, welded into the organism. The forms of bias
are not only inherited, but have been first made. Nothing
is so strong as long-established pressure in belief. The reference to the wheel suggests every side up at once. It represents revolution, many-sided opinion. What expresses
revolution better than a wheel ? Is not the former name
coined from the latter ?

It is the false steward that stole his master's daughter.
This is plain infidelity. An infidelity that has abused the
trust it has so long kept intact. Laertes replies—

> " This nothing's more than matter."

The above is difficult and incoherent. It is no apparent

answer. It may suggest materialism. Or it may suggest the conflict between materialism and spiritualism.

Laertes says the madness of Ophelia shall be paid in weight until—

"One scale turn the beam."

We see how divided society is by this expression. One which shows the preponderance of Laertes.

"*Oph.* There's rosemary, that's for remembrance; pray, love, remember: and there is pansies, that's for thoughts.
Laer. A document in madness, thoughts and remembrance fitted."

The above, we take it, signifies the effect of the Church upon Laertes. He is to remember his parentage. And he is to fit his thoughts to that remembrance. Religion is thus standing, with Laertes still as her support. Appeal to the past theological controversy supported by Laertes, and *vice versa*, is thus implied. We interpret the whole of these esoteric speeches of Ophelia's to mean different stages in the conflict between scepticism and orthodoxy. In it are contained every manner of opinion which such a conflict would bring about. Is not Laertes, at the present stage of the drama, all remembrance of his father? And his mode of thinking is fitted to his mode of remembrance. He is orthodox, and fights for the Church. He is thus orthodox literature, defence of orthodoxy, etc. And his love for Ophelia, and the alarm he feels for her state, makes him more in earnest against the cause of this state.

"*Oph.* There's fennel for you, and columbines: there's rue for you; and here's some for me: we may call it herb-grace o' Sundays: O, you must wear your rue with a difference. There's a daisy: I would give you some violets, but they withered all when my father died: they say he made a good end,—

[*Sings*] For bonny sweet Robin is all my joy."

Fennel signifies strength, worthy all praise.
Columbine, folly (plain).
Columbine, resolve to win.
Columbine (red), anxious and trembling.
Daisy, innocence.

Daisy, I share your sentiments.
Daisy, farewell.
Daisy, I'll think of you.
Rue, disdain.
Violets, faith and faithfulness.[1]

Now we are greatly perplexed in the choice of which signification we are to apply in the multiplied meanings of some of the same name-bearing flowers. Rue admits of no ambiguity. Ophelia will have to suffer disdain, and so will Laertes. Contempt is current of Ophelia, and also for Laertes. But on Sunday there is a reprisal. An outward attendance which may well be called "herb-grace o' Sundays." By a daisy Ophelia perhaps signifies that Laertes and herself share the same sentiments. She cannot give him any violets. Faith, so well thus expressed, withered when Polonius died. There is strength for Laertes, which is worthy all praise. An essay might be written on the above passages alone. Nay, a work—a great work; for it is the history of the rise and progress of rationalism in Europe. In the words—

"For bonny sweet Robin is all my joy"

—we might venture to suggest many ideas it gives rise to; but we prefer to leave it as it stands.[2] We will only remark as a hint that the robin is a bird connected by vulgar superstition with the Crucifixion, where a drop of blood is supposed to have stained its chest. Hence its general immunity, in comparison with the safety of other small birds. The last song of Ophelia is full of import:

"And will he not come again ?
And will he not come again ?
No, no, he is dead :
Go to thy death-bed :
He never will come again.

---

[1] We insert here a few of the significations of flowers as mere suggestions.

[2] The reader is begged to remember we deprecate anything further than suggestion.

> His beard was as white as snow,
> All flaxen was his poll :
>   He is gone, he is gone,
>   And we cast away moan :
> God ha' mercy on his soul ! "

Here we have the continued appeal to the question of certainty, as contained in tradition. And the result is *certainty* will never come again. It is the expression of the realization of the end of all certainty, upon religious questions, which we find in this last song of Ophelia. It is the finale of her madness. Nay, we are given to understand, reconcilement is found to this death of certainty. For she says :

> " He is gone, he is gone,
>   And we cast away moan :
> God ha' mercy on his soul ! "

And in the last words which we ever hear Ophelia speak we have this addendum—

> " And of all Christian souls, I pray God.   God be wi' ye."

Mere hope and speculation is here expressed. The whole song is one which implies the death and disappearance of certainty and tradition for ever. When we meet Ophelia again, a long period may have elapsed since the point we are concerned with now has passed. So we must understand how thoroughly our Poet grasped the slow evolution and progress of thought, and how tenaciously Laertes and Ophelia would stand by each other, and fight out every inch of ground of her madness.

We now return to Hamlet once more. The first intimation we have of him is through Horatio. And he gains his tidings of our hero through the instrumentation of sailors. We are sorely puzzled to find an expression for them.

> " *Hor*. I do not know from what part of the world
> I should be greeted, if not from Lord Hamlet."

We have hitherto considered Horatio, from all we could

gather, as the spirit of justice and scholarship, who is part of Hamlet, or the spirit of truth-seeking. We find him for a time absent from his friend; and it is during this period that our hero, though silently accumulating fresh force, which will presently show itself dramatically, is absent also from the dramatic action of the play. Hamlet, it must be remarked, never reaches England.

And in this we notice again our Poet's profundity. To England is left the mere work of killing Rosencrantz and Guildenstern. The banishment of Hamlet is probably meant as a relegation of truth-seeking to specific branches of inquiry alone. His absence from the play is the separation of these specific lines of thought, from any great work, with Horatio. We mean any historical crisis, as comprehended in an artistic sense. No doubt Hamlet has everything to do with the madness of Ophelia. But our Poet has not thought fit to dwell upon it. It is implied in Hamlet's forsaking that unfortunate lady; and it is implied in the death of Polonius. Now after the madness of Ophelia, we feel the necessity of the presence, in a dramatic sense, of Hamlet once more. The sea adventures of Hamlet are, in our mind, expressive of that pause, of that reaction and misgiving, which separates an age of certainty from an age of doubt. Hamlet is literally and truly at sea. And we shall have cause to find, further on, great probability of this being the truth. The Pirate who captures Hamlet, and thus saves his life, may be Discovery. That discovery may necessitate the assistance of Horatio. And a crisis may return the banished Hamlet as naked for the first time. The reader may naturally ask, why Hamlet does not proceed to England, find some mode of killing Rosencrantz and Guildenstern, and then, having enlisted England upon his side, return with an army to Denmark? But we have not reached a point advanced enough for this. England is as yet far too young and too weak to venture openly against the King. Besides, our Poet leaves England only to come in as a power at the end of the play. The whole being the apprenticeship of man, and not his travels, would be spoilt by making England too auto-

cratic, and allied too soon to Hamlet.[1] Sufficient that England kills slowly Rosencrantz and Guildenstern. In this
she plays an important part on Hamlet's side. She does him
the best service she possibly can. And his escape from the
two courtiers may be expressed well by the boldness of a
Pirate. A pirate is lawless and undaunted. Therefore
Hamlet, by the force of genius and of discovery, may be
returned naked to Denmark—

"*Hor.* [*Reads*] Horatio, when thou shalt have overlooked this, give these
fellows some means to the king: they have letters for him. Ere we were two
days old at sea, a pirate of very warlike appointment gave us chase. Finding
ourselves too slow of sail, we put on a compelled valour, and in the grapple I
boarded them: on the instant they got clear of our ship ; so I alone became their
prisoner. They have dealt with me like thieves of mercy : but they knew what
they did ; I am to do a good turn for them. Let the king have the letters I have
sent; and repair thou to me with as much speed as thou wouldst fly death. I have
words to speak in thine ear will make thee dumb; yet are they much too light
for the bore of the matter. These good fellows will bring thee where I am.
Rosencrantz and Guildenstern hold their course for England: of them I have
much to tell thee. Farewell.

He that thou knowest thine, HAMLET."

We are dealing with a text which bears directly upon the
escape of Hamlet from the two courtiers. And Horatio is
the first to hear of it, and to repair to him. It is through
Horatio the King receives the letter of Hamlet. It is only
through Horatio that Truth is once more in the ascendant.
And that Truth itself has first to react upon the spirit of
justice, of earnestness, and inquiry. The King soon hears
of it.

The sailors are truths themselves. They are the advanced
guards of Hamlet. And they soon carry Hamlet's letter to
the King.

This letter we have already commented upon. It is
a dramatic and artistic signification of the bare truth, and

---

[1] Goethe, in his novel, says : "All these circumstances and events (alluding
amongst others to the despatch of Hamlet into England, his capture by pirates,
the death of the two courtiers by the letter which they carry, etc.) would be very
fit for expanding and lengthening a novel ; but here they injure excessively the
unity of the piece, particularly as the hero has no plan, and are in consequence
entirely out of place."

nothing but the truth. The reader will understand us. The spirit of truth-seeking has thrown off its shackles. It is openly above board; it is direct to its point. It has neither equivocation nor shadow of turning. In freeing itself, it has confined the King. In proportion as the King is weakened, so Hamlet is strengthened. And this is the structure of the whole tragedy.

Hamlet has but one opponent now. That is Laertes. The King is contained in Laertes, and the latter in the former. And Hamlet knows it too. The King and Queen are belief in error and error in belief. They are fictions.

> " *King.* . . . The queen his mother
> Lives almost by his looks; and for myself—
> My virtue or my plague, be it either which—
> *She's so conjunctive to my life and soul,*
> That, as the star moves not but in his sphere,
> I could not but by her."

Thus we understand the relation of the King and Queen. They are one. They may both die, and yet we shall find no contradiction nor difficulty.

Now we must ask ourselves what is this union of Laertes and the King? We believe it to be the union of literature, and thus learning, against Hamlet. It is a union which has probably either a false method or a false criterion of things. To define it were absurd. We would call the reader's attention to the Norman, who makes such masterly report of Laertes. This *Lamond* we identify with *Lamonde*, or the world. Presently we shall find him to be identical with Osric.

> " *Laer.* Know you the hand?
> *King.*   'Tis Hamlet's character.   ' *Naked !* '
> And in a postscript here, he says ' *alone.* '
> Can you advise me ? "

The King, we see, relies upon Laertes. He asks him for his advice. And the answer of Laertes is full of point:

> " *I'm lost in it, my lord.* But let him come ;
> It warms the very sickness in my heart,
> That I shall live and tell him to his teeth,
> ' Thus didest thou.' "

Laertes is naturally much stirred up at the advent of a
naked Hamlet.   All his father's blood is roused in him.
He is indeed buried or lost in it.   We shall now find out
what accomplishments Laertes has been acquiring since his
travels.   Those are—

> " For art and exercise in your defence."

Thus we see Laertes is full of defence.   His position is one
that is passive.   He defends : Hamlet attacks.   How perfectly is the whole continuity of the tragedy expressed in
the following extract :

> " *King.* Not that I think you did not love your father ;
> *But that I know love is begun by time ;*
> *And that I see, in passages of proof,*
> Time qualifies the spark and fire of it.
> There lives within the very flame of love
> A kind of wick or snuff that will abate it ; [1]
> And nothing is at a like goodness still ;
> For goodness, growing to a pleurisy,
> Dies in his own too much : that we would do,
> We should do when we would ; for this *'would'* changes
> And hath abatements and delays as many
> As there are tongues, are hands, are accidents ;
> And then this *'should'* is like a spendthrift sigh,
> That hurts by easing.   But, to the quick o' the ulcer :—
> Hamlet comes back : what would you undertake,
> To show yourself *your father's son* in deed
> More than in words ?
> *Laer.*   To cut his throat i' the church."

In the appeal of the King to Laertes we have the
words, " your father's son."   In this expression the reader
needs no further explanation concerning Laertes.   He
sees he is a modified Polonius, allied to the King by
identity of interest and historical association.   We would
call attention to the metaphysical nature of the King's
speech.   It is almost a psychological one.   It is profound,
and putting aside all reference to our subject, shows
clearly how Shakespeare recognized the nature of law in
the human mind.   We see he recognizes that the *wish*

---

[1] The whole of this passage, and this line in particular, seems to indicate
modification of the principles of Polonius.

to do a thing changes, and is not dependent on ourselves. And the power of doing it depends upon the wish to do a thing. Therefore the power of doing anything (volition) is a thing which is the result of something we mistake for originality. We mistake the consciousness of consciousness, to be not alone a symbol of consciousness, but an entity, by which we fancy we have some occult power. What we wish we think. But that very wish is under law, and is the result of antecedents; but as the symbol of self-consciousness accompanies all thought, we labour under the pleasing delusion of separating effect into cause, the knowledge of thought into will or the resultant of thought.[1]

To return to the play. The King clearly recognizes the great change which has been effected in things. He dreads its effect also in changing Laertes any farther than he has already. His speech is a conservative re-action. It is alarm at the already rapid change, and self-argument, and self-reproach, to excite himself and Laertes against any further innovation.

The Queen now comes in to inform the King and Laertes of the death of Ophelia. There is a continuity of Ophelia as in Polonius. We can never say when they either exactly die. Their influence is so indefinite, and both will have adherents to such a length of time, that to bury them straight off is an error of the grossest kind. We must therefore temper the wind to the shorn lamb.

> " *Queen.* One woe doth tread upon another's heel,
> So fast they follow : your sister's drown'd, Laertes.
> *Laer.* Drown'd ! O, where ?
> *Queen.* There is a willow grows aslant a brook,
> That shows his hoar leaves in the glassy stream ;
> There with fantastic garlands did she come
> Of crow-flowers, nettles, daisies, and long purples
> That liberal shepherds give a grosser name,
> But our cold maids do dead men's fingers call them :
> There, on the pendent boughs her coronet weeds
> Clambering to hang, an envious sliver broke ;

---

[1] It is perhaps worth suggesting that this dualism we all feel is due perhaps to the *successive* character of thought. We cannot criticize a *present* thought, only a *past* one.

> When down her weedy trophies and herself
> Fell in the weeping brook. Her clothes spread wide ;
> And, mermaid-like, awhile they bore her up ;
> Which time she chanted snatches of old tunes ;
> As one incapable of her own distress,
> Or like a creature native and indued
> Unto that element : but long it could not be,
> Till that her garments, heavy with their drink,
> Pull'd the poor wretch from her melodious lay
> To muddy death.''

We are about to examine our crucial test of the text in relation to Ophelia. If we cannot rationalize this excerpt, all we have done goes for nothing.

To begin. The willow, and in this case the water-willow, signifies freedom and liberty. Running water is significant of instability—"unstable as water." The two together, namely, willow, which grows aslant, and the brook, are the freedom and liberty of progress, and *vice versa*. Ophelia expressed a state of sad scepticism, incoherence, and division from herself, prior to her death. Nothing is more natural than that these signs of the times should be the result of willow and water. And, of course, they increase. It is natural she should make fantastic garlands. We have met her before with straws (unions), as dissent and church associations, and flowers in her hair. She is, in fact, full of sentiment. We have her now hanging these fantastic garlands upon the tree of liberty. But the tree of liberty has its foundations laid over a brook. Of course this is an insecure spot to hang garlands upon. What are her garlands made of ? "Long stings of conscience," which others laugh at. Long pricks of remorse, which are laughed at by cold maids as the effect of the impress of things with no longer any life in them. Nettles are slander, in concert or union. The crow-flower may be the crow's-foot. If so, it is " Justice shall be done." Daisies are " Farewell," or "Sharing of sentiments." The application of these sentiments is of course left to the reader's choice. Climbing to hang this fantastic garland, the tree of liberty breaks, and casts her into the brook. Change is thus typified in this fall. Her " *weedy trophies* " are thus cast into the brook. And though her clothes keep Ophelia afloat for a time, and though she chants snatches of old songs, nevertheless she is finally drowned. How beautifully is all this rendered by our Poet. The snatches of old songs are expressive of a still lingering but expiring ritual and faith. The expression " muddy death " is full of truth. Every thing stirred up from the very bottom, or foundations, is thus well rendered. Laertes says:

"Too much of water hast thou, poor Ophelia."

He means that constant change of opinion, many diversities of thought, have divided the house against itself. A remark which is very applicable indeed to the present day. The dramatic death of Ophelia, like the dramatic death of Polonius, is not, however, her end. Ever bearing in mind that continuity, which we are always insisting upon, we find even after her death and burial the King saying:

" This grave shall have a living monument."

Even over the grave of Ophelia the fiercest fight is waged between Hamlet and Laertes.

And now we may perhaps be allowed to look back and see what the four acts have done for our hypothesis, and whether there is any contradiction which, meeting us, may be finally reconciled. We will therefore take the play in a pure relation of action, and of action in its relation to cause and effect alone. And we shall refrain from in any way making allusion to history. Let us suppose our Poet to have contemplated the construction of a tragedy, which was to form the subject of the conflict of Truth and Error. We might almost not be going too far to say Good and Evil, so far as results are concerned. For Hamlet gives us the impression of goodness. And the King gives us the opposite one of evil. The result of the tragedy in such a case might seem pessimistic. One in which destiny or fate overwhelmed good and evil indiscriminately. But we hope to clear this up by and by, and show how purely optimistic the whole tragedy is in its conclusion.

Shakespeare contemplating his idea of the conflict of

humanity, would first embody two characters to represent
the two ideas of Truth and Error in totality. All the rest
would be but so many followers, so many qualities, of these
two central figures. The latter must be in importance before
their inferiors. Therefore the one in possession has been
made a King, the one out of possession a Prince. He had to
make the relative importance of each character in harmony
with their order of time and their order of importance to
the central figure to which they belonged. Thus Hamlet
is the central figure on the side of truth. He is contained
by all his adherents. On the other side, we have the King,
who, being in possession, is wedded to human belief—the
Queen. In the next order of relative importance to the
King comes Polonius, who contains Ophelia and Laertes.
After Polonius, Voltimand and Cornelius ; next Rosencrantz
and Guildenstern ; and lastly Osric. All these characters
would have to be more or less moulded, so as to suit the
continuity of the action of the drama. And nothing could
have been more admirable than to make Truth a Prince and
a rightful heir to the throne, which is in possession of error
and injustice. But here must have arrived a difficulty.
How express the error of the King ? How express his
wrongful possession ? And how express Hamlet's right to
the throne ?

It is easy to reply, as we have the play before us. Simply,
our Poet made the King the perpetrator of a great crime.
In this is his evil nature. That crime is only unfolded by
time and by the detectives who set to work to scent it out.
And it added no little to the impressiveness of the play, and
to its ingenuity of construction, to make the murdered man,
as a Ghost, participate in the discovery ! And here was a
grand union possible. The father of truth is doubt. Error
had murdered doubt, by certainty of belief, by union with
custom ; whilst doubt was still asleep in the minds of men.
Thus we have a magnificent conception already laid down
in its skeleton form. But Hamlet is the son of doubt, and
by that claim has a just right to the usurped throne. The
discovery of this right, and the struggle to put it in force,

is the action of the tragedy. So far so good. But how is Hamlet to prove, dramatically, the King's guilt? By an introduction alone of the revelations of doubts, contrasted face to face with guilt. To show how the crime of the King had been committed, was to show error its own face, to expose it, and to show how it became error. In a mind like Shakespeare's the rest of the work was easy. To make support after support of the King fall before Hamlet, and to make Hamlet proportionally stronger, was indispensable. To make the groundwork one of time was also necessary of course. And to work the interest up to the point of discovery was dramatically necessary. After this the final catastrophe is brought bit by bit nearer and nearer. The play is so built upon the interdependence of antecedent and consequent, so under law, that it cannot fail to represent history, if the action is only considered. We see why Laertes and Ophelia are made the children of Polonius. We see that they depend upon him entirely. They take their very roots from out of him. And we see the absolute necessity of it being so. An able lawyer could make a case of Hamlet, which would defy contradiction. The action, the text, the succession, and the continuity, are so interwoven as to make anything of it but a philosophy of history an absolute impossibility.

The first act would necessarily be one in which the first rumours of a suspicious nature are made the subject of the opening scene. Doubt upon doubt, by means of those to whom doubt is accessible, go towards making a Hamlet. The second act would be an assemblage of all those scenes, which make the presence of a Hamlet and his suspicions uncomfortable to the King, through his representatives. Polonius is reached through Ophelia. The King through Polonius. The natures of the King's representatives are examined by Hamlet. They grow more and more offended at this scrutiny. They are gradually recognized by Hamlet. At this juncture, the means by which Hamlet may show error its own face, and how it became so, is furnished by the arrival of certain Players.

These Players are prompted by Hamlet. The result is a scene in which truth recognizes and exposes the usurpation and crime of the King.

After this there is no further fencing. All is open warfare. As if by accident, the first bulwark of the King dies. His death is made the opportunity of a division in the King's camp. For the Queen is able to listen to Hamlet's discourse touching the character of her husband. The result of the death of the King's right-hand man is a great change in the character of that right-hand man's daughter. And, lastly, Hamlet is so dangerous that all prudent people think his banishment an indispensable thing. But another result of the death of Polonius is the return of his son, to avenge his father's death. In this way our Poet has continued Polonius in his son. This son is a party,—a very large party,—allied by ties of blood to Ophelia, and bound to remain by his parent. Hamlet all this time has been steadily working, and at last succeeds in getting rid of another two of the King's supports. He returns, strange to say, alone, yet stronger naked than when clothed. So dangerous is he in this nude state, that the King and Laertes plan together to oppose him by fraud and trickery. Here we have arrived at the end of the fourth act. At this point we have dissension and scepticism in Church matters or religion, dissent, general unbelief, contained in the death of Ophelia.

CHAPTER IV.

WE are now at the most interesting part of the tragedy. We are about to discuss the famous churchyard scene. A scene so pathetic, so touching, and so solemnly striking, that we feel at once it is unparalleled in all literature. It has formed, indeed, a literature of its own. We feel how sublime, how magnificent, is this contrast of life and death. How deep, how profoundly inquisitive the mind which conceived it! Life and death are well contrasted by the light and shade of the clowns and death. It is painted by one who loved effect, yet knew how to deepen the tones, and blend the whole into an exquisite unity. But with all this we have nothing to do; we are architects who seek the principles of construction, the relation of architecture to thought, and we pass on with the knife of a dissector to the heart of the structure. Whatever we suggest here, as hypothesis of the meaning of this scene, is our own, and ours alone. We claim it particularly as a discovery. Goethe has nothing to say of it. Valuable even as the Wilhelm Meister's apprenticeship is to those who have already solved Hamlet for themselves, it contains nothing about this famous scene. At any rate we have no hint, no clue. If contained, it is part of the story, part of that detail which is found in Goethe's novel, not in Hamlet. And now, what is Goethe's novel? It would not be inappropriate to say here a few words concerning it. It is the apprenticeship of humanity in life and their travels. That

is to say, the first part is the development of Hamlet in
detail, often by means of Hamlet. The travels take up
the story where Hamlet leaves off. Goethe, of course,
plagiarized from Hamlet. He felt most likely he would
further his own genius and his fame better by a work of
art, than by plain exegesis of Hamlet. Exactitude is
required in the latter. Obscurity of vision may be sup-
plemented by obscurity, or originality. And it was a
grand conception to astonish futurity, first by an explanation of our Poet's spiritual unity, and secondly by a
philosophy of progress and history of his own upon the same
subject. Thus the two are blended — Hamlet and man's
travels. The novel is Goethe's prose conception of Shakespeare's Hamlet, and of a Hamlet of his own. How much
is Shakespeare's is of course contained in the whole idea.
But how much is in accordance with Hamlet, and how
much out of accordance, is another thing. Perhaps,
first, we must firmly decide in our own minds what Hamlet
exactly realizes. And that we believe posterity will not find
a difficult task. A knowledge of Goethe's novel, Wilhelm
Meister, will not assist much to the solution of Hamlet.
Witness in proof of this, that even the Germans have not
given us a solution of Hamlet. Dr. Gervinus says the
whole of Hamlet has been treated exhaustively by Goethe.
Has it, we ask? And if so, where is the key to Goethe's
novel? In England it is amusing to hear and read the
everlasting quotation from Goethe about Hamlet, in order
to explain his irresolution: "Here is an oak planted in a
vase, its roots strike out and expand. The vase flies to
pieces," etc. This is all that is ever gathered from Goethe.
Of course we see what Goethe meant. The expansion of
Hamlet is an expansion which bursts the vase, made of
King and company, to atoms. But it is not explained in
this light by the general run of critics. Hamlet is constitutional history.

Hitherto we have assumed a deduction of our own. Then
we have endeavoured to substantiate by induction, as far as
induction can be wedded to the text and to its connexion.

Our deduction is boldly the following. *The whole of this churchyard scene is a condensed chorus of time. Time and Progress, as clowns, epitomize much of that revolution which would interfere with the dramatic limits of the tragedy, if carried into actual detail.* What do we mean? the reader asks. We reply that Shakespeare has given us, in this churchyard scene, a continuation of the action of the drama as hitherto. The difference is, however, great, with one clown as Time and the other as Progress, a number of skulls can be dug up in a shorter period than if carried on as hitherto.

Time and Progress root up old institutions, and dig graves for existing ones. Hamlet and Horatio soliloquize over this strange scene.

Does the reader follow us? If he sees our drift, does he believe it? No—we answer for him. But we are nevertheless ready to stake everything upon the truth of this hypothesis.

Let us review some of the facts which make such an idea defensible. Hamlet having come back to Denmark naked, and having no opponent but Laertes, and his mad or dying sister, has things very much his own way. Not entirely, but of course the result must be one implying considerable reform and rearrangement in the institutions, opinions, and relations of men. Accompanied by Horatio, he would, of course, be at one with Laertes upon all but fundamental points. Those points being the character and sentiments of Polonius. There would be a sameness in all these reforms, and a tameness not indispensable to dramatic time and effect. But they must be represented in some manner. This scene is the short and striking way our great Shakespeare has solved the problem. Let us examine the characters first of the clowns. They are metaphysical, argumentative, and satirical. It has been well said, "nothing kills like ridicule." Discussion, satire, and philosophy, working by Time, are represented in these two clowns. We briefly call one Progress, and the other Time. They are burying Ophelia. That is, Christianity is slowly being sapped and put to bed by these jovial gentle-men.[1]

The first discussion is about Ophelia.

" Is she to be buried in Christian burial that wilfully seeks her own salvation ? "

And the answer from Time is

" She is. . . . . The crowner hath sat on her, and finds it *Christian burial.*"

The repetition of " *Christian burial*" leaves us no doubt, when taken in connexion with Ophelia.[2] The death of Ophelia may have meant a stage alone in the decay of the Church. It may have meant decadence and disestablishment, perhaps more—we will not venture to say. But now we have no equivocation. Our Poet has occupied so much time with the madness, death, burial and end of Ophelia, that we feel sure he realized the prominence, the length of time, and the slowness of the events which lead to her end and burial.

The above quotation seems to us the following: I tell thee she is, therefore make her grave immediately ; the owners (crowner) have sat on her, and find it her end.

" *First Clo.* How can that be, unless she drowned herself in her own defence ?
Sec. Clo. Why, 'tis found so."

This is exactly the case. Ophelia has drowned herself in her own defence, and " 'tis found so." In the constant change accomplished in the act of drowning, Ophelia has destroyed herself.

" *First Clo.* It must be ' se offendendo.' "

In this we read, It must be the end end of it.

---

[1] We have no hesitation in asserting that the proofs of this are beyond dispu-tation. Goethe has identified Ophelia with Aurelia, and the latter is the Church.

[2] We can realize the profound art of Shakespeare in thus obscurely discussing his meaning by means of a question of suicide.

The metaphysical discussions which follow show the philosophical and dialectic nature of the age. Indeed, Hamlet says:

". . . . . . We must speak by the card, or equivocation will undo us. By the Lord, Horatio, these three years I have taken a note of it; the age is grown so picked that the toe of the peasant comes so near the heel of the courtier, he galls his kibe."

We understand what this means. Rosencrantz and Guildenstern are dying all this time. It is an age of rigorous logic, of exactitude, of minute search, and of less and less trifling with words, and of a closer application of their meaning to facts, to induction, to cause and effect.

"*First Clo.* For here lies the point: if I drown myself wittingly, it argues an act: and an act hath three branches; it is, to act, to do, to perform: argal, she drowned herself wittingly.
Sec. Clo. Nay, but hear you, goodman delver,—
First Clo. Give me leave. Here lies the water; good: here stands the man; good: if the man go to this water, and drown himself, it is, will he, nill he, he goes,—mark you that; but if the water come to him and drown him, he drowns not himself: argal, he that is not guilty of his own death shortens not his own life."

The above, in our opinion, is a discussion over the nature of will and law—of necessity and free will. It is a discussion over time and the gradual recognition of law in the mind of man. For, as the Clown says, here lies the point, or as we read it, here is the contradiction—does man go to change, or does change come to him? An act is to do and to perform. Therefore Ophelia drowned herself wittingly or consciously. She did it spontaneously. This (mark) is the first decision of the Clown. But a little later he has blended the contradiction into the following.

Change is contradictory. If man changes his opinion, it is because he cannot help it, "it is will he, nill he, he goes." And if change comes to him and changes him, he is not responsible for his change. Therefore it is altogether out of his own hands. As the Second Clown asks—

"*Sec. Clo.* But is this law?
First Clo. Ay, marry, is't; crowner's quest law."

Thus are we let into the secret of the gradual recognition of law overlying the domain of thought. Various as the interpretation and clearness with which the above may be fought over by critics, the main point is evident: it is a discussion of whether man can help changing or not. We mean, of course, his beliefs. The conclusion is, we cannot. For change comes to him, and he goes to change; and neither are aught but antecedent and consequent. An antecedent and consequent traceable back to the first cause. Over which

> " There's a divinity that shapes our ends,
> Rough-hew them how we will."

We do not need to go into this discussion any further.

To those who recognize that man is part of nature, and that nature is under law, there is no escape from the conclusion—man is under law. And, indeed, it is impossible to realize man not under law. It is impossible to realize anything outside the chain of cause and effect. And even the conception of a God not under law is no conception. It is a negation.

We now will give our reasons for considering the Second Clown in the light of Time.

> " *First Clo.* Go, get thee to *Yaughan* : fetch me a stoup of liquor."

This word *Yaughan* is peculiar. It spells *any augh(t)*. From this we are inclined to think it may mean "any cipher." "Go, get thee to any cipher." Literally, let time multiply itself. Thus the chorus of Time going to Yaughan allows the First Clown to uproot all sorts of institutions, and reform them. We have first Politics, then the Court, next the Law. And Hamlet says:

> " Here's fine *revolution*, an we had the trick to see 't. Did these bones cost no more the breeding, but to play at loggats with 'em ? "

Loggats may be the artistic and obscure for *logic.* The First Clown digs and sings :

> " In youth, when I did love, did love,
>   Methought it was very sweet,
> To contract, O, the time, for, ah, my behove,
>   O, methought, there was nothing meet."

Presently he resumes—

> " But age, with his stealing steps,
>   Hath claw'd me in his clutch,
> And hath shipped me intil the land,
>   As if I had never been such."
>
> [*Throws up a skull.*]

In the first verse we have evidence of a contract. "It was very sweet to contract." There was nothing meet or fit for the time or times. And this contract and unfitness of the times was in the youth of the Clown, or of man's apprenticeship. The sum total of our interpretation of this verse is— Man recognizes by means of his changes the reality of progress. He sees that in early ages everything was a contract, only fit for such an age. Presently, however, Time, who is gone to Yaughan, alters him, as if he had no relation with his former state. There is little doubt this First Clown is an epitome of progress over a long period of time. The early discussion of the two Clowns is one respecting history, law, and the Bible. Ridicule is cast upon the latter in the reference to Adam. When the First Clown seizes his spade, he says :

> "*First Clo.* There is no ancient gentlemen but gardeners, ditchers, and gravemakers : they hold up Adam's profession.
> *Sec. Clo.* Was he a gentleman ?
> *First Clo.* He was the first that ever bore arms.
> *Sec. Clo.* Why, he had none.
> *First Clo.* What, art a heathen ? How dost thou understand the Scripture ? The Scripture says ' Adam digged:' could he dig without arms ? "

In the above there is direct satire and contradiction.

> " *First Clo.* I'll put another question to thee : if thou answerest not to the purpose, confess thyself—
> *Sec. Clo.* Go to."

In this reply of the Second Clown, "Go to," we recognize
the esoteric character of that Clown. It is "To go,"—that
is, Time.[1]

Presently we have the entrance of Hamlet and Horatio.
They only enter when the Second Clown has begun his
march to Yaughan. And there they stand by, and criticize
whilst the First Clown throws up skulls. Let us take the
great key of the play, given us in the following:[2]

"Ham. How long hast thou been a grave-maker ?
First Clo. Of all the days i' the year, I came to't that day that our last king
Hamlet overcame [sometimes o'ercame] Fortinbras.
Ham. How long is that since ?
First Clo. Cannot you tell that ? every fool can tell that : it was that very day
that young Hamlet was born ; he that is mad, and sent into England.
Ham. Ay, marry, why was he sent into England ?
First Clo. Why, because he was mad : he shall recover his wits there ; or, if he
do not, it's no great matter there.
Ham. Why ?
First Clo. 'Twill not be seen in him there ; there the men are as mad as he.
Ham. How came he mad ?
First Clo. Very strangely, they say.
Ham. How strangely ?
First Clo. Faith e'en with losing his wits.
Ham. Upon what ground ?
First Clo. Why, here in Denmark : I have been sexton here, man and boy,
thirty years."*

We have quoted here the very key of the tragedy.
If we fail to give a plain answer and to rationalize the
above in harmony with the whole of our conception, we
have only to apologize for throwing the reader's time away.
But if we can make the above as clear as we have the fore-
going part of the tragedy, and if, in addition, we can
rationalize it and harmonize it to our interpretation, then
we think our case made out, inasmuch as we have solved the
unity of idea in Hamlet.

---

[1] We have omitted the chief key to the signification of the Second Clown.
We find in this scene reference to the *gallows*, in connexion with this Clown.
This we believe to be symbolic for Time by a play upon words (all-ows). In
" Love's Labour's Lost " we find "five thousand years " termed " a shrewd un-
happy gallows too " (Act v. Sc. 2).
[2] We believe Shakespeare has purposely given us a key to the tragedy here.

What are the coincidences which strike us in the above conversation between the First Clown and Hamlet? They are *three* in number, and consist in an *identity* of origin or commencement. They are mutually interdependent. What are *they*? First, "the overcoming of Fortinbras" by the "last King Hamlet." Second, the beginning of the grave-making profession of the First Clown. Third, the birth of Hamlet. These three events are all started at one time.[1] To find the unity of this contemporary relationship is to solve the problem.

We have called Hamlet the spirit of truth-seeking. We have called the First Clown, for the sake of brevity, Progress. Fortinbras, we have said, is the spirit of liberty. Therefore the origin of Progress, and all that Progress implies in its grave-digging profession, would be begun on that day the spirit of truth-seeking was born, and *vice versa*. They are identical and interdependent. The first criticism, the first doubt, is identical with the first alteration—it is the same. And it is the same day that doubt begat (or o'ercame) or became (as we understand it) the spirit of liberty. *Truth, Liberty, Progress*, are all born at the same moment. They are all coheirs, and all co-partners. To recapitulate. *Progress* only commences when the spirit of doubt becomes the spirit of liberty, and they both are identical with the spirit of truth-seeking.

Every fool can tell when Fortinbras was overcome, or when the "last king o'ercame Fortinbras." On that day Hamlet was born.[2]

The reference to England, and the men being "as mad as he" there, strengthens our hypothesis upon the scientific character of that country. "'Twill not be seen in him

---

[1] Hamlet is Progress itself. The First Clown is an artistic and mere dramatic double to Hamlet. Shakespeare is clearly laughing at us when he says "Cannot *you* tell that? every fool can tell that." Hamlet is thus marvellously turned in upon himself.

[2] Hamlet and Fortinbras are part of each other. The Clown is also Hamlet himself.

there." And why? Because they all think the same way as Hamlet. The Clown cannot say why Hamlet is mad, or how he became mad. But we can understand how *England* signifies the *exact sciences*, which gradually kill Rosencrantz and Guildenstern, and are as mad as Hamlet.

Let us define our position. In this scene Shakespeare has given us progress of great length and great import. Hamlet and Horatio are actually studying that progress. They ask questions from it. The answers they get are interpretations of Hamlet himself. They recognize, for the first time, their own history. Hamlet learns, for the first time, from the First Clown, when he was born, why he was banished, etc., etc.[1] And, getting satisfactory answers, he questions still further. He studies how long beliefs are credited upon this earth. *And this leads him to study the whole of history.* The result is the repudiation of all history as a standard or criterion of truth. In this scene our Poet has pictured criticism of every kind, extending over the past; and historical criticism particularly. The scene opens with metaphysical or philosophical discussion over Ophelia. It leads to the question, whether the burial of Ophelia is to be the end of Ophelia or not? Time and progress decide in the affirmative. Next comes the nature of progress itself—is it under law or not? And again the answer is, Yes. Next we have the entry of Hamlet and Horatio, who begin to observe and comment over the Second Clown's doings. This is the study of progress. From this study Hamlet gets direct answers. Those answers are the history of himself— of man in his apprenticeship—of Hamlet's origin and development. Marvellously our Poet has turned Hamlet in upon himself. And by this means he gives us a key to comparative criticism of every kind. It is paralleled in the literature of to-day.

Lastly, Hamlet takes up *Yorick's* skull. Yorick is the

---

[1] Hamlet is actually studying himself. The First Clown and himself are one; only different dramatic aspects of the same meaning. Thus Hamlet is learning the nature of the rise and growth of Progress, or himself, from Progress itself.

King's jester. He is history. And Hamlet, criticizing him, represents criticism of history. Finally, Hamlet throws down Yorick's skull. In so doing our Poet signifies the repudiation of all past history as a criterion or standard of truth. The word *Yorick* is a compound of two words, *critic* and *history — ory*, *ick*. And, indeed, who could be termed better the King's jester than history? For it makes in the end all error a jest for time to laugh at. Whilst at the same time error in history has much on its side to laugh at. History is indeed the King's jester. It laughs at the King, whilst at the same time the King laughs mockingly through its means. Is not history a "fellow of infinite jest"? History indeed laughs at all things. Can we employ language adequate to such a conception? No. A silent awe is more in keeping, when we unfold the conceptions of a mind which was the epitome of all humanity before, now, and for ever! Again, how true is it history has borne Hamlet a thousand times on his back! And how true, too, it has drowned progress often in blood! As we read, he "poured a flagon of Rhenish on my head once."

It would be out of place to philosophize or make comments upon the tragedy and our Poet's genius here. It speaks for itself. We are occupied with unfolding the play alone. To proceed, or rather return :

> " *Ham.* I will speak to this fellow. Whose grave's this, sirrah ?
> *First Clo.* Mine, sir.
> [*Sings*]   O, a pit of clay for to be made
> For such a guest is meet."

Hamlet has here just commenced to study this Clown, who is Change and Progress. The lines of the Clown express his work. With pickaxe he roots up skulls. With that pickaxe criticism, discussion, philosophical and metaphysical, and with the chorus of his co-mate *Time*, he saps, kills, buries, and winds in a shrouding-sheet the past thoughts, the past beliefs, institutions and contracts of men. What a clown is this, who kills with ridicule! What a genius was that man, who, in the sixteenth century, could peer into the book of futurity! Who dares say he knows more

of the present, aye the future, than William Shakespeare?
And his statue stands at last for the first time in the
capital of that country he called his own.

> " *Ham.* I think it be thine, indeed; for thou liest in't.
> *First Clo.* You lie out on't, sir, and therefore it is not yours: for my part
> I do not lie in't, and yet it is mine.
> *Ham.* Thou dost lie in't, to be in't and say it is thine : 'tis for the dead, not
> for the quick ; therefore thou liest.
> *First Clo.* 'Tis a quick lie, sir ; 'twill away again, from me to you.''

How plain is all the above by the light of our interpretation !
How the contradictions, which seem mere verbal quibbles of
wit, vanish beneath the profundity of the spiritual meaning !
The Clown calls the grave he is digging "mine." And it
is his, for it is the result of change or progress. And
Hamlet tells him he lies in it. Hamlet is, be it remembered,
studying the Philosophy of History. And progress, at first
sight, seems to lie unremittingly and constantly. But the
Clown announces a paradox. He lies not, and yet it is his
grave. Progress seems to lie, yet it does not. Progress
has a law, which Hamlet is trying to grasp. It is a quick
lie which will away from Hamlet to the Clown, and from the
Clown to Hamlet.[1] For Hamlet plays a great part in this lie
of progress. As the Clown remarks : " You lie out on't, sir."
But Hamlet thinks this clown Change only digs for the past,
for the dead. The further study of the subject teaches man,
or Hamlet, that it is a quick lie, a living lie, which is existing, and always going forwards.

Hamlet has grasped the nature of Progress. Again,
" woman," throughout Hamlet, means belief :

> " *Ham.* What man dost thou dig it for ?
> *Clo.* For no man, sir.
> *Ham.* What woman, then ?
> *Clo.* For none, neither.
> *Ham.* Who is to be buried in 't ?
> *Clo.* One that *was* a woman, sir ; but, rest her soul, she's dead.''

It was a belief, but the belief is dead.

---

[1] Here again Shakespeare is laughing at us. Hamlet and the Clown are one.

There is a continuity and development, as in the rest of the play, throughout this famous scene. The whole scene is a study of man by man. That study is a study of sociology. Anticipating Mr. Herbert Spencer, anticipating Mill, and all the modern students of historical law, — Shakespeare has divined its existence three centuries ago. Let us notice one thing. The order of revolution : Politics first; the Court next, or, we should say, the kingly office, probably ; and then the Law. Again, the study of man by himself is full of apparent contradictions, and these our Poet has expressed. The first solution is a recognition of social law ; the next, a deep study of the past, or of Hamlet by himself. In this Hamlet, or man, recognizes the unity of progress, liberty, and truth. And this leads, of course, to repudiation of history as a standard for aught but the finding of law itself.

Time is indispensable to all this. So we have the introduction of Time, and his unrolling as he gets to Yaughan.

Let us note how Yorick's skull is made to turn up last, and how it has lain twenty-three years in the ground, and yet preserved. Who is a tanner ? He keeps out water or change a long time. Is he a curer of skins (of sins) ? Is religion the longest human institution to survive change ? How applicable to all times are the words :

"*First Clo.* I' faith if he be not rotten before he die—as we have many pocky corses now-a-days, that will scarce hold the laying in."

How beautifully is every fantastic theory, the thoughts of every day, the butterfly literature of an hour, here expressed !

Hamlet's speech about Alexander cannot be better dwelt upon than by a quotation to be found in the late Mr. Buckle's "Posthumous Works" : "You remember that wonderful scene in the churchyard, when Hamlet walks in among the graves, where the brutal and ignorant Clowns are singing, and jeering, and jesting over the remains of the dead. You remember how the fine imagination of the great Danish thinker is stirred by the spectacle, albeit he knows not yet that the grave which is being dug at his feet is destined to contain all that he holds dear upon earth. But though he wists not of this, he is moved like the great German poet; and he, like Goethe, takes up a skull, and his speculative faculties begin to work. Images of decay crowd on his mind as he thinks how the mighty are fallen, and have passed away. In a moment, his imagination carries him back two thousand years, and he almost believes that the skull he holds in his hand is indeed the skull of Alexander; and in his mind's eye he contrasts the putrid bone with what it once contained, the brain of the scourge and conqueror of mankind. Then it is that suddenly he, like Goethe, passes into an ideal physical world, and seizing the great doctrine of the indestructibility of matter, that doctrine which in his age it was difficult to grasp, he begins to show how, by a long series of successive changes, the head of Alexander might have been made to subserve the most ignoble purposes; the substance being always metamorphosed, never destroyed. 'Why,' asks Hamlet, 'why may not imagination trace the noble dust of Alexander?' When, just as he is about to pursue this train of ideas, he is stopped by one of those men of facts, one of those practical and prosaic natures, who are always ready to impede the flight of Genius. By his side stands the faithful, the affectionate, but the narrow-minded Horatio, who, looking upon all this as the dream of a distempered fancy, objects that ''Twere to consider too curiously to consider so.' O, what a picture! what a contrast between Hamlet and Horatio; between the idea and the sense; between the imagination and the understanding. ''Twere to consider too curiously to consider so.'"

Indeed all thinkers are convinced that this play of Hamlet is a history of humanity, an idealized philosophy of history. Every day this opinion is growing on us, and it only requires time to develope it most perfectly. Presently we have the entrance of the funeral party. The Priest says of Ophelia, "Her death was *doubtful.*" Here, again, we read the cause of Ophelia's death—scepticism. The introduction of the burial party, and the fight over Ophelia's grave between Hamlet and Laertes, signify one more, and the final controversy of humanity over Ophelia. It is the end of Christianity as a creed. Perhaps it is more. But we venture no comments upon that subject. Laertes is even resigned. Hamlet is sorry, nay, deeply grieved.

> " *Queen.* Anon, as patient as the female dove
> When that her golden couplets are disclosed,
> His silence will sit drooping."

His couplets are disclosed, and his silence will sit drooping. Hamlet has been the cause of all this. But still he is sorry, very sorry, over his own work. We find that, according to our Poet, " bell and burial are brought home." All this part of the play is such pure prophecy—belongs so much to the future—that we feel the great responsibility of hazarding any uncertain criticisms upon it. Hitherto we have found plenty of historical and contemporary parallelism. From henceforward we are plunged into futurity. Nevertheless, there is much here we cannot be mistaken about. We feel that in this fight over Ophelia's grave there is more concerned than the end of a particular form of belief. It is true, " violets may spring from her fair and unpolluted flesh " (violets = faith). But in those references to the Titans, and their efforts to scale the heavens, we read a profound meaning.

> " *Laer.* Now pile your dust upon the quick and dead,
> Till of this flat a mountain you have made,
> To o'ertop old Pelion, or the skyish head
> Of blue Olympus."

Again—

> " *Ham.* . . . . And, if thou prate of mountains, let them throw
> Millions of acres on us, till our ground,
> Singeing his pate against the burning zone,
> Make Ossa like a wart! Nay, an thou'lt mouth,
> I'll rant as well as thou."

Our interpretation of the above passages are the efforts of Hamlet and Laertes to scale the heavens. The reader will understand us. Man is making in the above every exertion to pierce that veil which hangs between mind and the

absolute. But in vain. No positive knowledge can ever
be gained upon such a subject.

The attack of Laertes upon Hamlet is in keeping with
the subject of it. Hamlet bears it quietly, even passively.
Laertes can do him no harm. And Hamlet wisely recognizes that Laertes must have his day out:

> "*Ham*. . . . . But it is no matter;
> Let Hercules himself do what he may,
> The cat will mew and dog will have his day."

How well Laertes is expressed as a dog! He barks at
everything Hamlet does. And like a cat, he is treacherous
and spiteful. Hercules may do what he will, and Hercules
is Hamlet; but still the scratching and barking will and
must have their day. How perfectly did out Poet recognize
the true character of the controversy, which would accompany the death of Ophelia, and the slow advance of man's
progress.

This is the last we hear of religion in the tragedy. We
have the hope of Laertes that violets, or faith, may spring
from Ophelia's dead body. And we have the testimony of
the King that the grave of Ophelia shall have a *living* monument. In these words we comprehend the good Ophelia has
effected. How she has given man a system of ethics, ideal
it is true, but a noble one, based upon the scientific and
true foundations of the utilitarian relations of man to man.
It is for the future to show the relation existing between
the optimism of Ophelia and the divine plan of Evolution.

We would here go back to Alexander, and make a suggestion, which seems not unworthy of note. Alexander may
perhaps be taken to represent the kingly office. An office fitly
represented by one of its greatest occupants. And the words
of Hamlet may signify the decay of that office into a mere
symbol, a mere cork, that might "patch a wall" "to keep the
wind away." We think beautiful as Mr. Buckle's idea seems,
it is rather far-fetched. For it is out of connexion with
the criticism of Yorick's skull. And nothing would be more
in keeping with that criticism than to follow it up with the

decadence of royalty.   And we read in the words of Hamlet
a continuity, to which we have called attention throughout
the play.   We may say of·Polonius or Ophelia, as Hamlet
says of Alexander—

> "*Ham.* To what base uses we may return, Horatio! Why may not imagination
> trace the noble dust of Alexander, till he find it stopping a bung-hole?
>
> *Hor.* 'Twere to consider too curiously, to consider so.
>
> *Ham.* No, faith, not a jot; but to follow him thither with modesty enough,
> *and likelihood to lead it: as thus: Alexander died, Alexander was buried, Alexander
> returneth into dust ; the dust is earth ; of earth we make loam: and why of that
> loam,* whereto he was converted, might they not stop a beer-barrel?
>
> > Imperious Cæsar, dead and turn'd to clay,
> > Might stop a hole to keep the wind away :
> > O, that that earth, which kept the world in awe,
> > Should patch a wall to expel the winter's flaw! "

The depreciation and contrast of the possible destiny of
two of the mightiest of rulers makes us inclined to believe
we are nearer the truth than Mr. Buckle.   As we have
already hinted, Polonius and Ophelia died, Polonius and
Ophelia were buried, Polonius and Ophelia returned to dust;
and why should not that office so well summed up in an
Alexander and a Cæsar go through the same process of
decay?   Is it not going through it now?

We have run over a great deal in a great hurry.   We
have hardly sketched a theory of Hamlet.   But what we
have done is rather in the hope of suggestion, of showing not what is true, but what a play like Hamlet may
possibly be.   The reader, of course, will reject much of
our hypothesis.   In the present state of Shakespearian
criticism, this is only to be expected.   But nevertheless in
so doing, thoughts and suggestions will enter his head never
conceived there before.   And we feel our work will not be
utterly cast upon sterile ground.   For there is a growing
appreciation in the public mind of the profundity and double-
sidedness of Shakespeare's art.   An art which will redeem
him a second time from the grave.   And an art which will
form the study of future generations.

CHAPTER V.

WE now approach the end of this stupendous tragedy. We are dramatically nearing the end of man's apprenticeship. But Hamlet concerns us alone at present. How far, in point of time, the dramatic situation is from its parallel in future times, we know not. Who can tell what to-morrow may bring but a Shakespeare ? And now we have next on hand, in the order of the text, a retrospect by Hamlet. This review and explanation by Hamlet concerning his escape from the Pirate and discovery of the King's commission, seems to us to supply the missing links of the tragedy. It thoroughly explains the position of Hamlet at the time he was at sea, and had no decided plans of his own :

> " *Ham.* Sir, in my heart there was a kind of fighting,
> That would not let me sleep: *methought I lay*
> *Worse than the mutines in the bilboes.* Rashly,
> And praised be rashness for it, let us know,
> Our indiscretion sometimes serves us well, ·
> When our deep plots do pall : and that should teach us
> There 's a divinity that shapes our ends,
> Rough-hew them how we will."

We must return to Hamlet's exile for an instant. That exile was one because he had no plans and no ends. After the death of Polonius, Hamlet was almost frightened at what he had done. He felt, as he himself says, worse than "mutineers who lie in fetters." This expresses the whole case. He had mutinied, and he was in fetters. His own

plans were even obscure to himself, but his very indiscretion
serves him well. What do we mean? We mean that
Hamlet, as represented in man's history, has had his doubts,
his fears; he has not defined his ends even. Progress is but
a recognition of to-day or yesterday. Parties with their
different hopes and aims are the products of eminently
modern history. Presently we find Hamlet groping "to
find his ends"—

> "*Ham.* Up from my cabin,
> My sea-gown scarf'd about me, in the *dark*
> Groped I to find out them ; had my desire,
> Finger'd their packet, and in fine withdrew
> To mine own room again."

If anything would convince a reader of the nature of
Hamlet, the above should be of a conclusive nature. Here
is Hamlet "in the dark," trying "to find out them." But
what are *these* which he terms *them*? Clearly Hamlet's
"*ends.*" And, thanks to his rashness and perseverance, he
succeeds in "fingering their packet." Nothing can be
clearer than all this. Reviewing his own history, he sees
the time when obscurity of vision made him feel like a
mutineer. He dared not stand still, he dared not look back.
And, praised be the rashness which casts the balance in
favour of progress, Hamlet finds his ends. Those ends are
the recognition that Rosencrantz and Guildenstern threaten
the very life of naked truth. He labours doubly accordingly, escapes from them by means of a Pirate (whatever that
may mean), whilst scientific proof slowly undermines evasion
and sophistry. Hamlet and Horatio are gathering their
forces together for the last struggle. Partly for the sake of
clearing ambiguities ; partly for the sake of showing how
man in Hamlet reviews his own history and gathers addi-
tional strength from it, we have this scene.

The whole of the first part of this scene between Hamlet
and Horatio is a review of their own position, of the history
of that position, of the thought of Divine law ruling social
action, and of the great evil of compromise, hypocrisy,
sophistry, and casuistry, which science is slowly killing.

Hamlet expresses this science so beautifully that we must quote again:

> "*Ham.* Being thus be-netted round with villanies,—
> Ere I could make a prologue to my brains,
> They had begun the play—I sat me down,
> Devised a new commission, wrote it fair;
> *I once did hold it, as our statists do,*
> *A baseness to write fair,* and labour'd much
> How to forget that learning, but, sir, now
> It did me yeoman's service."

Hamlet writes fair. This is a *naked* Hamlet who writes fair. This very fairness kills Rosencrantz and Guildenstern. Who are the statists who refuse to write fair, and consider it a baseness to do so? They are those who are for standing still. They are the statics of society, in contradiction to the dynamical principle represented by Hamlet. The word "statists" is perhaps related to the word *statics*.[1] This writing fair does Hamlet "yeoman's service." Nothing kills like truth. Errors are obliged to assume the garb of truth even to pass muster; but like all false coin, they get exposed sooner or later. England takes up the cue Hamlet devises. England, as science, is prompted by a spirit of truth. And this truth invades every domain of thought, until it gives Hamlet power to return, with ever-gaining strength, to kill and exterminate the King and all his myrmidons. What does Hamlet devise? Nothing more nor less than a rigorous logic, which is beautifully expressed by an imitation of syllogistic reasoning—

> "*Ham.* As England was his faithful tributary,
> *As* love between them like the palm might flourish,
> *As* peace should still her wheaten garland wear,
> And stand a *comma*[2] 'tween their amities,
> And many such-like '*As'es* of great charge,
> That, on the view and knowing of these contents,
> Without debatement further, more or less,
> He should the bearers put to sudden death,
> Not shriving-time allow'd."

---

[1] We are aware that the word *statist* signifies sometimes a legislator or law-maker. But we suggest the word may signify even more.

[2] The word *comma* seems to *suggest pause*, not *full stop*.

Hamlet writes this, and in writing this our Poet shows us how the spirit of truth inspires England to deal with Rosencrantz and Guildenstern. That method is one in which close reasoning and trenchant logic (like the logic our hero indulged in when first in conversation with Rosencrantz and Guildenstern), allowing of no equivocation, infects the thoughts of man, and slowly brings about an increasing desire for rationalism in all things. This we see at the present day, and the thirst for clear answers to plain questions will ever be on the increase, in proportion as men think, and thus in the ratio of their knowledge, liberty and love of truth—things which go hand in hand.

Hamlet knows the news will soon arrive from England. Our Poet here signifies the influence of England upon human thought. He sees, as we may at the present moment, the foreshadowing of the universality of science. Hamlet foresees its widespread influence. He foresees the unlimited sway it will have in the future destiny of man. And foreseeing this, he is determined to hasten it, to do all he can to bring things to that pass. He is acted upon by this knowledge, and it stirs him up to fresh resolution :

> " *Hor.* It must be shortly known to him from England
> What is the issue of the business there.
>   *Ham.* It will be short: the interim is mine;
> And a man's life 's no more than to say 'One.'
> But I am very sorry, good Horatio,
> That to Laertes I forgot myself;
> *For, by the image of my cause, I see*
> *The portraiture of his: I'll court his favours:*
> But, sure, the bravery of his grief did put me
> Into a towering passion."

How admirable is the above! Hamlet sees in the cause of Laertes the portraiture of his! Both grieve and fight for the sake of their fathers. Both believe in those fathers. Hamlet is always spurred on by doubt, to redress wrongs and kill error. Laertes is always spurred on by a fatal but useful bias of certainty to defend the King and uphold the past. Both are in earnest. One is liberalism, the other conservatism. Their mutual death is their final convergence and identification in equilibrium. Everything points in England at the present day to such a finale. Every day the Conservative policy becomes more like the Liberal. And such is the history of the "statists," that they only let go when forced, and they will only cease holding on when there is no longer anything left to hold on to.

Hamlet will court the favours of Laertes. He will benefit by the prudence of the latter. He will be prevented from committing any imprudence by the latter. And he will find criticism after all a useful ordeal. Laertes is indispensable to the successful apprenticeship of a Hamlet. · Were Hamlet not checked in the often reckless way he would compromise his health and conduct, he might sacrifice the terms of his indentures. The bravery of Laertes' grief puts Hamlet into a towering passion.. Hamlet evidently thinks the grief of Laertes as unavailing, as even unnecessary ; and this unavailing lament and fight over what Laertes can neither bring to life again nor stop decaying is well calculated to put Hamlet in a passion. At this instant we have the entrance of one who is part of Laertes. He is a biassed judge. And one in whom Hamlet recognizes this character as also that of the sciolist. Of all our Poet's creations in this play, not one is painted with so forcible, so delicate, and such refined irony, as the courtier Osric. We reserve him for a chapter to himself.

CHAPTER VI.

WE are now for the first time introduced to Osric. In Osric we easily recognize society, and in Osric we also recognize criticism. The great enemy and critic of Hamlet is Osric, a gentleman who is decidedly of a bias of mind in favour of Laertes. Osric is part of the continuity and succession of the tragedy. To have left him out would have been a gross error, and a gross neglect of the last and not the least enemy of Hamlet. He is a critic, but a critic who has stakes in the game over which he is judge. They are balanced more heavily on one side than the other. He has laid the odds upon Laertes. In the politeness of Osric we recognize society. In his parrot-like speeches and empty phrases, we recognize the pretender to learning. The mere sciolist.

The point we have reached dramatically is not far off the final catastrophe and end. And the real meaning of Shakespeare is that historically the last stage in man's apprenticeship is reached. The last stake at issue over which Hamlet and Laertes fight is one in which Osric is concerned. And it is a stake of "six Barbary horses" against "six French rapiers and poniards, with their assigns, as girdle, hangers, and so: three of the carriages, in faith, are very dear to fancy, very responsive to the hilts, most delicate carriages, and of very liberal conceit."

The whole of the latter stake of the bet is *imponed*, as

Osric terms it, against six Barbary horses. It is not very difficult to seize the side Hamlet is upon, or the side Laertes defends. Hamlet will work for the six Barbary horses. Laertes will defend the six French rapiers, etc. At present we will refrain from giving our opinion of the meaning of the above. We will take the text first.

> " *Osr.* Your lordship is right welcome back to Denmark.
> *Ham.* I humbly thank you, sir. Dost know this *water-fly* ? "

In this word "*water-fly*" an infinity of meaning is expressed. We are instantly reminded of those flies we see in summer skimming the surface of ponds. The *surface* of things is here suggested. One who hovers upon the mere outside and never penetrates. This is Osric.

> " *Ham.* Thy state is the more gracious ; for 'tis a vice to know him. He hath much land, and fertile : let a beast be lord of beasts, and his crib shall stand at the king's mess : 'tis a chough ; but, as I say, spacious in the possession of dirt." [1]

In the above we have, as usual, a complete key to Osric's character. He is rich, he is a possessor of land, *and this is quite enough to make him at one with the King.* Rosencrantz is evidently not dead yet. No, he "*goes to't,*" but he will not be dead until Hamlet's death. Osric is society, and that part of society which stands by the King. The whole of this part of the play is one which is concerned with the last struggle of man and man. It is one in which society is concerned. One in which the classes of society are at war with six Barbary horses. These latter are probably not unlike what is known in the present day by *Communism.* Property, capital, possession, social injustice, are allied with Laertes against the principle of progress. The whole of the politeness of Osric shows his society manners, and gives us a key to his elucidation. He praises Laertes. For Laertes is his backbone, his stand-by, his very life. And what is

---

[1] Osric is Rosencrantz. It is quite sufficient that he is a large *interested owner* to understand that he will side with the King. There is no escaping Shakespeare's meaning *here.*

Laertes? We have long ago identified him with learning of an orthodox kind. He is literature of a conservative character.

> "*Osr.* . . . . Sir, here is newly come to court Laertes ; believe me, an absolute gentleman, full of most excellent differences, of very soft society and great showing: indeed, to speak feelingly of him, he is the card or calendar of gentry, for you shall find in him the continent of what part a gentleman would see."

This is Osric's version of Laertes. Presently we shall have Hamlet's. Osric speaks *feelingly* of Laertes. He is part of Laertes himself, and no wonder he speaks feelingly. The quotation we have made is a revelation in itself. Laertes is the liberal education of a gentleman, as understood by himself or Osric. But it is an education which Professor Huxley and Hamlet hardly consider liberal in our days. Laertes is the "*card or calendar of gentry.*" In him you see the whole of a gentleman's education. Now let us compare Hamlet's definition of Laertes :

> "Sir, his definement suffers no perdition in you; though, I know, to divide him inventorially would dizzy the arithmetic of memory, and yet but yaw neither, in respect of his quick sail. But, in the verity of extolment, I take him to be a soul of great article; and his infusion of such dearth and rareness, as, to make true diction of him, his semblable is his mirror; and who else would trace him, his umbrage, nothing more."

It is extraordinary how the speaking characters of pieces like the above escape the keen eyes of critics, who are on the look-out for a hint. Here we have, with a few touches, the whole character and worth of Laertes. He is "*diction.*" He is a "*soul of great article.*" And he is multitudinous in his acquirements, which are very raw in consequence of his quick sail. His motto is, *Multa non multum.* And the result is the mere sciolist. Those that trace him will not find anything but the shadow of Laertes. "*His semblable,*" or what seems *to him* the Truth (which is only a reflection of himself), is all that is to be found in literature of this description. Laertes is thus epitomized in the shallow education and learning of what are called cultured men. A culture which is strengthened on the side of error by the wide extent of the study of the literature handed down by

Polonius. Logical truth is not sought by such men. Erudition, or *the soul of great article*, is all that is required. Authorities (as they are considered) already false help to sustain error deduced from that authority. This class of literature has its use, it is true; and those things which cannot stand its batteries are not worth their salt. But all followers of Hamlet must recognize its emptiness, and its boast of a strength which is in its very ignorance and the ignorance of others. "*His semblable is his mirror*,"—a fit motto for metaphysicians and transcendental philosophers generally!

To follow the thread of our fancy, and see a mirror in our imagination concerning Truth, has been (putting all science outside the question) the whole history of human thought. Laertes is a liberal education, and he is more, he is often profound scholarship and profound learning of every description. But it is a learning which believes we are in possession of Truth. It is an erudition which criticizes not the sources and springs of its own fountain-head. It is defensive, it is passive. There is no progress with such a literature, unless there is an opposing one. This opposing one must be inspired by a Hamlet, urged on by the revelation of a Ghost, and must continually alternate the appearance of the Ghost with the crowing of the cock. Thus Doubt and Certainty, being active, and not passive, are that pleasing and invigorating suspension of judgment upon all things until verified. Our scepticism is one which is satisfied and allayed with the truths of nature, and in the exposition of those laws. Nature is all things, God, man, time, space, and every question which can agitate the mind of man. The tragedy of Hamlet is the history of the rise of rationalism in Europe. And to this end liberty, knowledge, and inquiry, with Doubt, go hand in hand. Without knowledge there is no inquiry; without inquiry, no doubt; without doubt, no progress. And all interdepend upon an accompanying spirit of liberty, which we have in Fortinbras. All these conditions are fulfilled in the beginning of the tragedy. And they are fulfilled in an orderly and natural sequence. We have Bernardo relieving and recognizing Francisco.

And we have the rivals of this watch following. The sure accompaniments of the art of reading—Inquiry and Scholarship (Marcellus and Horatio). Doubt follows as a Ghost. Faintly, of course, at first. But increasing in power. The cock crowing signifies Certainty following Doubt. And, at the same time, we have the rise of Fortinbras and his suppression. Thus the spirit of liberty goes hand in hand in unity with the rest.[1]

But to return, after this digression. We have recognized the character of Osric and that of Laertes. Their cause is common. The stability of society, the conservation of the social hierarchy threatened by Hamlet (and ruin at the same time), necessitate the voice of Osric upon the side of Laertes. As we have before remarked, they are identical. Osric will both fight and be judge. Laertes is literature, and Osric is society itself. We shall see the result of the duel presently. Hamlet, and all those who constitute Hamlet, are, as in the present day, recognizing the worth of what has hitherto been dignified by the title of education, learning, etc. Hamlet has learnt some method of thinking, which puts him above or over Laertes. He sees what the *infusion* of Laertes is worth. Like his father, Polonius, Laertes clings still to words, and, under their cover, tries to make an escape from Hamlet, as the cuttle-fish does under cover of his ink. As Hamlet remarks:

" To know a man well, were to know himself."

This criticism of self is very rare and very difficult. Hamlet knows Laertes. But Laertes knows not himself. Nor does Laertes know Hamlet. Hamlet knows exactly his own strength and his own weakness.

The whole of this conversation between Osric and Hamlet is · a picture of beauty, truth, and rarity. It is the final duel of social man, being summed up in its causes, in its forces, and in its nature. The wrongs and evils

---

[1] We are only too sensible of the cursory manner in which all this is discussed; but until the nature of the play is clearly established, it were waste of time to go deeper into the subject.

of a social state, handed down from a feudal system, are in direct conflict with unvarnished justice. The daily labourer, or artisan, is well pictured in a Barbary horse. He works like a horse, and he is rough and uncultivated. He is thus barbarous. Certain classes of society are well pictured in the "rapiers and their hangers, carriages, assigns." The assigns look very much like a term in heraldry. The carriages, or hangers, are perhaps the aristocracy, the landed gentry, or plutocracy. They are of a very liberal conceit. And they are called by Horatio the *margent*. It is their anger, or (h)angers (?), which cause this duel. Property is perhaps the cause. We know not. But what Hamlet says is very true. Cannon would be more likely to settle the question, if the angers had their way. The whole bet is *imponed*. This word we believe to be from the Latin *impono*, "to beguile, to wheedle, or trick out of; to lay upon," etc., etc. The reader must apply his own reading of this word. The odds are placed by the King on the strongest side—on that of Laertes. And we would draw attention to the at first sight contradictory evidence of the bet. For the Barbary horses are wagered with Laertes. How is this to be reconciled? There is no reconcilement needed. If Hamlet wins, he wins the Barbary horses, or rather, to speak exactly, they (the horses) win, whilst the six French rapiers, etc., etc., lose. Does the word *imponed* signify *imperilled?* And if so, we understand Hamlet's question. But if not, it may mean "to be got out of stake," "out of pawn." We see that in the bet of the King the odds are twelve to nine upon Laertes. In fact, Laertes is to exceed Hamlet by three hits.

"*Osr.* The king, sir, hath laid, that in a dozen passes between yourself and him, he shall not exceed you three hits: he hath laid on twelve for nine; and it would come to immediate trial, if your lordship would vouchsafe the answer.

Ham. How if I answer 'no'?

Osr. I mean, my lord, the opposition of your person in trial.

Ham. Sir, I will walk here in the hall: if it please his majesty, '*tis the breathing time of day with me;* let the foils be brought, the gentleman willing, and the king hold his purpose, I will win for him an I can; if not, I will gain nothing but my shame and the odd hits."

The whole of Osric's message is a challenge and defiance. It is, "Do your worst, I am so safe with Laertes that the odds are all on my side." Hamlet says it is "the breathing time of day" with him. That is, Truth has an existence. The spirit of rationalism, of justice, has long been roused; and, as we know, Hamlet is a powerful party, who has but another party to contend against. Shakespeare evidently was determined to go as far as he could. A short dramatic period may be a very long historical one; and with these questions we are not concerned. Hamlet sums up the character of Osric in the following:

"He did comply with his dug, before he sucked it. Thus has he—and many more of the same bevy that I know the drossy age dotes on—only got the tune of the time and outward habit of encounter; a kind of yesty collection, which carries them through and through the most fond and winnowed opinions; and do but blow them to their trial, the bubbles are out."

In these satirical remarks of Hamlet we recognize our friend Osric still more forcibly as society. "He did comply with his dug, before he sucked it." Literally, "nothing is natural about him, *all is made up*, and is a matter of inheritance." Again, we may read in the above, "self-interest is before all things, and his circumstances are the result of accident." Hamlet calls it a "*drossy age*." Money is the ruling principle of this society. The words *yesty* and *winnowed* suggest froth, chaff, emptiness, nothingness, shallowness. If Osric is put to the test, "*the bubbles are out*." In short, we must make up our minds that this is rather a contemptible judge to decide between Hamlet and Laertes; particularly when we know how biassed Osric is in his own favour and that of his friend.

"*Lord*. My lord, his majesty commended him to you by young Osric, who brings back to him, that you attend him in the hall: he sends to know if your pleasure hold to play with Laertes, or that you will take longer time."

Thus we see the King is commended to Hamlet by Osric.

That is, Hamlet is going in again at the King, this time
represented in Laertes and Osric.

"*Ham.* I am constant to my purposes ; they follow the king's pleasure : if his
fitness speaks, mine is ready ; now or whensoever, provided I be so able as now.
Lord. The king and queen and all are coming down.
Ham. In happy time."

Hamlet never swerves from his purpose to kill the King
and avenge his father. He is indeed constant to his ends
when he knows them. Hamlet's purposes follow the King's
pleasure. And it is already realized that the fall of the
King and Queen are at hand. Hamlet says, "*in happy
time.*" The reconciliation of Laertes and Hamlet is only
skin deep. It. is the polish, the refinement, the for-
bearance and amenities of modern and future polemical
literature.

We would here pause before we proceed any further.
We are at a solemn point of the tragedy. We are un-
veiling, or blaspheming, our Poet's thoughts as to the
future conflict of man on earth. And we would first make
clear our opinion concerning some, at first sight, gross
contradictions to our hypothesis.

The reader has probably long wanted to know why
Hamlet does not succeed to the throne of his uncle ? Why
does he die ? Why should Truth be defeated in the
end ? Is it a dramatic necessity ? Or is it the limit of
Truth ?

We answer, neither one nor the other. The death of
- Hamlet is not the death of Truth. For Hamlet is not
Truth itself. Indeed, there never can be for man absolute
truth. Only relative truth. What is Hamlet then ? We
have all along identified him with Truth. *Yes, but Hamlet
is the spirit in man of truth-seeking alone.* Hamlet is the
spirit of *conflict warring* through man for truth's sake.
With the end of the apprenticeship of man Hamlet dies.
For his apprenticeship is done.

Let us clearly define our position. We have merely
employed the word *truth* as allied to Hamlet in the sense
of truth-seeking and progress. What is truth ? This

has been a question which has never been satisfactorily answered by man. We cannot discuss such a subject here. But we may as well define our idea of truth as regards Hamlet. Absolute truth can be for a God alone. But relative truth is for man. That truth is best exemplified in the laws of God, which have been beautifully termed by Oersted "the thoughts of God." To this Hamlet or man may attain. The rest is silence. But even in this we do not apply the same line of argument to Hamlet. For the tragedy of Hamlet is a social one. A conflict concerning man's opinions. And its end is the end of this conflict. The realization of harmony, liberty, justice, and science. Thus the death of Hamlet is the death of the autocracy of party. It is the finale of man's social antinomy. And as Goethe has far better expressed it, the termination of man's apprenticeship. Up to this point man has been divided in opinion, unlearning the mistakes of his youth, and gradually recognizing his place and the nature of himself in the order of nature. However, to prove that this is what Shakespeare intended, we will appeal to the text again.

If the death of Hamlet were in reality more than the death of mere conflict and difference of opinion, we should hear no more of him. But Horatio tells us his "*voice will draw on more.*"

> "*Hor.* Of that I shall have also cause to speak,
> *And from his mouth whose voice will draw on more.*"

Horatio thus tells us Hamlet is not dead. He is dramatically dead. And in this his after-continuity is on a par with that of Polonius, of Ophelia, after their deaths. The necessities of art are inexorable, when allied to rationalism. The latter cannot be applied to the letter, though it may to the spirit of the letter. Something, perhaps a good deal, is to be said upon the necessities of dramatic art in Hamlet. The grandeur of the tragedy is aided, nay fulfilled, by Hamlet's death. And we have a lesson on the indiscrimination of law between good and evil. Destiny is no distinguisher of persons. And thus the philosophy of

life is also true in Hamlet. But this does not necessitate
that Hamlet, as Mr. Tyler would have it, is a tragedy
whose philosophy is pessimistic. It is eminently optimistic,
for it points to an end of man's discord, to liberty, justice,
and progress of a different order to that of the play itself.
Nothing could be more hopeful, more utopian, or more
optimistic than Hamlet throughout. The progress and
strength of rationalism, and all that it implies, is long, it
is true; but as Hamlet says:

"These foils have all a length."

When reason is universal, and has taught social man what
is true here below, and what is false, then the tragedy
of Hamlet draws to its end on earth. Hamlet might be
termed the history of progress. It might be truly, as
Goethe thought, man's apprenticeship. Or, again, we
may call it a philosophy of history. There is little
philosophy, it is true, in the strict sense. But we can
find ourselves in it much historical philosophy. In the first
place, it recognizes social law. This is the root and keystone of a philosophy of history. Secondly, it implies, in
a remarkable degree, that discovery which Comte claimed
for himself. That is the law of mechanics applied to history
and sociology. It implies in Hamlet and his supporters
a law of social dynamics, in contradiction to the King and
his supporters, who represent social statics. Indeed, the
structure and continuity of the play inclines us to a belief
that our Poet thoroughly not only recognized this law,
but that he seized what we cannot—its secondary laws.
For how in heaven's name can we account for his marvellous
prophetic powers? Let the reader judge for himself. For
in our eyes history is paralleled line for line in this play.
Not only history, but contemporary, and the daily life even
of these our days are photographed in Hamlet. There
must have been intention or genius in this. To use the
latter word is to solve the whole question. And perhaps
the laws of progress may be better furthered by a study
of Hamlet than by aught else. There is not a principle in

Buckle's History of Civilization which is not grasped by our Poet. The relations of knowledge, scepticism, liberty, authority, religion, so insisted upon by Buckle, are here dramatically exhausted in a two hours' play. And this play was written when men did not seize even the idea of law as regards man. What are we to say to all this? Simply that genius is the power of ratiocination on an infinite scale : of following cause and effect into its remote sequences. And how does this speak for the existence of law, which foolish people still question? It proves it. It indorses it. For were law not there, where would be the prophecy which trusts to the invariability of that law in the future?

Now we shall endeavour to explain the finale of the tragedy as regards the catastrophe. It will be noticed Laertes wounds Hamlet, and then Hamlet in his turn wounds Laertes, with the poisoned rapier of the latter exchanged in scuffling. What does this mean? It means the death of Laertes by means of his own error. *It is turned in upon him.* In his conflict with Hamlet he probably uses a false method, a false criterion, which, being erroneous, when once exploded by Hamlet, puts an end to the party Laertes represents. And of course the King dies when Laertes dies. For he is the error for which Laertes fights;[1] and to prove this, Hamlet stabs the King with *the same rapier* he has stabbed Laertes, and by which he has himself been stabbed. That rapier, we have said, belongs to Laertes. Thus the King's death, Laertes's death, and Hamlet's death, are all the result of *one rapier.* And so the error exploded, the King dies through Laertes, the latter with his error, and Hamlet through the end of conflict. The death of the Queen is the death of the King. Both are wedded in belief. Both King and Queen drink the same potion ; that potion, poisoned and set for Hamlet, is like the rapier in the case of Laertes, again turned in upon themselves.

---

[1] The King is made up of his adherents. Thus he disappears with his last constituent. And Hamlet thus is acting and killing the King all through the play.

Belief in error and error in belief both die, with the explosion of their beliefs and errors. Thus the symbols of the play die, in harmony with our whole exegesis. The poisoned cup is perhaps a dramatic necessity, to get rid of the Queen. Hamlet says, as the King drinks off, or is supposed to swallow the poison:

> "Drink off this potion. *Is thy union here?*
> Follow my mother."

The union of the King and Queen is in the poison. It is union of belief and error (erroneous beliefs), and the poison represents the efforts they make to foist upon Hamlet those beliefs. Obliged to swallow their own words, and thus exposed, they die. In the death of Hamlet and Laertes we read the end of party. We read the union and mergence of Hamlet and Laertes. The former (Hamlet) represents social dynamics, the latter social statics. Now both are one in union. The social statics have become so weakened by the social dynamics that finally both are merged. Party is abolished. And identity of interests, of beliefs, springing from the unity of science alone, makes man at peace with man and self-governed. Individualism has conquered social authority, by the latter becoming identified with the former.[1]

Hardly is Hamlet dead or dying, when Fortinbras "with conquest comes from Poland." Liberty, coming from many, gives to the Ambassadors from England (science) "a warlike volley." How splendid is all this! And how thoroughly plain is the whole tragedy!

We now would go back to the text, and illustrate all those points hitherto left in obscurity. The madness of Hamlet is thoroughly identified with our conception of its nature in the following extract:

---

[1] That such is the prospect of party politics is only too plain at the present day. And the philosophic student of history will find that this is the destiny of all constitutional history.

"*King*. Come, Hamlet, come, and take this hand from me.
　　　　　[*The King puts Laertes' hand into Hamlet's.*
　Ham. Give me your pardon, sir : I've done you wrong :
But pardon't, as you are a gentleman.
This presence knows,
And you must needs have heard, how I am punish'd
With sore distraction. What I have done,
That might your nature, honour and exception
Roughly awake, I here proclaim was madness.
Was't Hamlet wrong'd Laertes ? Never Hamlet :
If Hamlet from himself be ta'en away,
And when he's not himself does wrong Laertes,
Then Hamlet does it not, Hamlet denies it.
Who does it, then ? *His madness : if't be so,*
Hamlet is of the faction that is wrong'd ;
His madness is poor Hamlet's enemy.
Sir, in this audience,
Let my disclaiming from a purposed evil
Free me so far in your most generous thoughts,
That I have shot mine arrow o'er the house,
And hurt my brother."

The whole of the above is Hamlet's justification of himself
and his deeds. The key-note lies in the utterance—

"Hamlet is of the faction that is wrong'd ;
His madness is poor Hamlet's enemy."

Here we have the essence of Hamlet. He is "of the
faction that is wrong'd." *And his madness lies in trying
to redress these wrongs.* In redressing these wrongs he
"shoots his arrow o'er the house, and hurts his brother"
Laertes. This falls in with our conception of Hamlet's
madness. His madness is his badness and his incoherence
in the eyes of his enemies. Dramatically Hamlet's madness
is a perfect expression of the stoical idea we have already
dwelt upon. Every reform, every progress, until it falls in
with the age, is first the scheme of a madman, next of a
theorist, and finally it is accepted, so that men wonder
they could ever have done without it. So with Hamlet :
" Mad for Ophelia's·love," is in reality " Bad for Ophelia's
life." And the end proves it so indeed. All those of
the opposite faction to Hamlet call him mad. This is
why "his madness is poor Hamlet's enemy." Literally the

great enemies of Hamlet are those who term him mad.
And his enemies and his madness are identified. The madness is in reality upon their side. They are in the position
of the lunatic who ascribed his own lunacy to the blindness
or madness of the world. There is not a shadow of doubt
that this is our Poet's exact meaning. He has made the spirit
of progress, in truth and justice-seeking, mad in the eyes
of those who cannot see aught but their own view of things.
Everything outside these views is madness. Hamlet goes so
far as to assert he cannot have wronged Laertes. If truth,
or Hamlet, be taken from himself, then untruth wrongs
Laertes, it is not Hamlet. Thus Hamlet, in the above
quotation, justifies his own deeds and character. First he
shows how impossible it is for truth to wrong anybody.
And if truth does wrong anybody, it must be simply his
enemies. And in this they are not wronged, but righted.
For as Hamlet wrongs his enemies, he rights himself, and he
rights his enemies. The madness of Hamlet is the madness
of Laertes. And Hamlet shows that this madness of
Laertes is his (Hamlet's) enemy. All the ambiguity which
arises from any other conception of madness utterly vanishes
with our explanation. The difficulty lay in reconciling
what appeared at times as madness and what seemed at
others profound method and sanity in Hamlet. The sane-
ness of Hamlet lay, in the eyes of critics, in our hero's
philosophy, and in his repudiation of madness ; as also in
his sanity of action. But his wild and incoherent words
to Ophelia, to Polonius, gave a direct contradiction to the
above. All this vanishes when we see this apparent incoherence is but profound meaning, hidden under artistic
unity. Shakespeare had ever a double plot to wed in
harmony—artistic and spiritual unity. How he has realized the harmonious working of this dual unity the reader
will see for himself. First, an artistic development, which
must in reality be the servant of the spiritual soul and
idea. Second, the spiritual development, to hide under an
artistic envelope. It is the peeping out of the former,
through the often thin dress of the latter, which has given

rise to every ambiguity and perplexity in the various criticisms upon this tragedy.

The union of the exoteric and esoteric sides are so perfect, that neither is developed at the expense of the other. "In Nathaniel Hawthorne's Transformation," Lord Lytton says, "we have the classical sensuous life typical through Donato; the Jewish dispensation by Miriam; and the Christian dispensation shadowed forth by Hilda. Those who do not follow the mysticism, of which the above are the exponents, can never understand the story; the conception is most grand; although the way it is carried out is imperfect."

We have quoted the above from the late Lord Lytton's Essays (Caxtoniana), to show what that great writer thought of the principles of art which underlie all works of the imagination.

We here again quote Lord Lytton on the duality of art: "The writer who takes this duality of purpose, who unites an interior symbolical signification with an obvious popular interest in character and incident, errs, firstly in execution, if he render his symbolical meaning so distinct and detailed as to become obviously allegorical; unless, indeed, as in the Pilgrim's Progress, it is avowedly an allegory. And accordingly he errs in artistic execution of his plan, whenever he admits a dialogue not closely bearing on one or the other of his two purposes, *and whenever he fails in merging the two into an absolute unity at the end.*"

Here we have a complete definement of the rules of what we might call double plot. Goethe has pointed out Shakespeare as the great master of them. It is the impossibility of recognizing and harmonizing one side without the other,—the artistic without the symbolical,—which has been the stumbling-block to critics. Both Shakespeare and Goethe have so marvellously brought their symbolical meanings under the dominion of art, that there is little or no conception of the very existence of the former in the minds of ordinary people. Imagine Goethe or Shakespeare writing plays, like a Sheridan or a Vanburgh, for mere histrionic effect, or to satirize an age! Their works of art are but the vehicles and the preservative wrappers of their thoughts, opinions, and prophecies. There is a rich mine for futurity in all Shakespeare's works, down to his very sonnets. It is Shakespeare alone who has so developed and perfected this great art of arts that three centuries have hidden his meaning, until the age recognizes in Hamlet its own knowledge. Thus we grow up to genius, and not until we have reached, by the aid of time, the level of genius, do we understand it. Dr. Maudesley remarks in his Essay upon Hamlet: "The right aim of a critic, who is conscious of the exalted scope of art, is to show how he has developed nature; to unfold the *idea* which inspires and pervades the wondrous drama."

This is exactly what we have endeavoured, though lamely, to effect in this short sketch. We quote from Professor Morley's History of English Literature the following as to Shakespeare's spiritual unities: "Every play of Shakespeare's has its own theme in some essential truth of life, which is its soul expressed in action, and with which every detail is in exquisite accord."

This is what a large body of Englishmen tacitly deny. They have devoted themselves to the language, and surface of the text, and have ignored, or refused to acknowledge, the very existence of quite another side of Shakespeare's works. In doing this the Poet is robbed of his true soul, and the principles of all true art are forgotten.

Coleridge, Malone, Johnson, and a host of English critics, have done nothing for Shakespeare's thought and soul. Their criticisms are with art, and art alone. The French mind seems farther off than even ours from a true conception of the meaning of Shakespeare. We must make one exception in favour of Victor Hugo, who, in addition to translating the works of our Poet, has written an admirable work upon him. Hamlet, he says, "c'est l'univers." But we have no direct light beyond this. The latest French critic is M. Taine, who, in his History of English Literature, of course discusses Shakespeare, and Hamlet in particular.

M. Taine recalls the dictum of Voltaire upon that play. The latter, who understood perfectly the uses of dramatic art, has immortalized himself in the following, which is not unlike M. Taine's criticism: "Hamlet is mad in the second act, and his mistress is so in the third. The Prince kills the father of his mistress, feigning to kill a rat. The heroine throws herself into the river. They bury her on the stage; the grave-diggers utter quodlibets worthy of them, holding skulls in their hands. Prince Hamlet replies to their disgusting follies with coarseness not less disgusting. During this time one of the actors makes the conquest of Poland. Hamlet, his mother, and his stepfather, drink together on the stage, they sing at tables, they quarrel, they strike, and kill!"[1]

M. Taine, in a similar manner, tells us "Hamlet talks in a style of frenzy." That the play is the produce of a "night's delirium." Skilled in generalizations, with the literature of Europe at his fingers' ends, M. Taine writes to the countrymen of Shakespeare in this manner. Does M. Taine understand his own *métier* of writing histories of thought, since he cannot comprehend the greatest master of that art? We must nevertheless acknowledge the candour of M. Taine. There are thousands who refuse to see a difficulty in criticizing Hamlet. They show incapacity in harmonizing the artistic development of the play, and refuse to own it is a problem. They thus shut their eyes to their own ignorance, and succeed in perpetuating this delusion.

To turn to the German mind, we find ourselves immediately in presence of our true masters, in respect to Shakesperian criticism. Goethe has been the true discoverer of Shakespeare's secret. In his novel, the Wilhelm Meister's Apprenticeship, we have an exegesis of Hamlet. The true value of that work is its interpretation of Hamlet. Hamlet

---

[1] The curious part of Voltaire's blindness to Shakespeare's meaning lies in the fact that he wrote his own plays upon similar principles. See Brutus, Mahomet, Alzire, etc., etc.

is incorporated with Wilhelm, Serlo with Polonius, Aurelia
with Ophelia, and Laertes remains Laertes.   The play is
used in the development of the novel.   That novel is a
prose Hamlet.   It would be easy to rationalize it thoroughly.
Philina is Philosophy, Mignon Poetry, etc., etc.   It is a
history of man, in which Hamlet is blended.   Thus an
interpretation of Hamlet is given in a detailed and lengthy
manner.   It is not our province or desire to solve the
Wilhelm Meister here.   We ourselves were only led to
its comprehension by a first and earlier conception of
Hamlet.   It has never thrown any distinct, or aught but
false light, upon the reading of Hamlet.   No one has solved
the latter by means of Goethe's novel.   To prove this, we
take a countryman of Goethe's, who is the latest and the
profoundest critic upon our Poet.   Dr. Gervinus, in his
Commentaries, adds nothing new to the criticism of Hamlet.
Let us see first what Professor Gervinus, speaking for
Germany, says of the latter: "It is a text from nature
of truest life, and therefore a mine of the profoundest
wisdom; a play which, next to Henry the Fourth,
contains the most express information of Shakespeare's
character and nature, a work of such a prophetic design,
of such anticipation of the growth of mind, that after
nearly three centuries it is first perceived and appreciated;
a poem, which has so influenced and entwined itself with our
later Germanic life, as no other poem even of our own age
and nation could boast, with the exception of 'Faust' alone."
This is a refreshing contrast to the extravaganza of M.
Taine, and a direct proof how Shakespeare is cultivated
and reverenced throughout Germany.   But with regard to
Hamlet, the Professor says: "Since this riddle has been
solved by Goethe in his Wilhelm Meister, it is scarcely
to be conceived that it ever was one, and one is hardly
disposed to say anything more towards its elucidation."[1]

---

[1] This shows how utterly unconscious Professor Gervinus is of the character
and nature of Hamlet.   The riddle of Hamlet will probably remain one of the
remotest and most difficult of sciences, since it embraces all other sciences.

Is this the way the Philosophy of History, by the greatest genius the world has ever seen, and written three centuries ago, is to be treated? Nevertheless, Professor Gervinus proceeds to discuss the play, suggesting much, and hinting much ; but still clearly no nearer the real solution of either Goethe or Shakespeare than he likes to confess. Thus we are driven from the Continent home again in a discontented frame of mind. We must help ourselves. And it is only right Englishmen should be first in this work. Dr. Maudesley, in his recently published Essay on Hamlet, truly says : "No one who sets himself anew to the earnest study of the drama is content with what others have done, but believes he can add something important from his own reflections." All that Dr. Maudesley tells us, however, is that "Hamlet is a poetical creation, and never was a living reality." His essay is deeply interesting, and full of valuable reflections on the play. He says truly, "Hamlet is so acted upon, that events rather prick him on than his own feelings." This is a profound recognition. For everywhere in Hamlet we recognize this "pricking on." No one realized better than Shakespeare how certain events, such as liberty, knowledge, and progress, go hand in hand. So much so that each monologue of Hamlet is hand in hand with either Fortinbras, the Players, or some movement which is indispensable to any further resolution, or action, on the part of Hamlet.

All that hitherto has been said in connexion with Goethe and Shakespeare is the criticism of Jeffrey in the *Edinburgh* upon Wilhelm Meister. That criticism was to the effect that the novel "is a most exhaustive criticism of Hamlet." It is the recognition of a certain subtle relationship, but a kind not easily rationalized.

The last notice we have upon Hamlet is Mr. Tyler's "Philosophy of Hamlet." Mr. Tyler is one who has suddenly been bitten with a Hamlet mania. He has been suddenly illuminated with a revelation. But though partial, it is a true one. And Mr. Tyler, believing that he of all mortals is the first to make this discovery, takes good care to let the public know of it. We are however little better off than before. There is nothing new in his demonstrating the relation of Ophelia to Hamlet. No one could help seeing who Aurelia was in Goethe's Wilhelm Meister, and one could hardly help seeing that she is only Ophelia in another guise. But is this sufficient to justify a claim to a great discovery? If so, we must also make that claim. But we thought any suggestions not in harmony with the whole play, action, text, etc., to be absurd in the face of Goethe's novel. And we have waited until, word for word and line for line, we have had the play partially revealed to us.[1]

---

[1] Nothing but a work of a lifetime could do justice to Hamlet, and it is probable that each century will see more exhaustive interpretations of the play.

CHAPTER VII.

THE first thing to be done in criticizing a work of art is to separate the main lines upon which it is built from the secondary and correlated parts. In doing this with Hamlet, we find the whole play to rest upon one first cause. That is, the unjust usurpation of a throne from its just heir by crime. The action will be then, first, the detection of this crime; secondly, the attempts to revenge, and turn the unjust occupant off his throne. Upon this discovery and action the whole play will revolve. All the rest of the *dramatis personæ* are but accessories to the discovery, to the revenge, and to the opposition to that revenge. First, we have a King in possession. This possession has been effected by crime. The rightful heir first discovers and then avenges the crime. The details of this discovery, and the struggle to avenge, and resist this revenge, is the action, the detail, the whole story of the tragedy of Hamlet.

The King is human error.[1] He is a mere symbol for every injustice as regards man. He is in possession. Prince Hamlet is the spirit of truth-seeking in man. He is the rightful King by every right. But though a prince

---

[1] Historically and philosophically alone. And he is the sum total of his partisans. He dies as they separately are destroyed.

and the rightful heir, he never succeeds to the throne. The King is married to the Queen. The Queen is human belief. She is wedded to error. But truth must be also belief. Therefore the prince is made her son. He laments her bad marriage. But it is some time before he detects crime to have been perpetrated, and that he has been not only robbed of a father, but tricked out of the throne. As long as he knew nothing of the crime of the King, he sees in the King's marriage to his mother a just claim to the throne. But when he discovers the crime of the King, he sees his mother must be spoken with, reproached, and induced to relinquish the King. To avenge the crime of the King is then his only thought. To oust him from the throne—to kill him by so doing—is the action of the play.

Now let us take this theory of ours as exemplified in history, and try and wed it to the structure of these main lines.

There was a time when man knew not that error was in dominion over him. Such times were the Dark Ages. The discovery of error is to recognize its unlawful dominion. To recognize that unlawful dominion is to wish to repair it, by getting rid of it. First, the discovery must be made. Then the efforts to carry it into effect. The last will be a work of time. It will be done only by successive stages. To render that discovery possible, we must have the means of discovery. To carry that discovery into action, we must have further means. And over time will be spread the battle, which must be represented by growth of power, implying loss of power on the other side.[1]

But this is the plan of the play. Characters inform Hamlet of his father's Ghost. The Ghost informs Hamlet of the King's crime. Hamlet then charges the King with the crime. And then we have, with the successive fall of the King's Lord Chamberlain and Courtiers, a successive

---

[1] Thus Hamlet is born, grows to manhood, and accomplishes his mission and destiny.

weakening of the King. Whilst with the means of Hamlet, as contained in the characters who lead to discovery, we have also the Players, the march of Fortinbras, and the address to the Queen. The whole history of progress and reform is one of time. So is the play of Hamlet. The history of man's progress (as exemplified in Europe) is one in which error is constantly weakened—injustice and error of course are the same. The spirit of truth gains at the expense of error. But time is required, and the spirit of truth is always lacking power to crush out every wrong at a blow. It only gains strength very slowly indeed. Thus Hamlet's want of power, or irresolution, is explained.[1] Time alone can give it to him. In the death of Polonius we read the first destruction of one of the King's bulwarks. What should that bulwark be? Certainty, we reply. For error only exists in proportion to its being believed in with certainty by men's minds. When this Certainty is dead, belief can be shaken. So we have Hamlet's address to his mother, and his direct charge to her for the first time after the death of Polonius.

The discovery of error is only effected by the unity and co-existence of three things. The spirit of liberty, knowledge, and doubt. But we have all this in the play. We have Bernardo relieving Francisco, as implying knowledge relieving ignorance by the art of reading. Next, Marcellus and Horatio, who are probably produced by the above two. Scholarship and inquiry result from printing and the diffusion of reading. Then the Ghost, or doubt, comes in the train of the above. Knowledge brings criticism, and criticism brings scepticism. And contemporary with these we have the rise of Fortinbras, who represents the spirit of liberty. Thus knowledge, liberty, and progress, enter the play almost hand in hand. All these will form the spirit of justice and truth-seeking, who is realized presently in Hamlet. They then *"go in together"* to set

---

[1] We cannot too much insist that Hamlet is acting all through the play, as he kills the King through his adherents.

the times, "*which are out of joint, right.*" That is to
attack error, the King, wedded to human belief. But how
are they to effect this? They must first prove the King is
guilty of crime. They must show he is error. And this
they effect by showing the King how he became the
occupant of the throne. They point out his crime, which
is a revelation from scepticism. *Error is only recognized
by showing how it is error.* And the King is only King
in virtue of error. Therefore the Player-scene embraces the
Reformation, and the first revolt of Hamlet or man.[1] Upon
this revolt and its proof the play must hinge. From this
time the King must continuously lose power. This he does
first by the death of certainty shaken by the Player-scene.
And mark how this is effected by the Player-scene. The
Queen only wishes to speak to Hamlet *in consequence of
that Player-scene.* And this leads to the death of Polonius.
Thus the Player-scene is artistically shown to be the cause
of the death of Polonius. The first blow at the King is
the death of certainty. From this time he continues losing
power, and Hamlet in gaining it. After the death of
Polonius, Hamlet can address his mother. Belief is shaken,
is divided, and, from this time, she gets less and less faithful
to the King, until she dies, which is merely the death of
belief in error, and error in belief.

Who are the next enemies to truth and justice-seekers?
Clearly those who are benefited by error, or by the King.
They will not care about Hamlet, since he seeks to rob them
of their possessions in destroying abuses.[2] They will be indifferent to reform. They must live in the lap of fortune.
They will therefore oppose Hamlet by every means in their
power. They must be pictured all this, and they are so
pictured. The weapons they use must be hypocrisy, cunning,
sophistry, indifference, and casuistry. The text will show
that the characters of Rosencrantz and Guildenstern are all

---

[1] It is impossible to separate truth from progress, or the latter from history.

[2] Those who understand history will see that Rosencrantz, by means of
Guildenstern, represents the chief opposition of authority.

this, and more. They will only be got rid of by time and by a system of thought, which will crush them out. England does this. And England is perhaps science. Science is truth, which admits of no equivocation and no sophistry. The action and growth of liberty, knowledge, and truth-seeking, must be expressed. It is so expressed in the march of Fortinbras, the speech of the Players, and by every soliloquy or self-reproach of Hamlet. The continuity and gradual death and lessening of certainty must find utterance. It does so in the faint continuation of Polonius by Laertes, who finally represents conservative literature. The growth of Hamlet must be also expressed. It is done by touches of the text. Such is the letter of Hamlet stating his naked-ness. The death of the King must be contemporary with the death of the Queen and the death of his last adherent. And the end of the conflict must be also pictured. All this is done by the deaths of King, Queen, Laertes, and Hamlet, almost simultaneously. Why must this be so? Because error lives by belief in error. And error lives by its representatives in the play. When injustice is dead, the work of Hamlet is done. The crime is avenged. Therefore when the Queen dies, error dies, and *vice versa*. When Laertes dies, the King or the error must die. And, as Hamlet's work of warring for truth is finished, he must die also.[1] And how is error found out? By turning it in upon itself. Therefore the same weapon must kill Hamlet, the King, and Laertes. And this is the case. The Queen dies by the same potion as the King also. Next, by what should the spirit of truth-seeking be best accompanied? By a spirit of liberty. And this is marching with Fortinbras all through the play. The next best friend to truth-seeking is the spirit of justice and in-dependence. And by knowledge, Horatio represents all three.

---

[1] If we go deeply into the subject, we find our Poet is obliged to kill Hamlet. Since truth is not an entity, but a movement, and the tragedy is concerned with conflict alone, with the end of the latter, the personality of Hamlet disappears, as he represents conflict alone.

And Horatio comprises Marcellus, Bernardo, and the Ghost. Thus Hamlet is only an expression of liberty, knowledge, justice, and truth-seeking. He is all in one. He is the symbol of progress. And the King is the symbol of error contained by his adherents. He is backed up first by cruelty, force, and despotism. Voltimand, Cornelius, and Norway express all these. When they die, he has Polonius, — certainty. Next Rosencrantz and Guildenstern. Then Laertes and Osric, who are inheritors of Polonius and his direct heirs. They are orthodoxy, literature based upon certainty, and society.

The Church must find expression. It does so in being pictured the daughter of Certainty. And as there is a period in history when she is autocratic, the first attack of Hamlet upon Certainty must be through her. Therefore she is criticized by Hamlet. She is supposed to be sequestrated from Hamlet. This is the recognition of their mutual antagonism. As liberty and all free thought is considered dangerous to the Church (who is one with Polonius and the King), the representation of this must be given. And we find it in Hamlet's supposed madness. Next, as difference of opinion arises between autocratic Certainty, through Intolerance, and the growing Hamlet, the text furnishes in Hamlet's letter to Ophelia the grounds of his madness. His madness is his badness in the eyes of his enemies. The growth of learning and criticism must be expressed. The arrival of the Players supplies it. And then we have the Reformation. The means Polonius takes to keep Laertes orthodox is found in Reynaldo. The Players are also to be prompted by Truth. How is this to be expressed? In the instructions given to them by Hamlet. How is general reform and progress to be represented? By an introduction of Time and Progress, in a scene effecting their ends. In this scene the progress of the age is represented by criticism of every sort and the recognition of social law. How is the decadence of the Church to be represented? By real madness or incoherence, by change in drowning, and by final burial.

And this is shown to be the result of the death of Certainty. What is the advice of Laertes to his sister ? The support of the Church by orthodox literature. How is the persecution of the spirit of reform to be artistically rendered ? By touches of the text. How is the growing criticism of authority and error to be portrayed ? By satire, irony, and mockery, under cover of madness. How is the continuity of the dead characters[1] to be portrayed ? By sometimes artistic reference to the body, and gradual burial, as in the case of Polonius and Ophelia. How is the weakness of progress to be expressed in the play ? By the irresolution of the spirit of progress, viz. Truth.

To do justice to Hamlet would be to take the tragedy line for line and word for word. Then to exhaust the historical parallelism of the History of Europe since the end of the Dark Ages. And finally to discuss the Philosophy of History therein contained. But before a work of this sort is attempted let us have a flood of criticism. For this is the ordeal of every truth, and the better the truth the worse for criticism. There are many points we have refrained from touching upon in the play. Such is the praying of the King, and Hamlet's thoughts of killing him. We think this is meant to illustrate the *weakness* of the King. A weakness springing from Hamlet's corresponding strength. We must never forget the great difficulties which art must encounter in expressing truth. Much *must* be taken as understood. Thus we see that the arrival of the Players is the arrival of Hamlet to a state of manhood. He has grown, and he has expanded into " Learning," which soon shows itself in the action of the Player-scene. Shakespeare has made actors artistically the type of true actions in the world. And the contrast between the *acted* upon and those who act is very striking.

The end of the tragedy is in perfect accordance with our efforts at interpretation. Fortinbras, though not seen, has

---

[1] And by the continuation of Polonius through Laertes.

been marching silently all through the play.¹ The death of
Hamlet is his signal to appear in *complete* conquest from
Poland.² Liberty, which we found expressed in abortive
revolt at the earliest part of the tragedy, has shown itself
once with forces marching in the middle of the play. It
then gave Hamlet a tremendous impulse. For he used his
reason with England ; and thus liberty and science, with
justice, have possession of the field. Every word of the
text is in harmony with the above.

How perfectly the death of Rosencrantz and Guilden-
stern is in harmony with our hypothesis as regards
England ! And we do not hear of their deaths until
Hamlet is dead !

> " *First Amb.*   The sight is dismal ;
> And our affairs from England come too late :
> The ears are senseless that should give us hearing,
> To tell him his commandment is fulfill'd,
> That Rosencrantz and Guildenstern are dead :
> Where should we have our thanks ?
>   *Hor.*   Not from his mouth,
> Had it the ability of life to thank you :
> *He never gave commandment for their death.*"

In the last lines we have an apparent contradiction. Did
not Hamlet give commandment for their death? Artistically,
yes ; truly, no. They died by the letter of the King. That
letter, being signed by Hamlet, was their death, *by their own
errors.*³ Rosencrantz and Guildenstern died of their own
" baser natures," by the progress of the systematization of
truth—science. Horatio says :

> " . . . . . Give order that these bodies
> High on a stage be placed to the view ;

---

¹ Fortinbras, it is plain, is *might and right*. The conquering march of Hamlet
is thus artistically expressed. *But this is liberty.*

² The sudden introduction of Fortinbras and the Ambassadors from England
exactly as Hamlet dies proves our theory, that Hamlet is conflict alone. For it is
only with the end of conflict that perfect liberty and justice can be realized, as
also science.

³ As in the case of Laertes, both Rosencrantz and Guildenstern die when their
errors are *turned in upon them*, by the contradiction of truth when contrasted with
the false.

And let me speak to the yet unknowing world
How these things came about: *so shall you hear*
Of carnal, bloody, and unnatural acts,
Of accidental judgments, casual slaughters,
Of deaths put on by cunning and forced cause,
And, in this upshot, purposes mistook
Fall'n on the inventors' heads : all this can I
Truly deliver."

The above is the history of history. One of conflict, of slaughter, and of accidental judgments, all at last to fall upon the inventors' heads. This is the history of man, identical with Pisistratus Caxton's intended history of "*human error.*" Hamlet is the history of human error—past, present, and to come. Horatio will deliver—"all this (can I) truly deliver." For Horatio is to Hamlet what Laertes was to the King—literature. And all through the last scenes Hamlet is warring through Horatio. We have a condensed history of history in the play of Hamlet. The name of Hamlet is not unsuggestive of MANLET, "A Little History of Man." It is the history of progress. And it is a sublime prophecy. The last words of the play should be written on the heart of every true lover of progress, " Go, bid the soldiers shoot."

The play is continuous, blended, and gradual. No abrupt halts. Insensible deaths and insensible progress. All dovetailed, all connected, until the whole conflict is over, and harmony and equilibrium are established in identity of interests and purpose. Thus man's apprenticeship ends, leaving complete liberty, complete justice and science to continue his travels. This is the tragedy of Hamlet. An eminently optimistic view of life, and without doubt the real one, which will arrive at some future day.

This is only a sketch—the briefest sketch—over a subject actually limitless and boundless. Every line, every word, could be taken as the text of a sermon, article, or essay upon humanity. It is, as a whole, the Philosophy of History in Europe. It is a solution of that Philosophy of History. Because, if true up to the present day, and that after three centuries of prophecy, everything pointing as it does to fulfilment of the rest, makes us inclined to believe Shakespeare before all men.

The subject of Hamlet is positively a limitless one. We leave the reader to read a volume between the lines of the text. He will find every word a revelation, every touch the work of a painter who has used up nature, and even the play upon words, to illustrate his deep meaning. Hamlet is the work of a great historian. It is the result of a great philosophy. And it is the prophecy of a more than inspired teacher. Artist, historian, philosopher, dramatist, prophet, are all contained in Hamlet. A god could have done no better than our Poet has in this marvellous work. For a god could but have been understood within the limits of human comprehension. Hamlet has a threefold unity. The unity of art, the unity of rationalism, and the unity of history.

To add to all this, the whole three are united in perfect harmony. Take the touches of the Churchyard-scene, and its succession. First, discussion as to progress, and its recognition. Then the surmisal of law, next the criticism of progress, and that of history. Finally, if Mr. Buckle is not far wrong, the reduction of all life to an eternal conservation and reappearance. Hamlet is indeed a little history of man. It is the microcosm of the macrocosm. No wonder Hamlet was a play our Poet constantly retouched and altered.[1] His conception of this tragedy must have gone through many slow processes and evolutions of thought. The length of Hamlet's address to his mother is in keeping with the importance of the Reformation. But we see how difficult, nay impossible, to realize the schism in the action of the play. For the Queen can only in words divide her heart in twain; not in action. But finally we have her drinking to Hamlet. Shakespeare has dwelt dramatically

[1] Knight, Delius, and Staunton give good evidence that Shakespeare constantly altered Hamlet. There is an earlier edition extant, in which the names of the characters are different. For example, Polonius in this first (quarto, 1603) edition is entitled Corambis.

alone upon the epochs and crises of history. The Player-scene, the revelation of the Ghost, the death of Polonius, all these are points upon which history and the play itself hinge. Every minor event, every gradual decay or growth, is in the text, or summed up in an appearance or return. Such is the grand chorus of Fortinbras, running like a thread all through the play. Another is the spread of education, by the revolution of Laertes. A third, by Hamlet's banishment to England. And over all this the insanity of Ophelia, in contrast to the one-sided mania of Hamlet, hangs like an unutterable pall, to heighten the contrast and the effect.

But before all this comes the exquisite beauty of the Churchyard-scene. The decay of what is dearer to men even than their lives (which they count as nought in its defence), is represented by the aptest of images, a church-yard. Death is indeed at its busiest when progress and beliefs are at stake. How many lives have been sacrificed over questions of policy and belief! And here we have the sharp contrast of mockery, ridicule, and laughter, with the dread end. Everything gives way before those arch-clowns Time and Progress. What genius, to represent Progress uprooting institutions as skulls! And how great the art, that could represent man interrogating Progress, and criticizing himself, by Hamlet's conversations with him-self.

Hamlet must be recognized as *the* History of Man. No-body recognized more distinctly than our Poet that Reason is the son of Time. We are told so in more than one play. Shakespeare was the most complete evolutionist that we can realize. He was a firm believer in science. And he was a Utopian believer in the future of man—an optimistic future—after the end of the tempests of Man's Appren-ticeship.

The words of one Leonard Digges promise to be fulfilled to the letter, aye, to such a degree as to make men believe that they have indeed shaken hands with Shakespeare, but have not known him until three centuries have passed over his head.   Those words are (speaking of his works): " *They would keep him young for all time, and the day would come when everything modern would be despised, everything that was not Shakespeare's would· be esteemed an abortion ; then every verse in his works would rise anew, and the Poet be redeemed from the grave.*"

CHAPTER VIII.

WE may now endeavour to realize the whole unity of Hamlet. That unity is the unity and prospects of history, when the latter becomes worthy of its name. For mere despotism and stagnancy is not properly history. Chronicles may hand down records of the deeds of kings and of nations, but progress[1] only exists with the first inspiration of the breath of freedom. Shakespeare has therefore very properly left out all irrelevant matter. The Dark Ages are the proper starting-point of modern history. As they broke up, so the history of Europe began to evince a growth and development, which is in striking contrast with the credulity, superstition, and ignorance of anterior centuries. The first thing to be represented dramatically was the breaking up of darkness and ignorance. Doubt illuminates itself by the light of the revival of learning. Increased liberty gives and takes fresh power from this movement, whilst out of it springs a force which is well represented by Hamlet. The latter, we maintain, like the King, is an attribute, not a personification. Hamlet represents the genius of truth and justice-*seeking*. He is the human symbol, which wars for righteousness on earth. He is well indicated when we use the word *Truth* in connexion with him.

---

[1] We mean progress in the sense of modern history. Evolution is progress, of course, and is identical with universal history; but we believe that in this cosmical sense Shakespeare has given us the " descent of man " in " The Tempest."

As the birth of Hamlet is contemporary with that of liberty, Shakespeare has opened his play with the feeble and abortive attempts of Fortinbras. At the same time Doubt and Certainty succeed each other at intervals, until Certainty is expressed by the revelation of the Ghost.[1] Hamlet recognizes evil, and sees that he is born merely to set things right. This is his sole mission, and, prompted by justice and reason, he makes up his mind to expose error, wrong-doing, or evil.

Side by side with Hamlet, we are presented with his enemies. These are expressed successively by despotism, tyranny, authority, bigotry, self-interest, and gradually modified into literary controversy. The principle of each side is never lost to view. And this principle is explained artistically by making the son of Polonius revenge his father. Guildenstern and Rosencrantz fill up the interval by personifying self-interest in power and the languid indifference of the world generally. Hamlet is pictured as first attacking and repudiating the Roman Catholic Church pictured in Ophelia. The result is the Reformation, which we must understand completed when he persuades his mother to cleave her heart in twain, and throw away the worser half of it.

With this act authority and the spirit of certainty is overthrown. Therefore it is contemporary with the death of Polonius. Soon after, we have the appearance of Fortinbras, which expresses the immense stride liberty has gained through the Reformation. The death of Certainty being gradual, we have Ophelia continuing this decay in phases of dissent and scepticism. She finally is buried. All this time Hamlet artistically seems to lack power to kill the King. But we maintain the King is only a fiction, or symbol of abstract error, necessary for the drama alone. Therefore the King is in reality dying all through the

---

[1] We have not sufficiently explained Hamlet's father. Our belief is that Christ or pure Christianity is typified through him. Thus the Ghost is a revival of purity leading to the Reformation.

play, as each of his supports and members of his court are killed by Hamlet. Irony, satire, and open ridicule also grow successively out of each other as Hamlet gains strength.

The banishment of our hero well expresses the apparent reaction of history. During this time forces are working silently, and they do not break out again until Laertes, or education, completes the revolution of authority from the hands of the State into the hands of the people. The return of Laertes is the complete revolution of politics. In it the State exists for the people, not the latter for the former.

But Laertes is still true to his principles. He expresses in the place of sovereign, or State power, the principles of a party. This party is of course the social and the stable one. This state of things is most favourable to the growth of Hamlet. Gradually, through reform, Hamlet escapes from the trammels of Rosencrantz and Guildenstern. He returns thoroughly accepted by the opposite, or liberal party of individualism. This is beautifully expressed in the word *naked*. The relations of Laertes and the King are still more beautifully insisted upon. And the questions at issue become fought in a literary arena. Those questions are ones beyond our age. They are social ones, which probably affect the interests of privileged classes alone.

In the meanwhile Shakespeare has given us a beautiful picture in the Churchyard-scene of progress generally, in thought and in historical criticism. Our conception of that scene is our particular claim to discovery. Much of what we have already pointed out may be easily believed to have been borrowed from Goethe. But this scene, which, un-rationalized, gives no force to our interpretation, is in our belief the very keystone of proof. Our conception of the first scene of the fifth act is that Shakespeare has here revealed the criticism of Hamlet by himself. The Clown whom we have termed Progress, or Change, is only Hamlet himself tracing his own genesis. Any fool can tell the day Progress was born, for Hamlet was born that day. Hamlet and the Clown are identical. In the progress of truth we recognize, not a particular and separate birth, but a progress synonymous with general progress. To trace the genesis of progress is to trace that of truth, and *vice versa*. Truth is an attribute, not a concrete something. It is a relation, not a thing. Shakespeare has thus magnificently realized, artistically and symbolically, the historical criticism of man by man. The answers of the First Clown are the direct results of historical criticism and retrospect grown scientific. In these days, when every science tends to grow historical and history scientific, we can perfectly comprehend our Poet's meaning. It is just at this point of the play that we should halt, and suggest the parallelism of our own times and progress in general. The very same Progress which was born with Hamlet, and which arose with liberty in Fortinbras, is artistically represented in the Churchyard-scene, as criticizing and uprooting institutions. In short, Hamlet is grave-digging in reality. The Clown is only an artistic double to Hamlet. Hamlet has begun to evolve the science of history. Law, at first ambiguous, appears in the simultaneous birth and growth of liberty, knowledge, and truth. But it is subtle law, which will away from the present to the past, and from the past to the present. In fact, whilst we are eliminating law, we are working under law. A procedure we do not venture to fathom. We certainly believe that the Second Clown is merely the symbol of time. For we have omitted perhaps the most important element in proof of it. It will be seen by the text that the Second Clown is termed "*gallows.*" We believe this to be artistic for all O's (OOOO).[1] This would well represent time. In Love's Labour's Lost we have a specimen of the same word, which can throw . great light here.

> "*Rosalind.* That was the way to make his godhead wax ;
> For he hath been five thousand years a boy.   ˙
> *Kath.* Ay, and a shrewd unhappy *gallows* too."

---

[1] See also " Cymbeline," Act v. Sc. 4.

Here we have five thousand years only applicable to time through the word *gallows*. If we are right, our Poet could nowhere have found a word more fitted to express in a hidden and esoteric way both symbolically and artistically *Time*.

The whole Churchyard-scene stands for progress and criticism of a searching and profound character. We are not inclined, upon second thoughts, to reject Mr. Buckle's interpretation of " Alexander." However that may be, " Yorick " is clearly history. Nothing could be more admirable than to represent Time and Progress as two clowns, who, by mockery, satire, and discussion, laugh at everything in their inexorable march together. The discussions between the two are often metaphysical, and would well signify the fierce discussion of philosophy through a length of time. We can understand how Time thus instructs Progress as to Ophelia's burial, and how Progress would evolve itself through Time. This we believe most religiously to be Shakespeare's intention, though we of course deprecate any intention on our part to give the right meaning to each line and word. The anomaly of clowns in a churchyard is thus easily rationalized. Shakespeare has distinctly realized the fierce and prolonged decay of Ophelia. Even in her very grave the fight is waged between Laertes and Hamlet. Truth is truth, and Hamlet is in the hands of higher law, of reason, and of evidence.

We have been forced by the nature of the problem in Hamlet to attempt to solve it historically and universally. Truth is not a thing ; it is an attribute. By itself it has no existence. We can find its birth and its growth alone in the history of humanity. The philosopher feels there is no real separation in life and history. Politics, rationalism, philosophy, art and religion, are all parts of one great whole, and are all related to each other in unity. When we speak of truth, it is only relatively that it can even have a meaning. And the only human signification it can have must be sought for in history. There we immediately recognize it in the presence of the great dynamical principle of progress. Within the dominion of thought it strives to show itself in action, until, accumulating force enough through time as a party, it enters into the heart of political, philosophical, and religious life, to reveal itself finally in the civilization of humanity. Truth is thus the principle which, by its appeals to justice, to liberty from the absolute or Divine in all things, manifests itself in religion, in politics, and in philosophy. Whence it comes, or whither it goes, is not for us to determine. Sufficient is it to us that this divine idea of truth is implanted within us. Satisfied it can never be, except in realizing God alone—an impossibility —which still as an ideal unrolls and evolves the godhead and essence of the divine in itself.

The whole of history is in reality the history of the progress of truth. Its life is a growth which manifests itself by political growth. The latter is the expression of how truth permeates each individual and unit of the community. Where individualism, which is self-knowledge and self-development, slumbers, we have despotism and tyranny. When it awakes, it begins to realize its manhood, first in self-government, afterwards in self-criticism. Thus we see how impossible it is to deal with a problem like Hamlet, and not treat it historically. For truth and error are only attributes of humanity, and the latter are fully expressed alone in history. Truth, justice, and liberty are the real incentives which lead Hamlet forward. But these require time to expand themselves through the growth of education and knowledge. The more knowledge spreads, the greater must be the latitude and force which truth has to express itself. Based upon the order of nature outside us, it can only find its expression and reflexion within us, by the spread of knowledge and rationalism. Science is thus the classification of the real relations and truths of nature. The growth of rationalism is the recognition of the nature of reason, and of its basis in cause and effect outside us. Knowledge and education depending upon liberty have slowly to wait upon the political development of the latter and the infiltration of themselves through the units. Liberalism is thus a growth of units of individualism, showing themselves as a force, and understanding more and more the nature of the past, present, and future of humanity. It is a pet theory of M. Thiers that, given the art of a people, we may surely infer everything else about them. And it is the truth. Art, philosophy, religion, politics, are so related and bound together, that we only lack proper data and knowledge to deduce one from the other. The science of history is based upon their interdependence. Politics, we can easily see, express the knowledge and liberty of a country. Religion, again, being a reflexion of past and present knowledge, will find its solution in philosophy, in rationalism, and in science, when complements to the absolute in thought.

Hamlet, striving to act, is a magnificent picture of the weakness of human thought, as it collectively begins to realize its force in European history. The long irresolution of man prior to the Reformation is thus expressed. And this irresolution finds its true strength in the march of Fortinbras [1] or liberty alone. Out of this political development of liberty all the rest ensues as a necessity. We cannot too much insist upon the co-partnership of liberty, knowledge, and progress. They are a triumvirate which spring naturally out of congenial conditions, and mutual interdependence. Liberty awakens individuality, and the latter the reason in each man. Again, political strife must be the first expression of this growth of liberty. The history of European civilization is the history solely of freedom, of individualism, and of truth. Truth is bound up with religion. It expresses itself in those ideals termed justice, liberty, equality, and goodness. The kingdom of Christ is an awakening and an endeavour to realize these ideas in Europe. Hearkening to this spiritual appeal through development, man has so far progressed, as is compatible with

---

[1] The reader may question our interpretation of Fortinbras as *liberty*. But, if he reflects, he will see that Fortinbras is intended to be *might and right*, and the growth or progress of Hamlet. What can this be but liberty?

the nature of force, to realize already some of these divine ideas, if even in a faint degree.

The unity of Hamlet is, as we have remarked already, to be found alone in the spiritual soul and interpreted symbolism of the play. For example, the abrupt introduction of Fortinbras has never been understood by critics who merely comment upon the artistic side of Hamlet. So great is the objection to this introduction, that it is frequently left out upon the stage. And we can quite comprehend the objections which arise solely from an apparent, not a real want of purport and unity. The sudden appearance of Fortinbras is on the merely artistic side an excrescence and an anomaly. It signifies nothing, and adds nothing to the beauty or the complication or development of the plot. But what a light it throws upon the unity and aim of the play, when we interpret and rationalize the whole in one idea and plan !

Then at once we see Fortinbras to be connected between beginning and end of the play. The underground thread is thus linked and pointed out as understood to be gaining stealthy ground all through the story. Besides, the death of Polonius being the result of the manhood of liberty, necessitates the artistic expression of this growth of liberty. And we see how it reacts once more with double strength upon Hamlet. Thus, what has hitherto been considered the great blot of the play becomes, by the light of reason, the great connecting thread and ground plan. The aim and end of the play is, that Fortinbras, as liberty, should finally conquer. Horatio, as justice, also conquers. The Ambassadors of England, representing truth in knowledge, also come in for the ultimate possession of the situation. This, we think, is Shakespeare's aim.[1] Hamlet and the King are symbols of a period of strife and conflict alone. Their death represents the end of the struggle and the solution of the problem. The dramatic situation is left in the hands of liberty, justice, and science. This is our firm belief. A

[1] Thus Hamlet's constituents do not die.

belief which Goethe indorses in terming the first part of his own work the Apprenticeship of Wilhelm Meister. Hamlet is Shakespeare's Apprenticeship of Man.

We would say something here as regards the profound knowledge portrayed in placing Ophelia's burial after the conversation of Hamlet with the Clown. Historical criticism is the great agent in theological change of opinion and in the decadence of forms of belief. Without a retrospection, which includes the rise and origin of creeds, there is no scepticism, no unorthodoxy, and no falling off in point of belief. Shakespeare has done well to make Hamlet's knowledge of his own progress and genesis the forerunner of the ultimate burial of Ophelia. Again, Shakespeare has plainly pointed out, by Ophelia's belief in Hamlet's madness, the disfavour in which the latter is held by the former. To represent this real enmity, and yet reconcile an artistic side, was Shakespeare's great problem. He has solved it, in making Hamlet abandon Ophelia, and artistically ascribing it to ambiguous madness.

The history of modern Europe is in a great measure the history of the decline of the temporal power of religion. As liberty and knowledge have expanded their wings into the realms of political life, so we trace the gradual segregation of theology to a position of less and less authority and power. Prior to the Reformation, we find the State another name for a religious hierarchy. Cardinals are prime ministers, and the Pope a king over kings. To trace the decadence of priestcraft would be to follow step by step the history of Europe to the present day. But we may ask ourselves the cause of this, and then we shall not have far to search. The growth of rationalism is antagonistic to the reign of superstition.

It is ignorance alone which can believe that one man holds a divine commission to govern the other. Bit by bit the sacred veil of reverence and fear, which shrouds the priest, shows him to be a man often less inspired than his lay brother. Shakespeare, in making Ophelia the ground and basis of Hamlet's madness, has only actually pictured history as it was. Ophelia and Polonius are bound by blood. Not less strong was the historical tie of authority and the Church at a period prior to the Reformation, if not later. The philosopher of history must take into account the criticism of Ophelia by Hamlet. And he is also bound to recognize the relations of Ophelia to Polonius. Before Polonius can be killed, Ophelia must be repudiated. In short, an attack upon one is an attack upon the other. They do not exist separate, but incorporated, and we must never forget, therefore, that Hamlet's relations and conduct to Ophelia are intended by our poet to signify his treatment of Polonius and the King also. This is the reason why we find Ophelia playing such a large part in the play. And this is why what passes between Hamlet and herself possesses such vital interest in the eyes of King, Queen, and Polonius. By herself, and deprived of support in her father, Ophelia sinks into insignificance. She becomes incoherent, she is forsaken by Hamlet, and she not unnaturally commits suicide.

The growth of Hamlet is one of the expansion of thought. His repeated soliloquies in solitude have the effect of clearing his intellect. He sees his way more clearly. And as all intellectual development is fatal to the growth of emotion and feeling, we find him becoming indifferent to the existence of his once great love.

Polonius represents the principle of absolutism. And as dramatic exigency necessitated his death, Shakespeare has continued the slow decadence of this power through Laertes. Ophelia and Polonius are one. Church and State for a time represent authority and absolutism.

The resemblance which the action of Hamlet bears to our modern conceptions of law is startling. Over the real course of events the hero has no control. Hamlet has to take his chance in his endeavours to kill the King. His will does bring it about in a way; but, let us mark, not in a direct way. Hamlet is acted upon powerfully by circumstances. The latter are completely beyond his control, yet they are parts of the chain of destiny which bring about the *dénouement.* However, we know that Hamlet's irresolution is not forgetfulness ; it is only weakness. And this latter well expresses the impotency of the human will over events, except in an indirect and unknown way. Whilst striving for the thing at hand, we are gradually bringing about something far off and undreamt by us. Unconsciously we evolve a divine plan, or a procession of events, which we understand alone historically. The human will, as depicted in Hamlet, is entirely the slave of time and circumstances. It is only by introspection, by knowledge of its own weakness, that it gathers strength. Again, it is entirely dependent upon others : only as a whole, as social unity, has the human will any power. In short, it is the conflict of opposing wills, of collective forces, which emerge in that resultant which we call history. The individual will by itself has no power. It becomes autocratic when it identifies itself with the social will. The contradictions of progress and history are the effects of our not being able to estimate the several values of the forces engaged, either in opposition or in influencing each other. The history of Hamlet is the history of his gradual growth from a small fraction to a great community of people. Fortinbras only comes with conquest from Poland when the majority and the most powerful are identified with him. Thus the idea of liberty and the progress of truth are growths which have their foundations in the amount of education and knowledge the units of a people possess. The more independent the electors, the more independent ought to be the constituents. And thus the institutions, the beliefs, and the general state of a country, are dependent upon the action and reaction of individualism and authority. If the latter were identical with the former, we should have realized Utopia. Each man would be self-governed; the wishes of the many, the wishes of the units. But as long as such is not the case, there must be an antagonism more or less between the majority who govern and the minority who are governed. Fortunately this minority is always altering, and promising to become the majority. Things are thus kept going, and each party lives to be somewhat satisfied.

12

Hamlet exemplifies this in a striking degree. His progress is one in which authority is always getting more nearly identified with individualism. The direct antagonism of the early portion of the play is substituted later for the graceful courtesies which pass between Laertes and our hero. It is the breathing time of day with Hamlet; and he has been long set naked in the kingdom. The march of Fortinbras has given Hamlet time to think and use "that godlike capability"—reason. . One of its consequences is the death of Rosencrantz and Guildenstern at the hands of England. The law of progress is one which admits of increasing exactitude and differentiation. This can come alone from individual effort in thought. The State as authority can encourage or depress these efforts—even quench them. So we see how essential it is that a Fortinbras should march hand in hand with Hamlet. Not alone is Fortinbras necessary, but the accompaniment of a ghost as doubt, which by means of an active scepticism should constantly enlarge our conceptions, and prevent us from falling into the delusion that our relative knowledge is absolute, or that it is incapable of extension. But here society steps in, and, as Rosencrantz and Guildenstern, offers its graceful and easy optimism in the teeth of all unpleasant and naked truths. The force of social opinion, of conventional thought, cannot be over-estimated. It is here Shakespeare has underlined his genius. The next great enemy to Truth, after special authority in Polonius, is public opinion, expressed in the social fitness of things, in careless indifference, in slothful optimism, and in conventionalities.[1] These are well pictured in Rosencrantz and Guildenstern. Their office is to run with the hare and hunt with the hounds. They alone banish Hamlet. With them he is indeed not naked. And we can alone imagine the death of these two courtiers by the hand of Hamlet through England. Truth, accompanied by an army under Fortinbras, gradually realizes its deter-

---

[1] Rosencrantz cannot exist without Guildenstern. The latter is method and weapon alone.

mination to use its reason. All this time it is banished, and working, as Fortinbras works, silently and very gradually. In the fulness of time it returns, without the two courtiers, naked. How has it attained this result ? We reply, by the rigid method of England. That is, an exposition of truths, through scientific method. Would religion and science ever have been at conflict, if the latter had not offered evidence at variance and unequivocal in the face of traditional contradictions ?

Guildenstern and Rosencrantz are safe upon the vague and shifting sandbanks of ignorance. As long as proof is wanting, sophistry can flourish. Verification is a deadly enemy to mere dialectic and casuistry. Indifference cannot maintain its light and careless air in the face of relentless science. The easy way with which science was once relegated to a few, and easily pooh-poohed, is now past. Guildenstern and Rosencrantz can no longer take a happy middle course. We speak out in these days; and we are forced not to ignore things, but to take our positions upon one side or the other.

It is essentially necessary we should realize the importance of Rosencrantz and Guildenstern. Everywhere they embarrass, and they hamper Hamlet. As long as he is with them, he is actually banished, and, in short, stifled under indifference and the self-interested by means of sophistry and evasion. Hamlet is simply out of court. And we have only to examine the play to realize everywhere this interpretation of the two courtiers.[1]

Shakespeare knew that there were two powers in the world—political authority and public opinion. He knew the latter would step in and fill up the place of the former when it had declined in autocracy. We therefore see the exile of Hamlet following the death of Polonius. Public opinion banishes Hamlet where before intolerance and persecution had acted.

---

[1] This is the period also when Hamlet is pictured at sea and groping for his ends. This is historical reaction and *pause*.

Shakespeare knew there could be no progress, unless the
majority of a people were for progress. That majority
would only become in time liberal. And since he also knew
how legislation in England would become more and more
the voice of the people, he saw that no progress would be
realized whilst the enemies to progress held power. This
he represents in Hamlet's irresolution and weakness, which
is a proof of the minority of Hamlet.[1] Rosencrantz and
Guildenstern represent not alone society, but political power.
As the interested in office, they have successively represented themselves as opposers of free trade, of Parliamentary
reform, and of every piece of just and righteous legislation.
They (Rosencrantz and Guildenstern) represent the continuity of Polonius, and are themselves modified in
Laertes.

Hamlet, we repeat, seems to us to embody man, stimulated
by a divine idea. That idea is the eternal which is implanted
within us, and which permeates our being in the craving
for liberty, justice, and truth.

It remains now to trace the artistic resemblance between
our theory and Hamlet. The latter is painted as a gloomy
and profoundly philosophical young man. So far we recognize the gloom as the result of a recognition by truth-seekers
of the corruption and pessimism of certain historical periods.
Without an ideal of good, of justice, and of progress, there
can be no pessimism. Hamlet is painted wretched, and his
misery arises from his being discontented and unsatisfied
with his surroundings. In his philosophical disposition we
recognize a mind satisfied with reason alone. Thought is in
him the governing principle. Disinterestedness and fidelity
to his father is his especial characteristic. The whole of his
character is a vindication of the beauty of truth. Alone and
by himself he manages to crush Polonius, Rosencrantz,
Guildenstern, Laertes, and King. It has been strangely

---

[1] It is plain Shakespeare did seize in his mind what we term constitutional
growth. There were signs enough since Magna Charta and Henry the Third's
reign, to show a genius like our Poet what the future might bring forth.

overlooked by critics, that, though Hamlet dies, he alone, by the power of thought, manages to crush an immense conspiracy against himself. It is extraordinary to notice, how in the play he destroys not only Ophelia and her father, but all his enemies. Yet he is termed repeatedly weak and unsuccessful. Let us also remark how his friends, Horatio and Fortinbras, survive him. It is for these latter and England that Hamlet becomes, strives, and accomplishes his destiny and himself.

Hamlet's grandeur consists in his patience, in his prolonged, but still determined purpose, and in his truthful thought and philosophy. Justice is his great aim, and his great desire. He lives for it alone, strives for it, and sacrifices himself in order to accomplish it. Justice and freedom are alone realized in his death. Thus his whole life is one vast sacrifice, which attains its end only at self-cost.

To many Hamlet may appear weak. To others unfaithful in his renouncement of Ophelia. But, merely looking at the play from the artistic side, we are struck with the unworthiness of the heroine. She has no individuality whatever. She looks upon her duty to her father as before her love to her lover. She is in all things servile to the former, never the heroine worthy of a Prince like Hamlet. As for our hero's forsaking her, it is a strong proof of the meaning of the play. For it proves to us Hamlet's madness, or it proves to us Shakespeare's signification. But Hamlet's madness cannot be even decided upon a purely dramatic and artistic side. We say it is one of those shadowy contradictions which symbolic art necessitates. The rationalism of the spiritual soul of the play cannot possibly find art to convey it, which can also bear on its side perfect consistency, and be free from ambiguities. In our belief these latter heighten the charm of the conception, and, by their mysteries, add to the effect.

Finally, we may remark that the Philosophy of History contained in Hamlet is, in our eyes, exhaustive as far as dramatism is concerned. What we gather from it is as follows.

Individualism finds its true strength in thought. The
growth of the latter is the growth of progress or of
man. The Divine idea unrolls itself as the psychological
principles gain in strength and in comprehensive powers.
The growth of rationalism is the unrolling of the cosmos. It
is the reflexion in the microcosm, not of the macrocosm, but
of how the microcosm is related to itself and to others.
Misery, oppression, and stagnation, are the direct results of
ignorance. The latter of bad government or want of
liberty. In political progress alone a nation first realizes its
individuality — itself. That is the reason England bears
such an advanced position in European thought and science.
Germany, in the growth of her national life, is an example,
different in degree, but not in kind. Progress is the realization of idea, and the birth of new ideas. These ideas are
always latent; they show themselves in the manhood of
nations. They are eternal, and find satisfaction alone in
metaphysical speculation, which, defeated, turns as a resource
to positive thought and action. They are the absolute as
conceived of God, as the infinite—the unity and equation
of all things. The next lesson from Hamlet is the reign of
law, which dominates the individual, and, through the latter,
social man. That law is defined by our desires and aptitudes. They are born, or inherited, acted upon by surroundings, and developed by circumstance. The social man acts
and reacts upon the individual man. The latter is kept within
his orbit by authority, which ought to be the voice of the
many units. The individual, in his turn, influences according
to his genius the social mass, and so affects his own life. Two
problems are presented in life. First, to secure freedom
without anarchy, and without stagnation. Secondly, to secure
order and law without violating individual freedom and happiness. This can alone be realized when the two terms are
identical—when each man's happiness is identical with social
happiness. But all this is within law. That law is to be
formulated alone by means of psychological analysis and
discovery. One thing is plain. We recognize law. We
know knowledge increases our liberty, for it enlarges our

aptitudes, our choice, and our alternatives.[1] And knowledge itself is verification, by means of substituting our rude guesses to the test of the order in nature. We thus discover order in ourselves, and order outside of us. The order outside of us has made order within us. That "divinity that shapes our ends" is not a Divine intervention, but a psychological growth by means of accretion and accumulation of knowledge. Facts are piled up, whilst the organism extends in its turn the neural groupings from particulars to generals. We thus bind the separate links of life together.

Hamlet bears some resemblance to Prometheus, and again to Œdipus Rex. There is the same savage grandeur about his character as we recognize in that of Prometheus. Like the latter, he is chained to the rock of necessity; like the Greek drama, the play exhibits the same inexorable character of fate. Hamlet has a fatal mission to fulfil, and that mission is one not of his own making. It is imposed upon him by the chain of life. And there is something about the way in which he goes to his own doom, whilst obeying his father's dread command, which reminds us of the story of Jocasta and her son. His weakness puts him within the pale of our sympathies; his lofty and ideal massiveness of thought, hurried along as it is by the cruelty of fate, impresses us with awe and solemn mystery. Like Prometheus, he is in the hands of the gods; like Prometheus, he sublimely bears his doom.

The whole life of Hamlet seems to us an accomplishment of purport. This purport is laid upon him by "that divinity that shapes our ends, rough-hew them how we will." And his whole character and aspect impress us with the belief that Shakespeare has painted him as an ideal of man fulfilling an historical mission. In his passionate love of truth, in his profound philosophy, in his weakness and his unselfishness, he

---

[1] Every man is free within the range of his *character*. But the latter is imposed upon him by heredity, circumstances, etc. We can do what we *wish*, but this latter is under law. Thus we never *feel* want of freedom, because we cannot get *outside* of ourselves. Law and the *feeling* of liberty are thus combined.

seems to portray the noblest part of human nature. His life is devoted to others; of his own happiness he takes no heed. A gloomy pessimism has its groundwork in his love of the good and true, and his whole life is to revenge the noble and root out the evil. Here we have the self-sacrifice of man, who lives not for himself, but for an idea, for truth, for liberty, or for humanity. Again, his whole development is one which is gained by inward introspection and thought. The strength and feebleness of the will has its ideal aspects portrayed in Hamlet. He recognizes his own irresolution, and he gains further strength from it. He merely falters— he never gives way nor forgets his father's command entirely. And the will, as expressed in Hamlet, is entirely at the control of circumstances; thus exemplifying the necessity of law. Nevertheless, he carries within him a freedom which finally finds sufficient strength to kill the King. He thus again idealizes human liberty, controlled under higher law.

There is no character in all literature, ancient or modern, which equals, in point of the sublime, that of Hamlet. We must never forget he is human. We must not pass over the fact that he is not a god. The sublime in the drama rests almost entirely with the conflict of man and destiny. Whether it be an Atlas bowed down under the weight of a world, or Prometheus chained to a rock, the grandeur of the story remains, not with rude conquest and illimitable power, but with the heroic, with the tragic, with destiny, and suffering. In Hamlet we have a character who realizes at once the profound questionings of Titan thought, and the weakness of human will, under the dominion of law. He appears, at one and the same time, human nature in the abstract, and human nature in the individual. The finiteness of knowledge, and questionings of genius, are face to face with mystery, with destiny, and with heroic suffering.

Hamlet seems to us the ideal apotheosis of thought, and of truth. It is his thought which constitutes at once his strength and his weakness. In his contemplations he discloses a power of mental action which endows him with the attribute of force, lacking opportunity. By the side of the King and his myrmidons he yet appears a giant, who draws his strength from fidelity and truth alone. We feel he represents the ideal aspects of humanity, yearning after the absolute, in justice, in liberty, and in truth. The whole world to him is an "unweeded garden." The glory of the firmament "a congregation of pestilent vapours." Everything is oblique. And he alone lacks power to realize the glorious ideal of which he is the true representative. His whole duty and mission is to set "the times right," which are "out of joint." And we immediately recognize strength of thought struggling against strength of physical force and injustice. In his philosophy we recognize a spirit of rationalism which is content with nothing short of pure reason. He is not carried away by his feelings. He forsakes Ophelia, to fulfil his duty, which speaks to him from his own conscience. Life to him has but one aim— extirpation of the King. Of himself he cares nothing. He easily detects the interested, the false, the mean, and the sophist. Patience sits crowned upon him like a dove, yet bears he for his motto—Death or Freedom.

A FEW WORDS

UPON

OTHELLO.

OTHELLO.

WE should like here to say a few words about another of Shakespeare's plays. We mean "Othello." That play presents difficulties to criticism, which are fortunately absent in Hamlet. The diversity of the latter favours satisfactory solution. For if we can find identity, which can satisfy every diversity, in one unity and one plan, we at once feel our proof more complete. In Othello there is little to apprehend. It is a simple story of the effects of jealousy alone. But none the less are we positive that it has a symbolical idea, of which it is the mere exponent. As in the case of Hamlet, Othello is borrowed from a foreign source. Cinthio's novel is now supposed to be the basis of Othello. The recognition that Shakespeare has borrowed from novels and stories plots for his plays, strengthens our idea of the symbolical character of all his works. If he sought merely plots whereon to hang his symbolical ideas and conceptions of great subjects, we can understand the secondary light in which plagiarism of this kind stands. But if, on the other hand, his plays are self-existent, and exhaustive on their artistic and exoteric side alone, we feel that his originality must seriously suffer in the thefts. Our own belief is that he was absorbed in his great conceptions of truths, and that, in reading Cinthio's novel, or Bellefôret's tales, he immediately saved himself further trouble by adopting the plot for his own uses. It would be only in character with genius if he did so. For the latter incorporates and embellishes all it comes across.

Goethe acknowledged his indebtedness to every one with whom he conversed. Thus Shakespeare, to save himself trouble and time probably, immediately recognized the apposite character of a story, in relation to an idea or a truth. We have already touched upon the symbolic character of all works of genius. Indeed, an appeal to this truth is absurd. Every work of genius is a living example of it. Goethe's poems are all symbolic, never direct and simple. Genius is genius, because it sees the many in the one, and the one in the many. Generalization is synthesis, and the latter is another name for unity of idea. Shakespeare, who has profoundly analyzed over everything human, could only have done so in disintegrating synthesis by analysis. Those who perform the latter process must perform the former also. The one is only the inverse of the other. The subtlest thinkers are not only the keenest to mark the finite and small, but the infinite and large as well.[1] Symbolism is the highest order of thought we possess. It is the algebra, of which mere feeling is the arithmetic. In conception and the highest order of thought we do not image concrete things, but formulate them. The imagery of imagination can give a concrete artistic idealism to this symbolism. Thus the artist in literature paints his conceptions in characters who image in their actions, etc., his profound conceptions. Shakespeare has undoubtedly employed his artistic genius in this manner. And it is the nature of genius to create in art; because it is not satisfied with cold logic and bald dialetic. It must have life, because its imagery is not successive as a chain of reason, but intuitive, instantaneous, and pictorial in consequence. A tableau is formed in the mind, not a sequence of syllogistic reasoning. This is why artistic genius is before all other genius. It satisfies the feelings which play such a great part in it. Cold logic has no feelings. None the less for all this is the rationalism

---

[1] We are quite aware that a power of deep and searching analysis is often accompanied by want of comprehensive power. But this is only found in scientific thought.

of symbolism in art absent. Intuition is to genius what necessary truths are to others. A flash, not a laborious process. For genius is born with inborn harmony — an organism which reasons unconsciously—without effort. This is why poets must sing. They cannot or care not to reason ; for they *feel* what others require explained, and they often sing what they could not rationalize themselves. We therefore claim for Shakespeare, in the name of all genius, and in common with all genius, symbolism under forms of art. Victor Hugo tells us he wrote his three novels, "Notre Dame de Paris," "The Toilers of the Sea," and "The Miserables," as vehicles of three aspects of life: Religion—Nature—Society.[1] Lord Lytton's novels are examples of the same principles; which, in an essay in "Caxtoniana," he has brilliantly explained under the title of "Principles which Underlie all Works of the Imagination." Again, what is George Eliot's "Middlemarch" but a picture of this nineteenth century ? We are very much mistaken if Casaubon is not a scholastic and metaphysical "witches' circle," and Ladislaw positive thought. If in selecting the name of Casaubon, George Eliot has selected one which recalls Isaac Casaubon (who, whilst adding nothing original to thought, represents well the barrenness of erudition and mere scholarship), why has she at the same time made the Casaubon of Middlemarch a fruitless Dry-as-dust also ? Are we far mistaken in the parallel? However, symbolism is and must be the true function of genius. Art is thus wedded to rationalism, and so blended as to delicately convey truths, which, in a less esoteric disguise, might do harm, and shake the equilibrium of those who have not intellectual force enough to think for themselves independently.

From this digression we turn to Othello. Here, as in Hamlet, the first question we ask ourselves is, where is the unity and plan of the play? If we take the latter solely as it

---

[1] It seems almost childish to dwell upon this question. What is Dante's "Divina Commedia" without a key ? Have "Rasselas," "Don Quixote," "Gulliver's Travels," no symbolic meanings ?

stands, in its simple "unvarnished" garb, as one of the fatal effects of love and jealousy, we find the unity of text and action, character and consistency, strangely conflicting. For example, the great stumbling-block to all critics has been the reference to Cassio in the opening of the play. Here he is called a "*great arithmetician.*" [1] Again, he is mentioned as married—

"Almost damned in a fair wife."

We never hear of Cassio's arithmetic in the play, nor can we imagine the necessity of it at all.[2] There is no mention of Cassio's wife, though there is of Bianca, his mistress. How are we to reconcile these anomalies? Are they anomalies? Is Othello, like Hamlet, something more than a tale of love and jealousy? Even supposing the latter to be all, we find it most difficult to carry any deduction of a philosophic character away from the play. We are deeply moved; but we are puzzled also with other things. For example, we cannot see why Othello should be so soon and unaccountably supplanted by Cassio. Nor can we understand the *rôle* of Roderigo. What part does he play, and why is he introduced at all? The song of Desdemona is also very ambiguous, as is Cassio's intoxication. Now we propose to offer a solution of the whole, merely as an hypothesis. We cannot even attempt to solve the question by aid of the text. All we do is to give a mere suggestion, that may find favour among some few profound thinkers, not, we know, the many.

Cassio is termed a *Florentine.* His name is *Michael.* He is called "*a great arithmetician,*" and one of mere "*theoric*" "*prattle without practice.*" *Galileo* was a *Florentine.* His name was *Michael.* He *was a great arithmetician.* Besides,

---

[1] "*Iago.* . . . . For, ' *Certes,*' says he,
' *I have already chose my officer.*'   .
And what was he?
Forsooth, *a great arithmetician,*
One *Michael* Cassio, *a Florentine,*
A fellow almost damn'd in a fair wife."
[2] Cassio as a soldier has no necessity in the play to be "*a great arithmetician.*"

he was a contemporary of Shakespeare's, being actually born the same year. Is it not just possible our poet has pictured in Cassio [1] *science*, or *knowledge of natural laws and discoveries*, which, through Galileo and others, were revolutionizing men's thoughts during *Shakespeare's life?* By the term "*theoric*" we can understand well the light science is held in by some people. And let us remember how all we have said in our essay upon Hamlet, in respect of the sixteenth century, is connected with the conflict of religion and growing science. Shakespeare must have seen, as did many others, that the whole question of the future lay in whether the autocracy of religious intolerance would stifle the discoveries of science, or be beaten and annihilated by the latter. It was a battle which needed no great intelligence to foresee its consequences. The Reformation had struck the first blow. Men's beliefs in tradition and in the certainty of the past were being shaken to their foundations for the first time. We have endeavoured to picture this in the death of Polonius.

The conflict between religion and science is magnificently centred and typified in the life and persecution of Galileo.[2] We suggest Shakespeare in Othello has pictured, through Cassio, science, or the growth of natural knowledge. Othello, as black, seems to us to personify human ignorance. Iago expresses perhaps the influence of the past, of tradition, upon men. His name easily stands for any number of years *ago*. If we insert noughts between the *I* and *ago*, we have 10 or 1000 (years) *ago*. We merely suggest this. Iago is termed *ancient* to Othello. The latter places infinite credence in him. Cassio is the lieutenant of Othello. That is to say, on our suggestion, he has supplanted by proof the claims of the past to infallibility and belief. But Othello will still be gulled, and believe in the past.

Suppose now we were to take Desdemona as truth. Her name sounds not very unlike *testimony*. Would not the

---

[1] The name of Cassio suggests that it may be related to *scio, scire,*—from which the word *science* is derived.

[2] Not alone by Galileo; but through Bruno also.

stifling of Desdemona by Othello well represent the way
that ignorance has stifled truth when gulled by the voice of
tradition ? The disgrace of Cassio is entirely on the back
of Iago. And the latter raises Othello's suspicions against
Cassio and Desdemona. Does not this well represent the
conflict of religion and science ? According to us, all
Othello's miseries come from his easy credulity. And half of
the ills of humanity, wars, persecutions, etc., come from a too
easy credulity. We have nothing in common with those
optimists, who see the right (like Guizot) in everything.
Those who hold such a theory destroy the freedom of
law within law, of moral choice, and vindicate error and
evil at once. History is the history of human error, or it
is not so. However, we can see a parallel (whether true or
not) between Othello's credence in Iago and in the beliefs
of humanity. The death of Desdemona, the disgrace of
Cassio, the torture and perplexity of Othello, are all upon
the back of that magnificent rascal Iago. He is well termed
an "*ancient*" indeed. Let us notice how Cassio supplants
Othello. The whole play is in reality the history and progress of Cassio. He finally rules in Cyprus. This has
puzzled critics sadly. Because, judging him by his intoxication, they cannot see the grounds of promotion. But do we
read the true idea of the play aright ? Is Cassio's drunken-
ness perhaps not the symbolism of religious conflict ? In
the play we find the song of Iago very curious and ambiguous. Cassio talks about "*souls that must be saved and
must not be saved.*" Again, it is through Desdemona's
influence Cassio is finally reinstated. Cassio seems to be
defeated, only that further promotion may be gained from it.
Othello doubting Desdemona is a true parallel of ignorance
ignoring the truth, and believing it false through science.
The belief of man in the past, in the voice of antiquity, is
well pictured in Othello's credence in Iago. The latter hates
Cassio, despises Othello, and sows mischief everywhere. He
not inaptly pictures Ultramontanism in the way he trades
upon Roderigo, who may well represent the foolish dupes of
superstition.

Othello says of Iago at the end of the play:

> "I look down towards his *feet; but that's a fable.*"

This not unreasonably suggests that Iago is in some way connected with the past. His feet would express the earliest history, and Othello may well say *"but that's a fable."* The whole conflict of history is one of two forces—past and present. The past, by its antiquity, custom, authority, and endurance, is always, like Iago, persuading and influencing the lives and beliefs of men. The present, born of knowledge slowly accumulated, throws light upon truths hitherto unapprehended, and which are at variance with the voice of the past. Until man clearly learns to comprehend the nature of progress and development, the discoveries of science are looked upon by many as dangerous innovations. Truth is rejected, and before truth can be accepted the nature of Iago must be thoroughly understood by Othello. In short, Othello is a phase of ignorance. With comparative criticism, and the intergrowth and dependence of all the sciences, the character of Iago is more clearly defined. Instead of looking back with reverence, we look forward with hope. And this is what we fancy Shakespeare has somehow pictured in Othello. It is a picture of one *"being wrought, perplexed in the extreme."* Shakespeare, without doubt, by the nature of his genius, clearly saw the relation of man to nature. That relation is pictured, we believe, in "The Tempest." And he must have accepted the discoveries of science before the voice of ignorance. Of course he saw also discoveries would accumulate; and he understood that for some time the greater part of men, and authority in particular, would throw the truth away, and believe the assumptions of tradition. This we believe he has pictured in Othello. Here we behold a noble man who, from a too easy credulence, is excited to murder his faithful wife, and lay traps for his weak but faithful lieutenant. The whole of the play is the triumphant march of Cassio. It seems as if his very weaknesses, at certain periods of the play, are historical expressions of

want of power. We may notice the way musicians are introduced; which- seems very much like the harmony of
gathering force. Shakespeare lived at exactly the time when
Cassio, as science, may be well represented as stepping into
Iago's shoes. The play opens with the non-suiting of Iago's
mediators. But the power of Iago, and the misery which he
entails upon Othello, seems also to symbolize the long conflict of religion and science (another term for the past and
present), which has continued from the sixteenth century
to the present day. How many truths have been post-
poned, laughed down, and stifled, because the past did not
agree with them? How often has truth been persecuted,
and oppressed, for the same reason !

It seems to us that Shakespeare has purposely allowed the
soul of his work to crop up in places devoid of artistic
covering and unity. For example, this association of Cassio's
name in Othello with arithmetic, seems to point directly to a
profounder meaning than has hitherto been surmised. It is
absurd, as well as most shallow, for criticism to try and overlook such a subtle hint. No one can calmly assert that
Shakespeare had no purport when he put these words into
Iago's mouth. Until we can reconcile every line and every
word of the text with the unity of idea which pervades the
play, we must acknowledge ourselves in fault.

~ Wondrous as is the play of Othello, we instinctively feel
that, like all Shakespeare's works, it is great on not alone
the purely artistic side. We are certain that something
more than the bare and vulgar effects of jealousy is pointed
at. We are bound, when we criticize Shakespeare, to allow
that it is possible his philosophy and art may be wider
and deeper than we dream. If Cassio represents, as we
surmise, science, then we claim for Othello a place only
second to Hamlet. We see at once that, taking Galileo
as a type and forerunner of the fiery trial which science
would have to suffer at the hands of the past, Shakespeare
has embodied, in the disgrace and final rule of Cassio,
the persecutions and triumphs of pure reason. Again, embodying in Iago the principle of absolutism and certainty,

arising from antiquity and tradition, our Poet has realized the long autocracy and tyranny of the past over the mind of man. In Desdemona's song of *Willow* we seem to hear a long sigh for liberty, which alone through Lodovico would realize her happiness. Othello, we repeat, seems the sum total of certain ages, "*perplexed in the extreme*," and believing, to their own ruin, in Iago rather than in Cassio. Of course with the detection of Iago, Othello, as representing a phase of human progress alone, must die. Othello believes his wife unfaithful to him, through Cassio. Plain symbolism is at once at hand. The truth, which man loves or pretends to love so dearly, is evidently untrue, since Othello believes Iago, whose evidence is at variance with that of Cassio. Simply Othello rejects such a truth (or dramatically stifles it) as a lie. He lives to find out that it is not Cassio who has done him wrong, but Iago, *who is a lying rascal—a fable*. With this discovery (which of course is an end of Othello as a phase of ignorance), he finds that Desdemona was really true, and not false. Thus long-rejected truth and persecuted science are pictured in Othello. At any rate, whether true or not, we would institute this parallel, for the sake of drawing attention to the nature of some of the problems which Shakespeare must have realized during his life, and which are being so wonderfully realized at the present day. Thus the question which distracts us at this moment is the comparative criticism of the characters of Iago and Cassio.

Shakespeare's century (the sixteenth) was the great critical period of European history. The past and the present were face to face for the first time. Science and religion, or reason and antiquity, were struggling for existence.[1] We believe Cassio represents, in his promotion over the head of Iago, an exact parallel to the growth of science during our Poet's life. Copernicus, Kepler, Bruno, Galileo, had clearly

---

[1] The sixteenth century will some day be looked upon as the turning point of man's intellect. Rebellion, misgivings as to the past, were born then, to grow into hope in the future.

stepped into the shoes of the past. But there was to be a terrible struggle, and revenge on the part of the Church and tradition, before this step would be consummated in men's minds. Shakespeare saw this plainly. In the martyrdom of Bruno he read the trials and triumphs of reason in the future. And he has therefore made the career of Cassio triumphant and successful. If we calmly ask ourselves whether Shakespeare believed in the past and antiquity, or in present discoveries of science during his life, can we hesitate for a moment in our answer? We have an only too clear exponent of Shakespeare's cosmical beliefs in "The Tempest." There we have evolution. For Caliban, Trinculo, Stephano, are undoubtedly three links, whose rise from each other is successive. They connect together the other and higher thread contained in Alonso, Gonzalo, Sebastian, and Antonio.

Prospero is probably Time, in which Shakespeare has put his whole trust. Ariel is perhaps Nature itself, through law and through reality, the servant of time and the worker of miracles. That Shakespeare has clearly realized through Caliban, Trinculo, and Stephano, evolution, is unquestionable. The name of Trinculo is clearly an intermediate stage (three in one) between Caliban and Stephano. The way Trinculo hides himself under the gaberdine of Caliban during the storm, is an artistic picture of a higher form evolved out of a lower. Stephano by his name—a-step-on-h(igher)—clearly realizes his mission. In the other characters Shakespeare has taken large syntheses of human epochs and progress. Gonzalo is Prospero's true servant and preserver, antiquity and continuity.

Of all Shakespeare's plays "The Tempest" is the plainest. Like Hamlet, it literally seems the tempest of man's apprenticeship, who is tossed about by time, without knowledge of self or aim. Time and nature land man at last on the enchanted island of futurity, when time reveals (as it does now to us) its character and its mission. With this knowledge Ariel is indeed free. In picturing Ariel as living in a "cowslip's bell," Shakespeare has exquisitely pictured nature.

Prospero or time teaches Caliban language, etc. Two
threads are noticeable in the play. One thread is that by
which we are let into the magic of time and nature; and
the other is a purely human side alone. Through the
masque Shakespeare has undoubtedly given us as a corollary
the different stages of man's progress. Agriculture alone,
the blessings of the union of mind and labour in knowledge,
are successively pictured leading up to the highest idealism
and Carlyleism. Those who fail to realize the nature of
Shakespeare's "Tempest" must be blind indeed. In Miranda
we have the human intellect, that "wonder," of which
Prospero is master in "a full poor cell." Thus Shakespeare has interwoven in his play several aspects of evolution. He has pictured mind as a psychological growth alone,
and led human development into something higher out of
a Caliban up to the finding of Ferdinand. But with all
this we are not concerned, except so far as they prove Shakespeare to have been an evolutionist and a Darwinian.
Therefore we may say, with some likelihood, that in Othello
Shakespeare has pictured that struggle between past and
present which was so wondrously commenced during Shakespeare's life, and which is still working itself out at the
present day.

APPENDIX.

A FEW GENERAL REMARKS.

We would here deprecate any too close interpretation being assigned to our interpretation of Hamlet. We rather wish to have exemplified the scheme, the plot, the subject-matter, than the exact Hamlet of our Poet. The latter would be too great an assumption. Whether we take Hamlet as the growth of rationalism, resulting from the revival of learning and the Reformation, or simply as truth, the principle involved remains the same. Hamlet is humanity, in historical continuity and development. This is all we insist upon. To affix too narrow a signification to any of the characters is not our intention; and when such a broad subject as History is in question, the mind must indeed fill up the vacuum. We have only called the *dramatis personæ* truth, error, certainty, or indifference, to illustrate what we believe Shakespeare's meaning. If we have gone into detail where we should not, it is rather in the hope of suggestion and of showing how every line *might* be rationalized. The characters of Shakespeare are far too collective in essence to be exhausted in any words.

As regards Ophelia, we can come to no certain conclusion. No more is heard of her after her burial in the play. Whether the hope of Laertes, that violets might spring from her unpolluted flesh, is fulfilled we know not. The play of Othello seems to us to deal more directly with this subject.

With regard to Hamlet's madness, we hope we have made its nature pretty clear to the student. In respect of Hamlet's banishment to England, his capture by a pirate, and his return to Denmark, we would venture to suggest that our Poet would have been clearer and (it seems) done better, to have made our hero accompany the courtiers to England, and, after having seen them killed by a slow and insidious death, to have returned with Fortinbras in conquest from England. We have as high an authority as Goethe on our side, who evidently took the same view. But probably Goethe erred, as we do, from want of real insight. And we believe further elucidation will only redound to Shakespeare's perfection in every detail.

HISTORICAL CHARACTER OF HAMLET.

The historical and real nature of the tragedy cannot be argued away. The student can say with Fabian in "Twelfth Night":

> "*Fab.* I will prove it legitimate, sir, upon the oaths of judgment and reason.
> *Sir To.* And they have been grand-jurymen since before Noah was a sailor."

The proofs of the historical nature of Hamlet are abundant.
First. The references to Wittenberg.
Secondly. The names of *Baptista, Lucianus, Bernardo.*
Thirdly. The introduction of Fortinbras, and the identity in the Churchyard-scene, of the birth of Fortinbras, Clown, and Hamlet at the same time.
Fourthly. Their *actual identity* of birth in the beginning of the play.
Fifthly. The harmony shown in the relations of Ophelia and Laertes to Polonius, by their continuity and their conduct and action towards Hamlet.
Sixthly. The steady progress of Hamlet and his irresolution. Also the incentives to action he gets from what really are impulses to progress in life, but which cannot be explained rationally otherwise, viz. the march of Fortinbras (growth of liberty).
Seventhly. The ready and easy way the play falls into historical parallelism; but refuses any rationalism otherwise.

HAMLET'S FATHER.

The murder of Hamlet's father is actually, in our eyes, the corruption of Christianity. Thus the Ghost represents the resurrection and revival of the pure Apostolic faith through Protestantism. This Ghost may therefore be well termed the spirit of doubt as regards its criticism of Roman Catholicism. We immediately recognize, therefore, in the Player-scene, the principles of the Reformation. Here we have a scene by which the King is exposed and detected, by acting or demonstrating the corruption he has effected through the ears of men. This is artistic for the famous protest itself, as the essence of the Reformation. Corruption is not only detected, but laid bare. Hamlet's father being the spirit of Christianity, is the subject of rumours and disturbances in the opening of the tragedy. And we can well understand our Poet's meaning. The play opens with those early disturbances (paralleled perhaps through the Waldenses, etc.) which foreshadowed the Reformation. Symbolically the Ghost typifies the shadowy revival and resurrection of the spirit of Christianity and truth which accompanied the revival of learning. The true sons of Hamlet's father are the Reformers themselves. In short they are young Hamlet. And Shakespeare has identified the spirit of Christianity with the spirit of truth-seeking all through the play.[1] We can now understand the allusions

---

[1] Readers may think the burial of Ophelia a contradiction in the teeth of all this. But possibly Christianity was more an ideal subjective revelation in Shakespeare's eyes than an objective fact. Christianity is more powerful and holds more true to the former position than to the latter.

of Horatio in connexion with the late King. And Hamlet's speech, where he says "*He was a king*," leaves us no doubt that Christ is here typified and pointed at as the representative and true symbol of Christianity itself. The Reformation was in reality a revival of Christ. And the Ghost is the artistic parallel, in our belief, of this rebirth. Gradually what first reveals itself by surmise and doubt, grows into certainty by the light of knowledge and liberty. Finally, corruption and error are exposed and denounced. Naturally this is followed by the death of Polonius, who represents so well certainty or infallibility, authority, bigotry, and interference. Thus we believe has Shakespeare artistically paralleled the Reformation.

THE FATNESS OF HAMLET.

In the following expression of the Queen with regard to Hamlet—

> "He's fat, and scant of breath.
> Here, Hamlet, take my napkin, rub thy brows:
> The Queen carouses to thy fortune, Hamlet"—

we read the prosperity and well-to-do circumstances of our hero. In fact, symbolically, things go very much his own way, with the exception of Laertes. That is to say, Hamlet is fat for want of exercise. The reader will understand us. And we believe this still further from the words of the Queen. She says she drinks to Hamlet. Thus belief is almost universally on Hamlet's side, or Progress. And this state of Hamlet is well expressed in the words "fat and scant of breath."

HAMLET ON THE STAGE.

It is only since this work has almost passed through the press that we have been made aware that Mr. Irving and Signor Salvini hold a copy of Hamlet in their hands, whilst striving (during the Interlude) "to catch the conscience of the King." This shows a thorough comprehension of Hamlet (up to that point) as History. It is possible (if our interpretation with regard to the Churchyard-scene is finally accepted) to add to the force of the play upon the stage, by still further histrionic symbolism. For example, if the First Clown (dramatic double to Hamlet) were *dressed as a second Hamlet*, it would distinctly symbolize Hamlet's self-criticism with startling effect.

HAMLET'S HISTORY.

The following is a brief analysis of the artistic and symbolic continuity, in respect of Hamlet's progress:

1. THE BIRTH OF HAMLET comprises: Bernardo, Marcellus, Horatio, the early revolts of Fortinbras, and the Ghost's revelation.
1. THE GROWTH OF HAMLET comprises: Hamlet's madness, his satire of Polonius, his persecution, his criticism of the Church, and the arrival of the Players.
3. THE MANHOOD OF HAMLET comprises: His determination to act in " *To be, or not to be,*" his mockery of Polonius, his inspiration and address to the Players, his action in getting up the Player-scene, and the Player-scene itself.
4. THE ACTION OF HAMLET comprises: Death of Polonius, address to his mother, banishment to England, death of Rosencrantz and Guildenstern, and finale of the tragedy.

RESULTS OF THE DEATH OF POLONIUS.

1. Death of Ophelia.
2. Return of Laertes.
3. Death of Rosencrantz and Guildenstern.
4. March of Fortinbras.
5. Address to his mother.
6. Death of Laertes.
7. Death of King, Queen, Laertes, and HAMLET.

THE SOLUTION OF HAMLET.

The interpretation of Hamlet should be the work of many. Each character, every line of the text, should be made the subject of special study. The same process employed in scientific discovery should be used in detail. Guesses should be made until they are wedded by induction with the text and the unity of the whole play. If half a dozen resolute thinkers would give their time to this work, we should soon understand Shakespeare. As for ourselves, the opinions herein contained are the results of *years* of patient thought.

THE END.

STEPHEN AUSTIN AND SONS, PRINTERS, HERTFORD.

www.ingramcontent.com/pod-product-compliance
Lightning Source LLC
Chambersburg PA
CBHW030311270326
41926CB00010B/1324